The Theft

Roy Moxham is the author of *Outlaw – India's Bandit Queen and Me* (2010), *A Brief History of Tea* (2009), an updated edition of *Tea – Addiction Exploitation and Empire* (2003), *The Great Hedge of India* (2001), and two novels, *The East Indian Company Wife* (2014) and *The Freelander* (1990). He was born and brought up in Evesham, England. After working for a while on a fruit farm, he went to Africa in 1961 to manage a tea estate in Nyasaland, now Malawi. He spent thirteen years in eastern Africa before returning to London to set up a gallery of African art.

Subsequently, Roy Moxham went to Camberwell College of Arts and qualified as a book and paper conservator. After a period at Canterbury Cathedral Archives, he became senior conservator of the Senate House Library, University of London. He also taught and examined in the Institute of English Studies on an MA in 'The History of the Book'. Following 'retirement', he devotes most of his energies to writing and giving talks. He spends half his time in London and the other half travelling, principally in South and South-East Asia.

www.roymoxham.com

The Theft of India

The European Conquests of India, 1498–1765

ROY MOXHAM

HarperCollins *Publishers* India

First published in India in 2016 by
HarperCollins *Publishers* India

Copyright © Roy Moxham 2016

P-ISBN: 978-93-5264-090-4
E-ISBN: 978-93-5264-091-1

2 4 6 8 10 9 7 5 3 1

Roy Moxham asserts the moral right
to be identified as the author of this work.

The views and opinions expressed in this book are the author's own and the facts are as reported by him, and the publishers are not in any way liable for the same.

All rights reserved. No part of this publication may be reproduced, stored in a retrieval system, or transmitted, in any form or by any means, electronic, mechanical, photocopying, recording or otherwise, without the prior permission of the publishers.

HarperCollins *Publishers*
A-75, Sector 57, Noida, Uttar Pradesh 201301, India
1 London Bridge Street, London, SE1 9GF, United Kingdom
Hazelton Lanes, 55 Avenue Road, Suite 2900, Toronto, Ontario M5R 3L2
and 1995 Markham Road, Scarborough, Ontario M1B 5M8, Canada
25 Ryde Road, Pymble, Sydney, NSW 2073, Australia
195 Broadway, New York, NY 10007, USA

Typeset in 11.5/15.1 Electra LT Std at
Manipal Digital Systems, Manipal

Printed and bound at
Thomson Press (India) Ltd.

Dedicated to all those across the world who campaign for equality of opportunity.

Contents

Preface		ix
One	The Portuguese *Spices, Christianity and Extreme Violence*	1
Two	The Portuguese *Conquest, Horticulture, the Church and the Inquisition*	22
Three	The English *Venture Capitalists and Adventurers*	44
Four	The English *Splendour and Disease*	61
Five	The English *Religious Freedom and Peaceful Trade*	88
Six	The Portuguese *Terror, Luxury and Decay*	121

Seven	The Dutch, the English and the Danes *The Triumph of Peaceful Trade*	139
Eight	The French and the British *Towards Conquest*	172
Nine	The British *The Seizure of Bengal*	204

Postscript — 227
Bibliography — 237
Further Reading — 244
Place Name Changes — 245
Acknowledgements — 247
Index — 248

Preface

Having spent some years in colonial and post-colonial Africa, I first visited India in 1992. It soon became apparent to me that the impressions I had formed of a benevolent British rule bore, as they had in Africa, little resemblance to the reality. The British had indeed improved education, irrigation and transport, but there was a much darker side too.

By chance I came across a reference to the Imperial Customs Line, a barrier that the British used to fence off the eastern part of India in order to impose a huge tax on salt. None of the standard histories of India mentioned this barrier. Following its path, and delving into its history for my book, *The Great Hedge of India*, I was shocked to discover that it had made salt, an essential commodity, prohibitively expensive for millions of Indians and that many had perished as a result. Similarly, while researching for my book *Tea: Addiction, Exploitation and Empire*, I discovered that hundreds of thousands of Indians had died unnecessary deaths because of the harsh conditions on India's nineteenth-century, British-owned tea estates. Again, this was not mentioned in the standard histories of India. On completion of these two projects, I began to research the impact of European colonialism on the Indian peninsula.

Accounts by early travellers of India's riches – its spices, gold and gems – had excited the imagination of the Europeans. Some of these luxuries had been brought to Europe by the Romans, but when the Roman Empire collapsed, the Europeans became reliant on supplies coming through Arabia and Persia. In the fifteenth century, Portugal and Spain developed ships equipped with powerful artillery that could travel beyond Europe. To avoid clashes between the two Catholic countries, the Pope divided the world into two spheres of influence. The East, which included India, would be explored by the Portuguese. In 1498, Vasco da Gama discovered the sea route from Europe to India. Thereafter, Europe would no longer be dependent on India's riches being supplied through the Middle East.

With their control of the seas, the Portuguese established a monopoly over trade between India and Europe. They seized Goa and several other enclaves. Events in Europe then began to impact on India. Portuguese naval supremacy was gradually eroded by the Dutch and the English, who themselves began to travel to India, and who eventually destroyed the Portuguese monopoly. The English largely confined their activities to trade while the Dutch, alongside trading, colonized parts of India. The Danes also established colonial enclaves. The French were the last great European power to arrive and set up colonial enclaves. The wars in Europe between the French and the British then spread into India. Eventually the British were victorious.

Rather than consult the usual history books, I sought out, for the most part, accounts written by eyewitness of all these events. Many of these have been published, with helpful editing, over the last century and a half by the Hakluyt Society. There were other memoirs too. I supplemented these readings with the study of academic papers, whose existence was hardly known beyond academia, by such outstanding scholars as C.R. Boxer. Gradually I built up a picture of what really happened.

The Theft of India highlights the terrible suffering inflicted on Indians by the European powers during the three centuries that followed Vasco da Gama's discovery of the sea route from Europe to India. For most Indians, life under the Mughals was considerably worse than is generally portrayed, but at least the Mughal spoils were generally retained in India. The Europeans, however, exported not only vast amounts of India's wealth but thousands of Indian slaves too.

European oppression began with a reign of terror by the Portuguese. Entire communities were massacred, and those who survived were often forced to convert to Christianity. Many of them were victimized by the Portuguese Inquisition and atrocities continued to take place under the conquests of the Dutch and French. All these European powers exported slaves, mostly to the East Indies. Finally, the British, who until the eighteenth century had largely confined themselves to peaceful trade, conquered Bengal. They imposed a chaotic administration and seized much of Bengal's wealth, which they then exported to Britain. The impoverished population, without money to purchase food from other parts of India, could not fend off famine as they had in previous years. Millions starved to death.

Numerous eyewitness accounts by both Indians and Europeans bring all these events to life.

One

THE PORTUGUESE

Spices, Christianity and Extreme Violence

> We took a ship from Mecca in which were 380 men and many women and children, and we took from it fully 12,000 ducats, with goods worth at least another 10,000. And we burned the ship and all the people on board with gunpowder.
> – A Portuguese companion of Vasco da Gama, 1502.

On 20 May 1498, Vasco da Gama anchored his ships just north of Calicut on the Malabar Coast of India. These were the first ships to reach India from Europe. Calicut was a haven of peaceful trade for the ships of the many nations that came to purchase India's spices. Only two years later the Portuguese would capture those ships, slaughter their crews, train their cannon on Calicut, destroy its houses and kill its inhabitants. The Portuguese terror would have started.

The Indian Ocean was not unexplored territory. Vasco da Gama's achievement had been in finding the route from Europe around the tip of Africa – an achievement that would transform the trade between Europe and Asia. Once he had reached the Indian Ocean he was in a sea that had been traded on for at least two thousand years. Spices from India were well known in Europe. They were much in demand, especially pepper, but they had usually come by sea to the northern ports of the Indian Ocean and then been taken overland.

Pepper had been used in ancient Egypt as a part of the armoury of spices used to embalm its rulers. The mummy of Ramesses II, who died in 1213 BC, is in the Cairo Museum. X-ray examination has revealed a peppercorn stuffed and sealed into each nostril. Pepper was the most important item imported from south India by the Greeks and the Romans. It is mentioned by Aristotle, and was recommended by the famous physician Hippocrates, when mixed with vinegar and honey, as a cure for an infected uterus. Much of this pepper probably travelled through Egypt, which came under Greek control in the fourth century BC. It seems to have been used solely as a medicine until the Roman emperor Augustus started to use it as a condiment. It was during his reign that the Romans annexed Egypt in 30 BC. The Romans transformed the trade across the Arabian Sea. In the middle of the first century they had become acquainted with the details of the monsoon – already well known to the Arabs – and had built large ships to travel directly from Egypt to southern India. Pliny the Elder tells us that the journey from Ocelis, at the mouth of the Red Sea, to Muziris on the Malabar Coast in south-west India, took one month. The Romans destroyed the principal Arab trading centre of Aden, and made treaties with the smaller ports on the Arabian coast so that they could dominate the spice trade. By the end of the first century, spices were no longer a scarce luxury for the Romans. Alexandria became the centre of the spice trade, with large pepper warehouses. The use of pepper spread across the Roman Empire. In Rome itself, Emperor Domitian built pepper warehouses, the remains of which are still visible. Pepper was used both in the kitchen and at table. Several exquisite pepper pots from this period have been discovered in France and in Britain.

It was not only goods of Indian origin that went from Malabar to Europe. From well before Roman times, there had been a flourishing trade in spices and other goods between south India and the East. Indian spices were exported to China. Spices from Indonesia, such as cloves and nutmeg, came to India. Quantities of these were then shipped onwards to Arabia and Europe. The spices from India were a heavy drain on the Roman exchequer. There was a market for some Roman goods in India – clothing, metals, pigments, drugs and cosmetics – and particularly for the red coral of the Mediterranean. Pliny the Elder, writing in the first century AD, observed that Roman coral enjoyed the same prestige with the men of India as did Indian pearls with the women of Rome. The coral was not only valued as attractive jewellery, but also as a charm against evil and disease. Most spices, however, had to be paid for with gold. Pliny, worried about the drain of wealth from the empire, estimated that imports from India, principally pepper, cost fifty-five million sesterces annually – the equivalent of over half a million English gold sovereigns. Numerous caches of Roman gold and silver coins have been found in southern India.

Much of our knowledge of the trade routes between Egypt and the Malabar Coast comes from the *Periplus of the Erythraean Sea*. This is believed to have been written as a guide by a Greek captain (many of the Roman Empire's ships were operated by Greeks) based in Alexandria around AD 79–84. It describes the journey from the Red Sea to a number of western Indian ports, stretching from the mouths of the rivers Indus and Narmada, all the way down the coast to Muziris – which 'abounds in ships sent there with cargoes from Arabia, and by the Greeks' – and beyond:

> They send large ships to these market towns on account of the great quantity and bulk of pepper and malabathrum [cinnamon leaf]...They make the voyage to this place in a favourable season who set out from Egypt about the month of July.

The trade between the Romans and the Malabar Coast continued for hundreds of years. As Rome declined, however, the trade diminished. Coin finds from the third and fourth centuries are progressively rarer. Nevertheless, some trade continued right up to the end of the empire. In AD 408, Alaric I, the Visigoth, laid siege to Rome. As part of the city's ransom, he demanded, and received, 3,000 lb of pepper.

With the collapse of the Roman Empire, the trade with India reverted to the Arabs. They totally dominated the trade of the Arabian Sea until the arrival of the Portuguese. Their first written accounts date from the ninth century. These describe journeys from Muscat to Quilon – which had become the main port of Malabar – as taking one month. They also mention the presence of Chinese ships in Quilon. Ibn Batuta, from Tangier, on his way to China in the fourteenth century wrote detailed accounts of his visits to Calicut, Quilon and many other places in Malabar. His writings, however, like those of the Arabs who had been visiting India for many centuries before Vasco da Gama, were unknown in Europe.

Europe, fortunately, had some chroniclers of its own. The most famous of these was the Venetian, Marco Polo, who returned by ship from China to the Persian Gulf via India, at the end of the thirteenth century. He described visiting Quilon; its pepper, sandalwood and indigo; its Christians and Jews. He also mentioned the trade with China and Arabia. Chinese ships were regular visitors to India until the mid-fifteenth century. The fleets were controlled by the eunuch faction at the Chinese court. When this lost power, the new favourites forbade all foreign voyages. Two travellers whose writings were known in medieval Europe were the French Dominican missionary Jordanus and the Italian Franciscan missionary Odoric of Pordenone. Both visited Malabar in the early fourteenth century. Jordanus wrote detailed descriptions of life in Quilon, where he wanted to set up a mission, with accurate descriptions of its spices:

> Ginger is the root of a plant which hath leaves like a reed. Pepper is the fruit of a plant something like ivy, which climbs trees, and forms grape-like fruit like that of the wild vine. This fruit is first green, then when it comes to maturity it becomes all black and corrugated as you see it.

He also urged the Pope to establish a Christian fleet on the Indian seas.

As the Dark Ages gave way to the Middle Ages, the demand in Europe for spices increased. In early medieval Europe spices were so expensive as to be the preserve of the very rich. They were used by monarchs and prelates to impress. In 1256, the Scottish king, Alexander III, visited Henry III of England, and celebrated the Assumption at Woodstock with a great feast that used fifty pounds weight each of ginger, cinnamon and pepper. As the Middle Ages progressed, the price of pepper dropped, opening up consumption to a larger class of the moderately wealthy. It has been said that the phenomenal demand for spices, particularly for pepper, was because of the putrid food served up to the medieval populace. It seems unlikely that this was a major factor, since the link between stinking food and disease was well known. More likely it was used to mask the pervasive taste of the vast amounts of salt used to keep food through the winter months. Most importantly, it was used because it was the fashion – used at first by the rich for ostentation and then imitated by others as the prices fell. Whatever the motive, the demand was huge.

The merchants of Italy controlled much of the distribution. They traded from Constantinople, Beirut, Aleppo, Alexandria and Cairo. With the fall of Constantinople, the markets at Alexandria and Cairo became the most important. Spices continued to flow into Europe, but only after massive profits had been creamed off by Muslim rulers and traders. For, although the Venetians dominated the spice trade within Europe, the Arabs controlled the sea trade to the source in Malabar.

Two European merchants, Afanasy Nikitin and Niccolò de' Conti, who travelled to India in the fifteenth century, brought back useful information about its riches and trade. Nikitin was a merchant who left Russia in 1468 and later crossed the Caspian Sea to Persia. From there he went to the island of Ormuz and took a ship to Chaul, a port on India's western coast. He went to the Sultanate of Bahmani in southern India, where he stayed for three years 'The land is overpopulated with people, but those in the country are very miserable, while the nobles are extremely opulent and delight in luxury.' In addition he visited Cambay, Dabul and Calicut:

> The country produces pepper, ginger, colour plants, muscat, cloves, cinnamon, aromatic roots ... and every description of

spices, and everything is cheap, and servants and maids are very good.

Nikitin was unreserved in his observations:

> It is the custom for foreign traders to stay at inns where the food is cooked for the guests by the landlady, who also makes the bed and sleeps with the stranger. Women who know you willingly concede their favours for they like white men.

More important than Nikitin, since Italy was the European emporium for spices, was the earlier Venetian traveller Niccolò de' Conti. He journeyed to the Middle East, India, South East Asia and perhaps China from about 1419 to 1444. In Damascus he learnt Arabic and from then onwards passed himself off as a Muslim. On his return the Pope made him do penance by relating his travels to the papal secretary, who then wrote them down and circulated the manuscript. This first went into print in 1492. It is probable that Conti's account encouraged the Portuguese explorers later in the century. It certainly influenced cartographers and early sixteenth-century travels.

Conti sailed from the Gulf to Cambay in Gujarat, and then went on to the mighty Vijayanagar Empire in the south before ending up on the east coast and taking a ship to the Far East. He then sailed back to Bengal from where he travelled up the River Ganges to Varanasi. He then travelled overland through Burma. From there he took a ship to Java and returned via Vietnam to India. He visited Cochin and Calicut before going to Cambay, and back again to Calicut before leaving for the Middle East and Venice. Conti described India as:

> 'Great abundance of aloewood [used as incense], gold, silver, precious stones and pearls.' He was most impressed

by 'Calicut abounding in pepper, lac, ginger, a large kind of cinnamon, myrobalons [dried fruits and kernels used in medicines] and zedoary [dried roots popular with pharmacists].'

These tales of plenty excited the imagination of the Europeans.

Vasco da Gama's vessels left Portugal on 8 July 1497, rounded the Cape of Good Hope, and sailed up the east coast of Africa to Malindi. From there, with the help of a pilot given to them by a local ruler, they had taken the wind to southern India. It took only twenty-three days to cross from Africa to Malabar.

Vasco da Gama commanded a flotilla of three ships and a store ship, with a total complement of about one hundred and seventy men. The ships were small by modern standards and even by the standards of the time. Da Gama's own ship, the *São Gabriel*, was the largest. It carried six sails on three masts, but had a total length of only eighty-four feet. The large forecastle and tall stern made the ship relatively high. This height gave additional range to its twenty cannon. The ship was unwieldy but powerful.

The fleet carried a few convicts who had been purposely taken to do dangerous tasks. One of these, probably a converted Jew who knew Arabic, was ordered ashore to seek information. After landing, he was taken to meet two Muslims traders. They were from Oran, on the Mediterranean coast of Africa, and were reported to have surprised the visitor with a greeting in Castilian:

'The devil take you! What has brought you here?'

To this the convict replied:

'Christians and spices.'

The Portuguese had a long history of conflict with Islam. The Muslims of North Africa had finally been driven out of Portugal in 1249, but out of adjacent Spain only in 1492. Meanwhile; the rise of the Turkish Empire in the eastern Mediterranean had continued apace. The conquest of Constantinople by the Turks in 1453 had deeply alarmed all Christian Europe. Portugal was strongly Catholic and saw the battle between Christianity and Islam as a battle between good and evil.

From the twelfth century onwards, rumours had circulated in Europe of Christian empires in the east. An emperor, Prester John, who was reputed to be descended from the Magi, was said to be the overlord of many other eastern Christian kings. These rumours were probably fuelled by the existence of a real Christian kingdom in Ethiopia. In the early fifteenth century the Portuguese prince, Henry the Navigator sponsored a series of voyages along the West African coast to find a river route to the kingdom of Prester John. Although unsuccessful, these led to the expedition, under the command of Bartholomew Dias, which had found the southern tip of Africa. This discovery has inspired the king of Portugal to despatch Vasco da Gama further east. Little is known about da Gama's background or why he was chosen. He seems to have been born in a tiny village of fishermen on the south-west coast of Portugal where his father, who was a knight in the service of a duke, was the civil governor. In 1492 Vasco da Gama had been sent by the king of Portugal, John II, to seize French ships that were attacking Portuguese shipping.

It is presumed that his conduct recommended him to the king. Vasco da Gama's year of birth is not known but he was probably under forty when he left for the East.

Following Columbus's discovery of the way to the New World, Spain and Portugal – the two great European naval powers – had concluded the Treaty of Tordesillas in 1494. With the blessing of the Pope, this had divided the world into two spheres of influence – the Spanish and the Portuguese. The dividing line was demarcated about 1,000 miles west of the Cape Verde Islands, which lay off western Africa. Territories west of that line went to Spain; east of it to Portugal.

The king of Portugal hoped to form an alliance with the successors of Prester John to fight Islam. If it was also possible for the Portuguese to buy spices, this would be especially welcome – for the spice trade would bring wealth to Portugal, and simultaneously deprive the Muslims of one of their main sources of revenue.

The Hindu ruler of Calicut, the Zamorin, was away from the city when the Portuguese arrived, but agreed to meet Vasco da Gama on his return. He also sent a pilot to take the flotilla to a safe anchorage at Pantalayini Kollam, fifteen miles to the north. It was from there, a week after reaching India that Vasco da Gama finally stepped ashore.

Da Gama and his dozen companions were met by a representative of the Zamorin and an armed retinue. They then proceeded by palanquin, watched by crowds of curious onlookers, towards Calicut. Halfway there, they stopped for a meal at a local noble's house, and then proceeded by boat on a backwater to the city. After disembarking, they were taken to a temple.

Spices, Christianity and Extreme Violence

It is quite clear from an account written by one of da Gama's men that the temple was Hindu. It notes that the priests wore threads across their upper bodies and that 'saints were painted on the walls wearing crowns. They were painted variously with teeth protruding an inch from the mouth and four or five arms.' Nevertheless, Vasco da Gama and his men were so expecting to find Christians, even if deviant, that they thought they were in a church. They fell on their knees and prayed. They also took away 'some white earth which the Christians of this country are wont to sprinkle on the forehead and chest, round the neck and on the forearm'. Incredibly, Da Gama and his men continued to believe they were in Christian territory, under a Christian king, for the whole of their time in India. They would return to Portugal to affirm this to their own king.

The Portuguese were taken through Calicut with pomp, accompanied by drums and trumpets. The roofs and balconies were thronged with spectators. There was such a crowd at the entrance to the palace that scuffles broke out and several bystanders were injured.

Within the palace, they found the Zamorin reclining on a couch of green velvet under a gilt canopy. He held a gold spittoon in his left hand and was being served with betel nut from a huge gold basin. He offered the Portuguese food – bananas and jackfruit – and then asked da Gama to explain his mission to a courtier. Vasco da Gama insisted that as he was the ambassador of the king of Portugal, he could only deal directly with the Zamorin. The Zamorin then listened as da Gama told him that in Portugal:

> There reigned a king now whose name was Dom Manuel, who had ordered him to build three vessels, of which he had been appointed captain-major, and who had ordered him

not to return to Portugal until he had discovered this King of the Christians, on pain of having his head cut off. That two letters had been entrusted to him to be presented in case he succeeded in discovering him, and that he would do so on the ensuing day.

As the Zamorin was a Hindu and da Gama knew nothing of the local language, da Gama's words were presumably corrupted in translation.

Da Gama did not return the next day for he was involved in acrimonious discussions with the Zamorin's ministers concerning to the gifts he intended to present. They laughed when they saw the washbasins, hats, casks of oil, honey and cloth he had brought from Portugal. They told him these were unacceptable presents and that he should give gold or nothing.

The following day, Vasco da Gama met with the Zamorin. It was a strained encounter for the Zamorin was unable to reconcile to da Gama's boasts that he came from a rich country with the absence of any gifts. He did, however, allow one of the letters carried by da Gama, which had been written in Arabic, to be translated to him. Perhaps mollified by the flattery it contained, he gave da Gama permission to land the sample goods his ships were carrying and to sell them.

The Portuguese returned to Pantalayini Kollam, where was then more tension. The Zamorin's officials feared that if they allowed the Portuguese to return to their ships they might depart without paying port dues; the Portuguese feared that they were being held as hostages. After two days, matters were resolved when the Portuguese landed some merchandise as surety and da Gama and his companions were allowed to return to their ships.

Calicut and its adjacent coast were predominantly Hindu, but also housed many Muslim merchants. Some were visitors from Arabia, others were Moplas, Indians who claimed descent from thirteen Arab merchants who had settled on the nearby River Beypore in the ninth century. Calicut itself was not a particularly good harbour. It had become the chief port of the Malabar Coast by guaranteeing safe and cheap facilities to all traders, irrespective of their nationality or religion. As one Arab visitor observed:

> Security and justice are so firmly established in this city, that most wealthy merchants bring thither from maritime countries considerable cargoes, which they unload, and unhesitatingly send into the markets and the bazaars, without thinking in the meantime of any necessity of checking the account or of keeping watch over the goods.

The majority of Calicut's trade was with the ports on the northern shores of the Indian Ocean. The Muslim traders were extremely hostile to the Portuguese. It may be that they had already learnt of the several clashes between da Gama's fleet and their fellow Muslims on the African coast, but they were also fearful that they would lose their monopoly of the lucrative spice trade. The Portuguese, of course, had no love for the Muslims. The result of this mutual hostility was that the Portuguese merchandise found no buyers among the Muslim trading community at Pantalayini Kollam. As one of the sailors recorded: 'When one of us landed, they spat on the ground saying, "Portugal, Portugal." Indeed from the very first they had sought means to take and kill us.'

Da Gama protested to the Zamorin, who sent some other merchants to view the Portuguese goods. These merchants were also critical of the goods on offer and bought nothing. The Zamorin then agreed to transport the merchandise to Calicut at his own expense for it to be sold there. Some sales were then made, but at a poor price. However, enough money was raised to purchase some cloves, cinnamon and precious stones. In addition the Portuguese crews were able to go ashore in twos and threes and make private sales of their own.

On 13 August 1498, nearly three months after his arrival, Vasco da Gama sent some presents to the Zamorin and announced that he wished to leave for Portugal. He suggested that if the Zamorin sent some emissaries with him, he himself would leave behind some Portuguese men who were looking after the unsold merchandise. The Zamorin then demanded the customary port dues on the landed goods. Fearful that da Gama would abscond, he put guards on the Portuguese men ashore, and prohibited any boats from going out to the Portuguese ships.

Some merchants, however, ignored the Zamorin's edict and went out to trade with the Portuguese. Da Gama seized eighteen of them as hostages. At the end of complicated negotiations, an exchange of hostages and the return of Portuguese goods were agreed. The Zamorin also sent a note to be carried to the king of Portugal:

> Vasco da Gama, a gentleman of your household, came to my country, whereat I was much pleased. My country is rich in cinnamon, cloves, ginger, pepper and precious stones. That which I ask of you in exchange is gold, silver, corals, and scarlet cloth.

The Portuguese, did not honour this agreement. Leaving some of their merchandise behind, they set sail for Portugal on 29 August 1498 while still holding six of the Indian hostages. The following day, their fleet was becalmed off Calicut. About seventy of the

Zamorin's boats came out to attack. The Portuguese kept them at bay with cannon until a fortuitous thunderstorm erupted and they managed to escape.

The winds were very unfavourable for Vasco da Gama's return voyage. The journey across the ocean to East Africa took nearly three months. Many of the sailors died of scurvy. Others were so debilitated that there were only a few fit enough to work the ships. At Mombasa, in East Africa, da Gama was so short of able-bodied men that he destroyed one ship to better crew the remaining two. Only a third of his original sailors survived to reach Portugal.

Vasco da Gama and his men returned to a rapturous reception. They had found the sea route to India, they had found Christians (or so they thought), and they had brought back valuable spices. They had encountered no great fleets to oppose the Portuguese Navy. It seemed, therefore, that Portugal could easily seize control of the shipping and trade of the Indian Ocean. The king of Portugal was delighted. He assumed the additional title of 'Lord of Guinea and of the Conquest, Navigation and Commerce of Ethiopia, Arabia, Persia, and India'. Even though da Gama's expedition had not been intended for immediate profit, the sale of spices and other goods, which had mostly come from India raised a huge amount of money – said to be sixty times the entire expense of the expedition! With the prospect of great riches accruing to Portugal, as well as the opportunity to strike a blow against Islam, the king immediately commissioned another expedition. He wrote to King Ferdinand and Queen Isabella of Spain:

> The Christian people whom these explorers reached are not yet strong in the faith … but when they have been fortified in the faith, there will be an opportunity to destroy the Moors of

those regions. Moreover we hope, with the help of God, that the great trade which now enriches those Moors ... shall be diverted to the natives and ships of our own realm.

In March 1500, only six months after Vasco da Gama's return, a Portuguese fleet of thirteen powerfully armed ships sailed for India. This fleet was under the command of Pedro Álvares Cabral and it was dogged by misfortune. Some ships were blown off course to South America; four ships sank in a storm at the tip of Africa and all on board were lost. The remaining six ships anchored off Calicut on 13 September 1500. The Zamorin, a successor to the ruler who had met Vasco da Gama mindful of the power of the expedition, allowed the Portuguese to set up a trading post, or 'factory'.

Once again, however, there were disputes between the Portuguese and the Arabs. These were exacerbated when the Portuguese claimed they had been given the sole right to buy pepper. Events came to a climax when the Portuguese seized an Arab ship in the harbour. A riot ensued and thirty or forty Portuguese were killed. Cabral then ordered his fleet to bombard Calicut. He also seized some of the ships in the harbour, took their goods – including three elephants, which were later killed and salted for the homeward journey – and slaughtered their crews. The bombardment of the city lasted two days. Many of its wooden houses were destroyed, and many of its inhabitants were killed. Fortunately for the people of Calicut, however, the violent recoil of the guns began to damage Cabral's ships. He was forced to suspend hostilities, and left.

Cabral then sailed one hundred miles south to Cochin. The Raja of Cochin was a rival of the Zamorin of Calicut, and he saw advantages in being hospitable to the Portuguese. He allowed them to buy spices and establish a factory. Within a fortnight, Cabral's ships were almost fully loaded. Then came news that the fleet of the Zamorin of Calicut was moving down the coast to attack. Cabral hurriedly slipped away by night – so hurriedly that he left behind the thirty Portuguese at the factory. Next day, Cabral's and the Zamorin's fleets came into sight of each other, but before they could engage in battle they were becalmed. When the winds rose again, Cabral escaped.

Before sailing home, the Portuguese paused at Cannanore, eighty miles north of Calicut. At the invitation of the ruler, they topped up with more spices. Another ship was wrecked on the journey back, Cabral reached Lisbon on 31 July 1501. Although only five of the original thirteen ships had returned from India, the spices they carried were valuable enough to more than pay for the losses incurred. The Franciscan friars who had travelled with the expedition had discovered the difference between Hindus and Christians. Cabral advised the king that, since there were no Christian kings to make alliances with (although in places there were Syriac and other Christians, and two Christians from Cranganore had travelled to meet Cabral), the Portuguese would need to come to an accommodation with the Hindu rulers of the Malabar Coast.

Cabral had seriously ruptured relations with the Zamorin of Calicut. He had, however, made allies of the Raja of Cannanore and the Raja of Cochin. While Calicut lacked a proper harbour, that at Cochin was superb. In addition, Cochin had better communications with the pepper country. Moreover, the Raja of Cochin was mindful of the superior strength of Calicut and keen to align with the Portuguese. Cochin was set to become Portugal's most important base in Malabar.

Six months after Cabral's return, Vasco da Gama set sail again for Malabar. He left Portugal on 10 February 1502 with fifteen ships and was joined by another five ships while off East Africa. Now that it was clear that there were no powerful Christian kingdoms in Malabar, the motive for the voyage was largely commercial. This expedition, nevertheless, had been despatched by the king of Portugal himself, for he was determined that the commerce with India would remain a Crown monopoly.

Sailing down the Malabar Coast, Vasco da Gama's fleet intercepted the *Miri*, a ship carrying pilgrims returning from Mecca. When the Portuguese boarded the ship, some rich merchants tried to make a ransom deal with da Gama, but he refused. Some valuables were handed over to the Portuguese and they also seized some of the ship's stores. After these had been offloaded, Vasco da Gama ordered his men to set fire to the *Miri*. Her crew and the pilgrims managed to put out the flames, but da Gama's men returned to torch the ship again. One Portuguese eyewitness described how the women waved their jewellery, offering it up in exchange for their lives, and held up their babies 'that we should have pity on their innocence'. Another Portuguese eyewitness gave the bare facts:

> We took a ship from Mecca in which were 380 men and many women and children, and we took from it fully 12,000 ducats, with goods worth at least another 10,000. And we burned the ship and all the people on board with gunpowder.

The Portuguese fleet then anchored off Calicut. The Zamorin, remembering the damage Cabral had inflicted on his city and knowing what had happened to the *Miri*, sent a message offering peace. In reply, da Gama demanded compensation for the goods Cabral's men had lost and the expulsion of all the Arabian traders. The Zamorin replied, reasonably enough, that it was Calicut which had suffered the most and that the treasure from the *Miri* was worth far more than the goods that the Portuguese had lost. He ignored the demand to expel the many thousand Arabs. Da Gama then announced that, unless the Zamorin met his conditions, he would bombard Calicut the next day.

The Portuguese had captured a number of small boats and their crews. At midday on 1 November 1502, they began to hang their prisoners. Thirty-four sailors were executed. As the dead men were taken down, their hands, feet and heads were cut off. These body parts were then piled on a boat, which was floated into the harbour together with a message saying that the actual killers of Cabral's men could expect an even crueller death. The truncated bodies of these innocents were then thrown into the sea so that the tide would carry them ashore. The bombardment of Calicut then began.

European ships of the early sixteenth century did not have heavy guns. Their barrels were forged from thin bars of wrought iron, bound with hoops. Such guns could not take a large charge of gunpowder, so their range was limited to about two hundred yards. The Zamorin, having already been bombarded by Cabral, had erected a stockade of palm tree trunks to protect the town. He had, however, very little artillery. Da Gama was able to take his ships in very close to the shore with impunity. They wrought great damage that day and the next. Da Gama then left six ships behind to blockade the port and sailed for Cochin.

As da Gama departed, a ship arrived with a message from the Raja of Cannanore. It seemed that an Arab merchant had left the port without paying dues. Da Gama sent one of his ships to intercept the absconding merchant, who then paid what was owed, but cursed the king. The Portuguese then flogged him until he fell unconscious. He was then sent back to his ship with his mouth gagged and stuffed with excrement and bacon.

At Cochin, Vasco da Gama went out of his way to establish good relations with the raja. The Muslim merchants, well aware of what had happened in Calicut, were hostile. Da Gama ingratiated himself with the Hindu ruler and further alienated the Muslims by saving a cow. Some Muslims had sold a cow for slaughter to some of the Portuguese. The Hindu raja, protested to da Gama. When the Muslims returned to sell another cow, da Gama arrested them and gave them up to the authorities. They were then executed.

Da Gama did not, however, confine his barbarities to the Muslims. While he was still at Cochin, a Hindu priest arrived with a message from the Zamorin of Calicut. After being burnt with red-hot embers, he confessed to being a spy. He then offered to commit suicide. Da Gama declined the offer, saying that he needed a messenger to take a reply to the Zamorin. The Brahmin was then sent back to Calicut. His lips had been cut off and his ears replaced with ears taken from one of the ship's dogs.

At Cochin the Portuguese managed to buy spices and repair their ships. They used Cochin as a base to collect spices from Quilon and other southern ports. They also went to Cannanore and came to an agreement with the ruler to use the port. Before Vasco da Gama finally left Cochin, he entered into a formal agreement with the raja to build a Portuguese factory. A factor was left behind – together with clerks, workmen and guards – with instructions to buy pepper for future expeditions.

On the way north to collect ginger at Cannanore, Vasco da Gama's ships were attacked by a large fleet sent by the Zamorin of Calicut. This fleet had thirty-two large ships, each carrying several hundred men and a host of smaller boats. If the

Zamorin's ships had managed to get alongside the Portuguese, they would have easily overwhelmed them. The heavier guns of the Portuguese, however, once again kept their enemy at bay. Many of the Zamorin's ships were sunk. Other ships were set on fire. They drifted into Calicut harbour to burn under the eyes of the Zamorin.

Da Gama sailed on to Cannanore. There he loaded spices, and left behind more of his men to operate a factory and buy more spices for the future. He also left behind five ships under the command of his uncle, Vincente Sodré, to guard both the factory at Cannanore and that at Cochin. On 28 December 1502, Vasco da Gama left for Portugal.

———•———

Vasco da Gama would return briefly to India in 1524 as viceroy. He died after only three months and was buried in the church of Santo Antonio, later renamed after St Francis, in Cochin. His body was returned to Portugal in 1539.

Two

THE PORTUGUESE

Conquest, Horticulture, the Church and the Inquisition

The greater the number of fortresses you hold, the weaker will be your power: let all our forces be on the sea; because if we should not be powerful at sea (which may the Lord forbid) everything will at once be against us.

Dom Francisco de Almeida to the
King of Portugal, c. 1508

Soon after Vasco da Gama departed from India in 1502, his uncle Vincente Sodré sailed north, hoping to capture rich Arab ships. His fleet was caught in a storm off Arabia and he was drowned. The Zamorin of Calicut saw his opportunity. He ordered his nominal subject, the Raja of Cochin, to surrender the men da Gama had left behind at Cochin. The raja refused and war broke out. The Zamorin's army took Cochin and then burnt it. The Portuguese, and what was left of the raja's army, escaped to the nearby island of Vypin. Fortunately for them, a squadron of Portuguese ships under the command of Afonso de

Albuquerque came to their relief. The raja then gave authority to the Portuguese to build a fort at Cochin. A square fort was constructed, made of double rows of palm trunks with earth rammed between. At each corner there was a bastion with cannons and the whole area was surrounded by a moat. On 1 October 1503 a Franciscan monk christened the first European fort in India. It was named, in honour of the king of Portugal, Fort Manuel. Many other forts would follow, but first the Portuguese had to secure control of the Arabian Sea.

When the Portuguese first arrived in Malabar, neither the Arabs nor the Indians had powerful navies in the Indian Ocean. The Arabs came only to trade, not to conquer. The Indian rulers had large fleets of small ships, but these were for suppressing piracy, patrolling the shoreline and for transporting armies. The ships were galleys. Sometimes they had auxiliary sails, but they relied on oars and were unsuited to the open sea.

The arrival of Portuguese warships soon provoked an Arab response. The Egyptians had a fleet in the Red Sea. In 1507 it sailed into the Arabian Sea to do battle with the Portuguese. It headed for Diu, an island off Gujarat, whose governor, Malik Aiyaz – a Russian convert to Islam – welcomed them. There it joined forces with the ships of the Zamorin of Calicut. The combined fleet then headed south to engage the Portuguese. The Portuguese, under the command of the viceroy's son, Lourenco de Almeida, sailed north. The two fleets met off Chaul. The Portuguese were outfought and fled. The viceroy's son was killed.

The viceroy himself, Francisco de Almeida, had assumed office two years earlier. He was the first of the Portuguese to be given the pretentious title of 'Viceroy of India'. He had been given total power over Portuguese affairs east of Africa, with the authority to make treaties and war. When told of the death of his son, he was reported to have said, 'Those who have eaten the cockerel must eat the cock or pay the price.' He collected all the ships he could and sailed north. On 3 February 1509 his ships met the Egyptian fleet at Diu. The governor of Diu, betraying his fellow Muslims, secretly sided with the Portuguese and deprived the Egyptian fleet of supplies. When battle commenced, the Portuguese artillery devastated the Zamorin's galleys. The Egyptians, realizing that they could not defeat the Portuguese, turned tail and never returned. Thereafter, although they sometimes encountered resistance close to the Indian shoreline, the Portuguese ruled the high seas.

Almeida sailed back to his base at Cochin. He had taken many captives. On the way south, these were executed in batches, dismembered and then their parts blown by cannon over the Muslim towns.

Francisco de Almeida, although a soldier, was acutely aware that Portuguese power came from its superior ships and their firepower. 'If you are strong in ships the commerce of the Indies is yours, and if you are not strong in ships, little will avail you any fortress on land.' He was a shrewd tactician and strategist. He took advice from a Hindu privateer, Timoja, who harassed Muslim shipping on behalf of the Raja of Honavar. This raja was himself a vassal of the king of Vijayanagar, who was the overlord of the huge Hindu empire, which took in almost all of India, south of the Rivers Krishna and Tungabhadra. Almeida saw that if he was conciliatory to the king of Vijayanagar, the two of them might divide the forces of the Muslim states to their mutual advantage. This policy was adopted and developed by Almeida's successor, Albuquerque.

Afonso de Albuquerque, after a dispute with Almeida who refused to hand over power, assumed the grandiose title of governor of India in 1509. It was him, rather than Vasco da Gama, who was the true architect of Portuguese India. Upon taking office, he immediately began to plan the conquest of Goa.

The name 'Goa' was derived from that a port in the south of the island of Tiswadi, Govapuri. When this harbour started to silt up in medieval times, a new port developed north of the island. This also became known as Goa, later as Old Goa. It had excellent deep-water access along the River Mandovi and was well sheltered from the monsoon. The river was stocked with crocodiles to deter illicit entry or escape. The island had changed hands several times between rival Hindu and Muslim dynasties during the fourteenth and fifteenth centuries. After 1470 it came under Muslim control and in 1510 it was ruled by the Bijapur sultan, Yusuf Adil Shah.

Yusuf Adil Shah was a legendary figure. He was said to be the younger son of an Ottoman Emperor. When his father died, Yusuf's elder brother decided to remove any potential rivals and ordered that Yusuf be strangled. His mother substituted a slave and Yusuf was spirited away to Persia. From there, inspired by a vision, he took a ship to India. He became a slave soldier, rose to high office in the cavalry of the Bahmani emperor and, following the break-up of the Bahmani Empire, became the first king of Bijapur.

Albuquerque sailed north from Cochin to Goa early in 1510, with a fleet of twenty ships. At Honavar he rendezvoused with Timoja who commanded a number of galleys. Timoja also brought intelligence that Goa was defended by only 200 Turkish mercenaries.

In mid-February the combined fleet reached the mouth of the River Mandovi and attacked the fort at Panjim. There was little resistance. The garrison fled to Old Goa where the inhabitants decided to surrender. Albuquerque arrived in state, guarded by pikemen and wearing his finest armour. He was met by eight of the leading citizens who knelt and offered up the keys of the city. He then mounted a horse they provided and entered the city where he was showered with flowers. The remaining Turks fled and Albuquerque became ruler of Goa.

Two months later, Yusuf Adil Shah arrived with an army, which eventually numbered 60,000. The monsoon, which normally arrived in mid-June, was early. On the night of 15 May 1510, in heavy rain, Adil Shah's soldiers crossed from the mainland on rafts. The island was quickly taken, and the Portuguese became besieged in the fortress town of Old Goa. Within the fort some Muslims, sympathetic to Adil Shah, harassed the Portuguese. After a week of fighting, Albuquerque realized that he could not continue to resist and prepared to leave. First he massacred the Muslims of Old Goa. A few children were kept for conversion, a few rich men kept as hostages; a few women kept to become wives. All the rest were killed – men, women and children.

The Portuguese, with their prisoners, managed to escape to their ships, but the ferocity of the monsoon made it impossible for them to cross the bar at the mouth of the Mandovi. They anchored off Panjim where they were raked with cannon fire from their own captured guns. Soon they were short of food. It is said that Adil Shah sent a boat, under a flag of truce that was loaded with food, and that the Portuguese rejected it with a mock banquet of their own food kept for the sick. Certainly, the Portuguese used some of their hostages to buy food, and certainly, they were reduced to eating rats. It was early August before the monsoon abated sufficiently for the fleet to sail away. Albuquerque was, however, determined to return.

Eighty miles south of Goa, Albuquerque came upon some Portuguese ships. Overruling the protests of their commanders, he requisitioned many of these vessels. Eventually, he built up a fleet of twenty-eight ships, together with 1,700 Portuguese soldiers. Once again, Timoja joined him with a large number of galleys and Hindu soldiers. The combined fleet returned to Goa in November 1510.

Meanwhile, Yusuf Adil Shah had died and been succeeded by his son, an infant king, Ismail Adil Shah. His huge army had withdrawn from Goa, leaving behind a garrison of 8,000 Persian and Turkish soldiers.

On 25 November 1510, the Portuguese attacked. They first assaulted the arsenal between the River Mandovi and Old Goa where a large number of the defenders were trapped and killed. Then they scaled the fortress walls and descended into the town. It was a total rout. Hundreds of defending troops were put to the sword. The Portuguese then celebrated with a Catholic service of thanksgiving. When the service was over, Albuquerque gave the order to kill all the remaining Muslims. It took three days to hunt them all down. Men, women and children were burnt alive as they prayed in their mosques. The final death toll was forty Portuguese and 6,000 Muslims.

Over the next few months, Albuquerque rebuilt the city walls and started the construction of a new fort within. A hospital was endowed, a mint established and a small chapel built – dedicated to St Catherine on whose feast day Goa had been taken. Most of these buildings were constructed with stone taken from Muslim cemeteries. Much of the administration, including the police and collection of revenue, was leased out to a relative of the Raja of Honavar, the Hindu overlord of Timoja.

In April, leaving a strong garrison of Portuguese troops behind, Albuquerque sailed for the Far East. He captured Malacca and built a fortress there. Control of Malacca gave the Portuguese control of the eastern approaches to the Indian Ocean as well as much of the trade that came that way.

Albuquerque returned to India in February 1512 to learn that the armies of Adil Shah were once again besieging Goa. They had captured Banastarim, on the eastern side of the island, and built a fort to guard a ford that led from the mainland. The ford was protected on each side by rows of stakes driven into the river bed. From the fort, the Adil Shah army – 6,000 Turks and 3,000 others, together with heavy artillery – had crossed the island to lay siege to Old Goa. They had been joined by a number of Portuguese deserters, some skilled in the use of artillery. These forces were kept supplied from the mainland, through Banastarim. It was thought that the waterway leading to the sea was too shallow for Banastarim to be at risk of attack by Portuguese warships.

Albuquerque arrived from Cochin with sixteen ships. He commandeered a small Indian boat and led five of his smaller ships up the shallow waterway to Banastarim. Under heavy cannon fire, they broke through the stakes that crossed the river at Banastarim and cut off the supply and escape route of the Adil Shah army. They anchored beneath the fort and commenced bombardment. Despite being peppered with arrows from above and raked with shot, the Portuguese managed to continue to bombard the fortress for eight days, and eventually silenced the Adil Shah artillery.

In the meantime, the rest of Albuquerque's ships and men had gone to the aid of the garrison in Old Goa. This tipped the scales against the besiegers, who fled to the Banastarim fort. Once there, they were trapped between their pursuers from Old Goa and Albuquerque's ships at the ford. Nevertheless, Adil Shah had a huge army in comparison to the Portuguese and, while the Portuguese might have eventually captured the fort, it would have cost the lives of many of Albuquerque's men. Albuquerque decided, therefore, to permit the retreat across the ford of the Muslim army. He insisted, however, that the Portuguese deserters be surrendered, although he promised not to execute them. He kept that promise, but cut off their noses, their ears, their right hands and their left thumbs.

The conquest of Goa was the first European annexation of Indian territory since the invasion of Alexander the Great. It transformed Portuguese influence in the East. Goa was one of the finest harbours in the world, protected from storms and easily defensible. From this safe base the Portuguese ships, with their superior firepower, could range along the western Indian coast and dominate its trade. Other ships would be allowed on the high seas only with the permission of the Portuguese. The Portuguese would corner much of the trade in spices and in horses.

Warfare on the Indian mainland was dominated by cavalry. Horses were essential for the armies of the Indian rulers. Very few good horses, however, were bred in India and there was a large trade in Arab imports. Albuquerque saw his opportunity. He wrote to the king of Portugal:

> I have decided that all the horses of Persia and Arabia should be in your hands, for two reasons: one being the heavy duties that they pay, and secondly, that the King of Vijayanagar and those of the Deccan may recognise that victory depends on you for he who has the horses will defeat the other.

Albuquerque gave instructions that all horses coming from Arabia and Persia should be offloaded at Goa. His ships intercepted those that carried horses and escorted them to the island. Those who voluntarily brought horses to be sold at Goa and those who purchased horses there were given customs concessions on their other cargoes. There was no import duty on horses, but a heavy tax on their export – a tax that eventually brought in over half the total revenue of Goa.

The king of Vijayanagar and Albuquerque's former enemy, Adil Shah, sent ambassadors to Goa. The southern Hindus and the northern Muslims were often at war with each other. Both offered friendship to the Portuguese and tried to secure a monopoly over the purchase of the horses at Goa. Albuquerque played one off against the other and sold horses to both.

Having secured the financial and political future of Goa, Albuquerque was determined to transform a garrison of a few hundred troops into a self-perpetuating colony. Albuquerque was not married, but he had a son by an African mistress. He encouraged his men to marry the Muslim and Hindu women they had captured, and endowed these couples with property. Many women committed suicide rather than proceed with these marriages, which involved conversion to Christianity. Many others, however, accepted the offer of a less bleak life. These mixed marriages – which mostly involved the poorer Portuguese – produced a class that monopolized the minor offices of government. Outside the city of Old Goa, Albuquerque allowed the thirty village communities to continue to administer themselves much as before. Preferment was given to Christians, but Hindus were allowed to continue their worship. The practice of sati, the burning of widows, was forbidden.

Albuquerque was in his fifties – with a beard that reached down to his chest – but still fired by ambition. He made plans to divert the Nile to starve Egypt, to capture Alexandria and Suez; to burn Mecca. In 1513 he sailed for Aden, hoping to capture the fortress that guarded the entrance to the Red Sea. The operation was a disaster. The Portuguese suffered heavy losses.

In 1515 Albuquerque sailed for Ormuz, an island city famous as a bazaar, which commanded the entrance to the Persian Gulf. Here, Albuquerque played the diplomat. A dynastic struggle was in progress. The king had been imprisoned by his nephew who had then assumed power. Fifteen princes, who might have had ambitions, had been rendered harmless by holding a red-hot bronze bowl to their eyes to make them blind. Albuquerque's arrival prompted the nephew to release his uncle. Albuquerque invited the nephew to negotiations and then assassinated him. The king was reinstated as a Portuguese puppet. Albuquerque then built a fort to control the trade between Persia and India. His health, however, had begun to fail. Wracked with dysentery, he decided to return to Goa.

On his return journey, Albuquerque overhauled a ship carrying a message from the king of Portugal ordering his replacement. Enemies in Lisbon had conspired to arrange his downfall. As the ship entered the River Mandovi, Albuquerque rose from his sickbed to view Old Goa. As the ship came to anchor, he died.

Albuquerque was buried in the church of Our Lady of the Mount. The king of Portugal, who had already regretted and countermanded his decision to remove the viceroy, gave instructions that the body should remain in Goa as a talisman. It required the intervention of the Pope for the family to finally bring the bones back to Portugal in 1566.

Albuquerque's policy of being helpful to the Vijayanagar kings proved extremely useful to the Portuguese. Vijayanagar forced Adil Shah out of much of the mainland adjacent to Goa and then encouraged the Portuguese to occupy it. The Portuguese were then able, by backing one of the contestants for the throne of the Adil Shahs, to obtain a formal treaty giving them the territories of Bardez and Salcete. These acquisitions more than quadrupled the area of Goa.

The Catholic Church did all it could to aid the Portuguese conquest. It was common for Portuguese soldiers to be given communion together before they went into battle. They also received free indulgences from the church so that, if they were to die, their passage to heaven would be all the swifter. Although the spread of Christianity was supposedly one of the main aims of Portuguese policy in India, it was some years before it was given any priority. The first bishop arrived in Goa in 1538 and this signalled an end to the easy relationship between the Portuguese Christians and the Indian Hindus. In 1540, proselytization began in earnest with the destruction of all Hindu temples. The following year the Church expropriated all temple land.

In 1542, the first Jesuit arrived at Goa. Francis Xavier was a man of extraordinary charisma. In his ten years in India and the Far East, he made many Christian converts. In one month he was said to have converted over 10,000 villagers in southern Malabar. In Goa he supervised mass conversions of hundreds in a single day. He reorganized the religious administration and schooling. His efforts were aided by Portuguese official discrimination against Hindus and the rewarding of converts, particularly those with influence. A huge programme of construction of religious buildings was inaugurated, with the construction and enlargement of many churches, monasteries and convents.

Francis Xavier died off the coast of China in 1552. He was at first buried in Malacca. Following a rumour that his body was miraculously preserved, it was shipped back to Goa in 1554 and was eventually interned in the Basilica of Bom Jesus. It became an object of great veneration, particularly after Xavier's canonization in 1622. The body has been put on exposition many times over the years, with increasing frequency in recent times. It no longer seems to be defying decomposition and at various times parts have been removed – a toe was bitten off and taken away at the first exposition; the right arm was sent for by a pope; parts of a shoulder blade are in Cochin, Malacca and Macao; the upper arm is in Japan; the internal organs have been distributed as relics; several other toes have been lost during the ritual kissing at expositions.

Before Francis Xavier died, he asked the Pope to establish the Inquisition in Goa. It arrived in 1560 – a year after five men were publicly burnt alive for sodomy – and took over the old palace of the Adil Shahs. Although it only had authority over Christians – and non-Christians who were considered obstructive to Christianity – there was much work to do. Many Hindus had converted to Christianity and mass baptisms on the Feast of the Conversion of St Paul became a feature of life in Goa. Some Hindus, particularly from the oppressed lower castes, converted voluntarily. Some Hindus, since land could only be inherited by those who could prove they were the offspring of a Christian marriage, encouraged some of their family to convert. Other Hindus were converted by force. It has been recorded by Portuguese friars that, a few days before the mass baptisms, Jesuit priests would go to the Hindu quarter with their slaves to seize Hindus. These victims would then have their lips smeared with beef. Having lost caste and become 'untouchables', they would have little option but to convert.

Many of these converts to Christianity kept some of their old customs and beliefs. There were also converted Muslims and Jews. Not only was irregular worship forbidden by the Inquisition, but it also became an offence to retain non-Christian customs – to cook rice without salt, to refuse to eat pork, to arrange feasts at funerals, or to strew flowers at weddings. The Inquisition investigated 16,172 cases before it was abolished for the first time in 1774. It was revived in a modified, less draconian form, in 1778 before being finally abolished in 1812. Most of its records were destroyed – probably deliberately. It is not possible to calculate either how many 'heretics' were burnt at the stake or the much greater number that died in the dungeons. It is certain, however, that the Inquisition in Goa destroyed the happiness of many thousand.

In 1674, Gabriel Dellon, a French doctor, was captured by the Inquisition at the Portuguese fort of Daman. The governor had asked Dellon to bleed his son. In order to do this, Dellon had asked the boy to remove an ivory figure of St Antony that had been attached to the boy's arm. The boy had refused, saying he needed the figure to prevent any mishap during the bleeding. Dellon had then unwisely upbraided the boy for believing in superstition. Dellon was arrested and transported to Goa for trial. He spent two years in prison being interrogated. Conditions were so bad that he attempted suicide. Eventually, he was sentenced to five years in the galleys and shipped off as a prisoner to Portugal. Through the intercession of a French physician to the queen, he was unshackled and released in 1677. He then wrote an extensive account of his ordeal in Goa:

> During the months of November and December, I every morning heard the cries of those to whom torture was administered, and which was inflicted so severely, that I have

seen many persons of both sexes who have been crippled by it and, amongst others, the first companion allotted to me in my prison.

No distinctions of rank, age, or sex are attended to in this tribunal. Every individual is treated with equal severity; and when the interest of the Inquisition requires it, all alike are tortured in almost perfect nudity.

Nor did the Inquisition restrict its activities to the living. Garcia d'Orta belonged to a Spanish family that had left for Portugal when Spain expelled the Jews. These Jews were forcibly baptized in Portugal and became known as 'New Christians'. D'Orta qualified as a physician and then moved to Goa in 1534. He was highly regarded and even given a lease over the island of Bombay, now Mumbai. His renowned book on Indian medicinal plants was printed at Goa in 1563. This volume is also famous among bibliophiles for having possibly the most typographical errors of any book. D'Orta died in 1568. Almost immediately the Inquisition moved against his family. His relatives were tortured. In 1569 his sister was burnt at the stake. In 1580, Garcia d'Orta's body was dug up and put on trial. He was convicted of not being a true Christian and his remains were burnt at an *auto-da-fé.*, a ceremonial burning to death of those found guilty.

The extremes that the Portuguese priests went to in order to suppress Hindu ceremonies is well illustrated by what happened at Bassein, a fort north of Bombay, in 1564. It was the custom for the Hindus to gather at festivals and bathe in Bassein creek. To deter this, the Jesuits planted the entire length of the waterway with crosses. The worshipers then decamped to a nearby lake. But, urged on by the clergy, the captain of Bassein dispersed them with soldiers and cavalry. Furthermore, the lake temple and its idols were demolished. Not content even with that, the Jesuits had a cow killed and its blood sprinkled over the sacred lake.

Despite the oppression, Goa remained largely populated by Indians: Christians and Hindus. Reputedly, 2,000 Portuguese a year came out to India. There was a proverb: 'Of the hundred who go out to India not even one returns.' Many did not even survive the journey out and mortality in India was dreadful. At the end of the sixteenth century, the population of Old Goa was about 75,000. Less than 2,000 of these were of Portuguese, European or mixed blood. Of course, this small group controlled all the power and the wealth. It has been said that the British Empire in India was a form of outdoor relief for the upper classes and this was certainly true for the Portuguese. Those who came out to high administrative or ecclesiastical appointments arrived with a host of poor relations and followers who expected rich pickings. It was a favourite destination for the illegitimate sons of the aristocracy. Those who survived often did make their fortunes, for Goa was the hub of the Portuguese empire and accumulating money was easy.

For the majority of the Portuguese who came out to India, however, life was far from easy. Great difficulties were encountered in finding enough men to crew the ships and man the army. Few respectable peasants or working men volunteered for a life where death was common and rewards uncertain. To find enough men for the overseas empire, convicts were allowed to work out their sentences in the colonial army; murderers imprisoned in Portugal were allowed to avoid execution by volunteering for banishment to the East. Wages due to these and more regular volunteers was deferred until after they arrived in India, and then, often for many

Conquest, Horticulture, the Church and the Inquisition 37

extra months. These penniless unfortunates became thieves and pirates in order to live. Many entered the private service of the administrators to become thugs or agents of bribery and corruption. In 1539, the viceroy wrote to the king that of 16,000 men on the payrolls only 2,000 were to be found on duty.

Very few Portuguese women came to India and fewer still that were respectable. The men took concubines – some of whom they married – and women slaves. Goa relied on a huge population of slaves. A relatively low-ranking Portuguese might have had twenty slaves, while a man of substance might have had hundreds. Women slaves were sold semi-naked at auctions and fetched more if they were virgins.

The Portuguese were the dominant power in the Indian Ocean for a century. The only major challenge came in 1538 from a Turkish fleet, which the Portuguese defeated. After the Vijayanagar Empire was overrun by the Muslims in 1565, the Muslim rulers united to attack the Portuguese forts. This culminated in a ten-month siege of Goa in 1570. The Portuguese survived and continued to control much of the Indian Ocean and much of the spice trade.

Portuguese mastery of the sea was enforced by the *cartaz*. This was a written permit allowing safe passage. In addition, the cartaz specified what route the ship should follow and what commodities could be carried. The Portuguese reserved certain monopolies, such as that on spices, to themselves. Some cargoes had to be offloaded at specific ports; horses, for example, had to be taken to Goa. Any ship without a cartaz, or found to be contravening its conditions, was liable to seizure and confiscation. To enforce the cartaz system, the Portuguese established a number of heavily armed fleets.

The strongest resistance to the Portuguese came from Calicut. After early efforts to effect a truce with the Portuguese, the Zamorins of Calicut became their greatest adversaries. In this, they were helped by a dynasty of able naval commanders, the Kunjali Marakkars. The Zamorins had originally hoped for help against the Portuguese from the Arabs who traded at Calicut. This had not materialized. In 1506, many of these Arab traders, fearful of the Portuguese, sold up the long-established businesses they had in the Zamorin's domain. As they embarked for Arabia at Pantalayini Kollam, a Portuguese fleet swooped down. The Portuguese captured a huge amount of gold. It is said that 2,000 Arabs were killed.

The Kunjali Marakkars were Moplas, local Muslims, who had become rich merchants. Unlike the foreign Muslims, they were keen to resist the Portuguese. They offered their services to the Hindu Zamorin, became the admirals of his fleet and began to harass Portuguese shipping.

The old Zamorin died. His successor was more sympathetic to the Portuguese, thinking he could come to an arrangement with them. He concluded a treaty with Albuquerque and allowed the Portuguese to build a fort at Calicut. All went well until the death of Albuquerque. The Portuguese then began to violate the terms of their treaty. They used force to obtain preference for their spice exports and they also seized some Indian vessels. In 1522, this Zamorin who was friendly to the Portuguese died. The new Zamorin instructed his navy to attack the Portuguese. The Kunjali Marakkars and in particular one of their captains, Kutti Ali, did this to great effect.

Realizing that they could not compete on equal terms with the Portuguese warships, the Zamorin's commanders built large numbers of small boats, rowed by thirty or forty men, to make guerrilla attacks. Bags of cotton were hung over the sides of the boats to give some protection from small arms fire. The heavy cannon of the Portuguese were designed to attack ships similar to their own and they found it difficult to pinpoint the smaller vessels. Even a successful hit only disabled one boat in a swarm. The Indians hid hundreds of these little boats along the Malabar Coast. They posted lookouts on vantage points to spot Portuguese shipping that came close to the shore. An elaborate signalling system was established to link these points with each other and with the flotillas of boats below. The Portuguese were particularly vulnerable when the winds dropped. The Indian boats would be rowed out at speed to the becalmed warships. They would send fire arrows into the enemy's sails, then board on all sides. The Portuguese would usually be heavily outnumbered and cut to pieces by the Indian swordsmen.

Sometimes the Indians were victorious in battle; sometimes the Portuguese. Neither side was able to gain ascendancy over the other. Meanwhile, considerable quantities of spices evaded the Portuguese blockade and made their way to Arabia and Europe.

The battles between the Portuguese and the Zamorin's admirals, the Marakkars, went on until the late sixteenth century. Towards the close of that century, however, relations between the Zamorins and the Marakkars deteriorated. A weak Zamorin tried to come to terms with the Portuguese and he allowed them to build a fort at Ponnani where the Marakkars were based. The Marakkars then moved their base to the north of Calicut. On a peninsula just inside the mouth of the River Kotta, they built a fortress from where they attacked Portuguese ships on both the western and the eastern coasts of India. However, Mohammed Kunjali Marakkar then overreached himself. He began to operate independently of the Zamorin and finally declared himself Raja of Kotta.

The Portuguese saw their opportunity and began negotiations with the Zamorin to launch a joint attack on Kotta. It is probable that, by entering into these negotiations, the Zamorin merely meant to frighten Marakkar into resuming allegiance. However, Marakkar decided instead to insult the Zamorin. He took an elephant from a royal stable and cut off its tail. The Zamorin then amassed an army to attack Kotta from the mainland while the Portuguese prepared an attack from the sea.

It had been agreed that the joint attack would begin on 4 March 1599, just before dawn. The signal would be given from the top of a prominent landmark, the Iringal Rock, by a burning lance. For some reason, the man to whom this task had been assigned did this at midnight – five hours too early. In the ensuing confusion the Portuguese and the Zamorin suffered heavy losses and had to abandon their assault.

At the end of 1599, the Portuguese and the Zamorin returned to mount a fresh siege. The Portuguese had been reinforced by fresh recruits from Lisbon; the Zamorin had amassed 5,000 soldiers, 1,000 workmen, timber and fifteen elephants, plus some ships to guard the river. Meanwhile, a Portuguese sea blockade of Kotta had further weakened the defenders.

Marakkar had ships in place to seal the mouth of the river, but the Portuguese, with the help of the Zamorin's men and elephants, dragged some ships overland into the river. Heavy cannon were installed on the riverbank to bombard the fort. The Portuguese managed to capture some of the fort's outworks and install themselves. Their artillery was then able to move forward to batter the fortress. It was an unequal battle. Marakkar was soon reduced to a few hundred men and decided to sue for peace.

The Zamorin merely wanted Marakkar's surrender, but the Portuguese wanted his life. Marakkar knew this and was only prepared to give himself up to the Zamorin who had promised not to kill him and his men. Secretly, however, the Zamorin had agreed to allow the Portuguese to abduct Marakkar.

On 16 March 1600, Marakkar surrendered. The Portuguese and the Zamorin's men lined up on either side of the main gate. Four hundred men marched out between them and submitted to the Zamorin, who let them free. Then came Marakkar with a black cloth on his head and a sword with the point lowered in his hand. He went up to the Zamorin, presented him with the sword and fell at the ruler's feet. The Portuguese then grabbed Marakkar and began to take him away.

The Zamorin's warriors were appalled at this treachery. A fracas ensued, but the Portuguese managed to hold on to their prize captive and forty of his followers. Kotta was sacked and burnt. A week after the surrender, the Portuguese sailed for Goa with Marakkar and his men in chains.

In Goa there were great celebrations. The victors were welcomed with gun salutes, together with 'drums and fifes, bagpipes and trumpets'. The first of the captives was landed and stoned to death. Marakkar was taken to the Tronco, the prison used by the Inquisition. At a show trial he was sentenced to death. A great crowd, presided over by the viceroy and the archbishop, came to see Marakkar executed. He was beheaded with an axe. The body was quartered, and then exhibited on the beaches. Then, 'his head was salted and conveyed to Cannanore, there to be stuck on a standard for a terror to the Moors.' Afterwards, all his surviving companions were executed.

By combining with the Portuguese to defeat Marakkar, the Zamorin secured his own eclipse. The last great power to oppose the Portuguese on the coast of Malabar no longer had an effective navy.

During the sixteenth century, the Portuguese built an extraordinary number of factories and forts in India. These forts were there to protect the factories and enforce a monopoly on the purchase of spices and other designated goods. Many were huge and had large garrisons. Working in coordination with the Portuguese navy, these forts were able to monitor virtually all shipping arriving and departing from India's ports. They enforced the rule that all ships on the Indian Ocean must carry a Portuguese permit, a cartaz.

After the construction of the small fort at Cochin in 1503, came others in rapid succession. There was, of course, a cluster of major forts in Goa. On the west coast there were also huge forts at Diu, Daman, Bassein, Chaul, Cannanore and Cranganore, plus a massive complex at Cochin. There were more forts on the Coromandel Coast; others skirting the Bay of Bengal. All together, there were at least fifty major Portuguese forts in India and many other minor fortifications. Garrisoning these forts – and others in the Far East and Africa – as well as finding men for its ships, was not easy for a country such as Portugal, which had a population of only a million. Moreover, the Portuguese were ploughing many of their resources into the development of Brazil. Nevertheless, as long as Portugal could enforce its monopoly in the East, it was just possible to sustain the edifice. Any serious breach of that monopoly would bring disaster.

Despite its control of the high seas, the Portuguese failed to achieve total control over the spice trade. The merchants of Malabar found it advantageous to take some of the crop inland and have it transported on the backs of animals and men to the Middle East and Europe. Or they would move the spices clandestinely, well away from the closely monitored main ports in small boats up the western coast. Gradually, these new routes became very significant. As a result, Venice partly recovered the trade it had lost to Portugal. The Portuguese, however, were still amassing wealth. Not only did they ship huge quantities of spices and other goods back to Portugal but, with their cartaz, they also levied a toll on the large trade between the territories which bordered the Indian Ocean. All this was set to change with the arrival of the Dutch and the British.

Three

THE ENGLISH

Venture Capitalists and Adventurers

If you will profit, seek it at sea and in quiet trade; for without controversy, it is an error to affect garrisons and land-wars in India.

Sir Thomas Roe
Letter from the court of Emperor
Jahangir to the East India Company, 1616

An expedition to the Arctic seas was the unlikely precursor to the foundation of the English East India Company. The English economy had blossomed in the early sixteenth century with large exports of wool to continental Europe. There had been a rise in imports too, even from the East. These, however, had mostly been purchased from Italian merchants who had established Mediterranean and overland trade routes. The price of spices had fallen as the century progressed. Simultaneously, the market had grown in volume. No longer was pepper the preserve of the upper middle classes. The English warship, the

Mary Rose, sank in 1545. When it was raised in 1982, it was found that most of those on board, even the poorly paid ordinary sailors, possessed a small amount of pepper. In the middle of the sixteenth century, there was still a great deal of money to be made out of pepper and the other spices and riches of the East. Some London merchants were convinced that the time had come for England to seize a share of these profits.

In 1553 some of these merchants financed a fleet of three ships to find a passage around the north of Russia to the Indies. Voyages through such a passage would help avoid a confrontation with the Spanish and Portuguese who controlled the southern oceans. It was an extremely hazardous venture. All aboard two of the expedition's ships 'for lacke of knowledge were frozen to deathe'. Those on the third ship failed, of course, to find the non-existent route to the East. However, they did manage to reach the White Sea from where they travelled to Moscow and met the Tsar. He agreed to grant them trading rights throughout his empire.

In the previous centuries, the English merchants had operated under guilds and other associations. These had regulated their trade and behaviour. Within these set limits, however, the merchants had either traded on their own account or in partnership with others. They personally made the investment and then took the resulting profit or the loss. The merchants who financed the expedition to find a north-east passage were pioneering an entirely new English financial structure. It was to be an enterprise where the capital would be subscribed by its members, its profits distributed in proportion to their subscription and the business carried out in the name of a company. This new type of organization was considered necessary to raise the large capital investment required to set up trading posts in distant lands – a risky investment that might take several years to recoup.

It also made it easier for investors to subscribe new capital as and when required, and to transfer their shares.

The London merchants behind the expedition to the north-east had obtained the royal licence necessary for trading abroad, but formal incorporation had been delayed by the illness and death of King Edward VI. They had raised £6,000 in shares of £25 each to finance the three-ship enterprise. A charter was finally granted to a company of 199 men and two women 'marchants adventurers of England' in 1555. It became known as the Muscovy Company or the Russian Company. In appreciation for the risk being taken, the company was given a monopoly of trade with Russia and other markets it might open up. Just after it was incorporated, news came through of the successful meeting with the Tsar and the loss of the two ships. Obviously, more money would be needed to develop the business. Within ten years, the existing shareholders found themselves asked to take their stake up to £200 each. The company traded hesitantly at the beginning, successfully for many years, gradually declining, and only expired with the Russian Revolution of 1917.

In 1575 two London merchants sent out agents at their own expense to Constantinople. This resulted in the sultan of Turkey making a promise to open his markets to the English. There were negotiations between the sultan and the English queen, Elizabeth. In 1581 the Levant Company, similarly structured to the Russian Company, was granted a charter giving it a monopoly of trade with the Turkish Empire. Many of the richest London merchants subscribed its capital and the queen herself loaned the company 10,000 lb weight of silver.

From the start it was 'very gainful'. The Levant Company soon had a huge business with Constantinople, Syria and Egypt. It became the most important conduit to England for the spices from the Far East and India.

In 1587 Sir Francis Drake captured a Portuguese royal ship, the *San Felipe*, off the Azores. It was fully laden with goods from Goa. When it was offloaded at Plymouth, the cargo that was declared to Drake's financial backers was not particularly valuable – velvet and silk with some gold and jewels. However, rumours rapidly spread that 300,000 ducats in cash had also been taken and secretly spirited away. These rumours, possibly true, fanned English ambitions. (In order to simplify matters, 'English' is used sometimes when 'British' might be more appropriate. The East India Company was incorporated in England, but many of its employees came from elsewhere in the British Isles to seize the eastern riches of the Portuguese.)

The Crowns of Portugal and Spain had been united in 1580. When the English defeated the Spanish Armada in 1588, it was also seen as a victory against Portugal. If the English could defeat the Spanish navy, it was argued, they could challenge the supremacy of the Portuguese ships in the Indian Ocean and seize some of their trade.

English ambitions had also been aroused from another, unlikely sources. Thomas Stephens, the son of a wealthy London merchant, had gone abroad and become a Jesuit priest. In 1579 he had gone from Lisbon to Goa. He became an outstanding scholar of the local language, Konkani, in which he composed a series of Christian epics. He also wrote back to his father about the life and riches of Goa. This excited an interest in India among the London merchants.

Things did not start well for the English. A year after the victory over the Armada, some merchants, whose names have been lost but who were probably involved in the Levant trade, decided to finance an expedition around the tip of Africa to India and the East. They petitioned successfully for a royal warrant and pleaded that 'Great benefitte will redound to our countree, as well as for the anoyinge of the Spaniards and Portingalls'. It was clear that they intended to act not only as traders but also as privateers.

The *Edward Bonaventure*, the *Penelope* and the *Merchant Royal* left Plymouth in 1591. The fleet was becalmed for a month and by the time it reached the Cape many of the men had died or were severely ill with scurvy. The *Merchant Royal* was sent back to England laden with the sick. The two remaining ships, with 200 men on board, continued east. After only four days, they hit a storm and the *Penelope* sank with the loss of all on board, including the leader of the expedition, George Raymond. The remaining ship, the *Edward Bonaventure*, was commanded by James Lancaster. He was both a merchant and a sailor, and had commanded the ship against the Spanish Armada. East of the Comoro Islands, the *Edward Bonaventure* was struck by lightning. Four men were killed and many others injured. Finally, however, the ship reached port on the Malay Peninsula. Death, lightning and disease had so affected the crew that only twenty-two men were still fit. Nevertheless, Lancaster went to sea again and managed to capture three Portuguese ships loaded with pepper and other riches. With its booty, the *Edward Bonaventure* sailed back west. Lancaster became very ill and when the ship reached Ceylon his crew mutinied. They insisted on immediately setting sail for England.

Ill fortune continued to dog the *Edward Bonaventure*. Strong winds blew it to the Caribbean where it lost its sails in a storm.

Getting some canvas from a French ship, it tried to make for Newfoundland, but was blown back to the Caribbean. Then, while Lancaster and many of his crew were ashore on the island of Mona, the *Edward Bonaventure* was blown out to sea. There were only five men and a boy on board. They were attacked by Spaniards from Santo Domingo and the ship and all its booty were lost. Lancaster and his men managed to return to Europe on a French ship. The expedition had been a total disaster – two of the three ships had been lost and there was nothing to show for it. It would be a while before English merchants financed another expedition to the East around the tip of Africa.

The driving force behind the foundation of the East India Company was Thomas Smythe. He was one of the London merchants – a group of only two or three hundred – in foreign trade. His father was involved in the collection of customs duty, some said corruptly, which had left his son enormously rich. Significantly, Thomas Smythe was a member of both the Russian Company and the Levant Company. He had plans to colonize Virginia and had backed attempts to find a passage to the East around the north of the Americas. In 1599, or possibly earlier, Smythe began to plan an expedition to the East, going round the tip of Africa. He had probably achieved informal backing from his colleagues before the first recorded meeting of 22 September 1599. At this meeting, attended by the Lord Mayor of London, 101 merchants formally subscribed from £100 to £1,000 each. They promised £30,000 in total to equip an expedition to the East Indies and to obtain the necessary charter for this from the queen.

The prospect for the charter looked good at first. On 17 October 1599, however, a deputation was summoned to attend the Privy Council. They were told that negotiations for peace with Spain might be compromised by the expedition and that their application was suspended. Negotiations between England and Spain then broke down. The London merchants' cause was given impetus by the arrival in Holland of six Dutch ships from the East, laden with spices. In September 1600, the Council gave permission for the merchants to proceed with preparations as their privileges would soon be granted and their expedition would be allowed to depart. Four ships were bought and work commenced on refitting and provisioning them for the voyage. The merchants were keen to make up for lost time. A barrel of beer a day was supplied 'for the better holding together of the workemen from running from ther worke to drinke'.

The charter of 'The Governor and Company of Merchants of London trading into the East Indies' was finally signed on 31 December 1600. The Company would be managed by a governor and twenty-four committees (directors). The charter gave the Company a monopoly over trade with the East Indies. It would be allowed to export bullion as well as goods – a rare privilege. It was emphasized that the Company was to restrict itself to trade and was not to attempt colonization or conquest. The Company's ships would be armed, but only for protection. This was in marked contrast to the practice of other European nations trading beyond Europe. It was this emphasis on peaceful trade that would, by the end of the century, make the Company more successful in India than its rivals.

Thomas Smythe became the first governor of the Company. He had also just become governor of both the Russian and Levant Companies. Smythe was rather grander than most of the merchants. He had been MP for Aylesbury and was master of a great city guild, the Haberdashers. His house was in Philpot Lane, near Fenchurch Street in London. It must have been large, since it is recorded that in 1619 a French envoy stayed there with his 120-strong retinue. It had a great hall, in which Smythe had commemorated his interest in finding a north-west passage to the East by hanging an Inuit canoe from the ceiling. In this hall the early meetings of the East India Company took place. It was from this house that sailors were recruited and paid; that the wives left behind went for assistance. He was popular at all levels of society and his seamen would often bring him back curiosities from their travels. The early sailors with the East India Company were given a share in the profits of the enterprise equivalent to two months' wages. When Thomas Smythe invested, others followed; when Thomas Smythe planned an expedition, seamen hastened to enlist.

The Company was administered in a very frugal manner from Smythe's house. He loaned the use of one of his own men to be part-time secretary. The only other member of staff was the beadle who carried the subscription book and advertised meetings. Purchasing the ships, provisioning them, recruiting their crews, supervising the accounts and conducting important correspondence was done by Thomas Smythe himself, or by the other subscribers to the Company. The London merchants were past masters at reducing overheads. They would also have had in mind that the Company's charter could be revoked by the Crown at only two years' notice and that, unless renewed, it would expire in 1615. The other threat hanging over the merchants was that discovery of a north-west route to the Indies, which many thought imminent, might undermine their endeavour.

Thomas Smythe was careful to confine his activities largely to business. In Parliament he concentrated on trade matters. Although he was well regarded at court, he did not, as many others did, give out bribes or loans to the royal circle. He lived, however, in dangerous times. In February 1601, he was seen talking to the Earl of Essex. He was subsequently suspected of being implicated in Essex's abortive coup and was imprisoned in the Tower of London. He managed to extricate himself with only a heavy fine. It must have been wonderful to be knighted in 1603 by James I in that very same Tower. With a few small breaks, Sir Thomas Smythe continued as governor of the Company until 1621. Much of the credit for successfully steering the Company through its turbulent first years goes to him.

James Lancaster – the man who had sailed to the Malay Peninsula in 1591 – was appointed to command the Company's first expedition to the East. Although his earlier voyage had been financially disastrous, he had gained much useful experience and information – information that had proved invaluable when making the case for the Company's charter. Moreover, he had put his own money into the Company as one of its subscribers. Those at court had tried to have a 'gentleman' put in command, but the London merchants had stood firm and successfully petitioned 'to sort ther busines with men of ther owne qualety'.

Initially, the Company had no permanent capital, as it had been agreed that each voyage would be subscribed for separately. Eventually, the bookkeeping for separate and overlapping voyages became too complicated and a more permanent system of subscription was adopted. It would be fifty years before it became the genuine joint stock company it had originally pleaded for. The 101 first subscribers had grown to 218. Nevertheless, costs exceeded receipts and each subscriber became liable for 10 per cent more at first, and another 10 per cent afterwards. Some subscribers were slow in paying what they had promised and it took threats of imprisonment by the Privy Council to collect all the money. Eventually, the Company amassed over £68,000. This was a huge sum at a time when a skilled craftsman in London would be lucky to earn £10 a year. A sum of £40,000 was spent on purchasing the ships and provisioning them; £7,000 on goods to take out for sale or exchange; £21,000 on providing money for the purchase of goods in the East.

Accumulating the right money was a problem. Exporting English coin was illegal. The standard currency used in the East by the Portuguese and others was Spanish, in particular the silver coins of eight rials – the 'pieces of eight' of pirate tales. England was still at war with Spain, so obtaining them directly was out of the question. Some were available from the hauls of English marauders, such as Sir Francis Drake. Others were obtainable on the continent. The Company gathered some of these by encouraging its members to pay their subscriptions in Spanish coin. However, there was still a substantial shortfall. The Company asked if the royal mint could perhaps manufacture some Spanish coins. Unsurprisingly, Queen Elizabeth was not keen on producing the coins of her enemy. Eventually, however, some coins were minted. Superficially, they resembled the Spanish coins. On one side was the royal coat of arms; on the other they were adorned with a portcullis. The experiment was not a success. As there were various forgeries of the Spanish coins about, people in the East proved reluctant to accept the new coinage. For its future expeditions, the Company ensured that somehow or other it found enough Spanish rials.

The four ships of the East India Company – and a supply ship that was subsequently discarded – sailed in 1601. All returned successfully from Sumatra and Java in 1603. Lancaster's own ship, the *Red Dragon*, which had been named *The Scourge of*

Malice by its previous owner but had been renamed to reflect the peaceful intent of the expedition, lost very few men. Lancaster had dosed them against scurvy with lemon juice to great effect. It took nearly 200 years for this treatment, which would have saved countless lives, to be adopted by the Royal Navy. The other three ships lost over a third of their complement. Overall, the expedition was judged a resounding success. It brought back 500 tons of pepper. It had also captured the cargo of a large Portuguese ship loaded with riches from India. However, neither this expedition nor the one that followed actually went to India. The Indonesian archipelago, with its cloves and nutmeg as well as its pepper and cinnamon, was seen as a better source of profit.

India was finally selected as one of the destinations for the Company's third expedition. Its main task was to collect spices from the eastern islands, but it was also instructed to investigate the market for English woollen goods in exchange for spices at Aden. In addition, it was to assess the possibility of buying textiles in India to exchange for spices in the Far East. Its three ships left England in 1607. The *Consent* left early and caught the trade winds. The *Dragon*, captained by the expedition commander, William Keeling, and the *Hector*, captained by William Hawkins, missed the wind and lost six months as they were blown to Brazil and then back to West Africa. There, while they waited for a good wind to round the Cape, Keeling's men gave performances of *Hamlet* and *Richard II*. In the Indian Ocean, the winds for Aden were unfavourable. It was decided that the *Dragon* should go directly to the East and the *Hector* go to India.

Hawkins, whose background is not known with any certainty, investigated the trade potential of India with great zeal against formidable obstacles. He sailed the *Hector* to Surat, the largest of the Mughal ports, anchored offshore on 24 August 1608 and took rowing boats up river to the town. The administrator of Surat was in league with the Portuguese and seized the English goods. He also allowed the Portuguese to capture two of the English boats and send some of their crews to Goa as prisoners. The *Hector* sailed for the East, leaving only Hawkins and his companion, William Finch, behind. The two of them tried to get recompense for the seized goods and permission to trade, but without success. The Portuguese tried to kill them. Unbowed, William Hawkins then recruited a bodyguard of Pathans and travelled 700 miles to Agra to plead directly with the Mughal emperor.

At the beginning of the seventeenth century, the Mughals controlled a huge portion of India. Their empire stretched from Persia in the west to Bengal in the east; from the Himalayas in the north to the River Godavari in the south. It was still expanding southwards. When Hawkins arrived at Agra, the Mughal throne had just been inherited by Akbar's son, Jahangir. The two men became very friendly and drank together. Jahangir found Hawkins an Armenian Christian wife and offered him a post at court. At first Hawkins was promised trading privileges at Surat. However, his position was later undermined by jealous Mughal officials and Portuguese priests, and finally by the arrival of some drunken English sailors from a wrecked Company ship, the *Ascension*, who had 'made themselves beasts and soe fell to lewd women that in shorte time manie fell sicke'.

Hawkins was in Agra for over two years but left without any concessions for the Company. At Surat he met up with another English expedition, under the command of Sir Henry Middleton, which had also failed to open trade with India. Hawkins joined Middleton when he left for Java in February 1612. In the East, some five years after relinquishing his command, Hawkins met up with his old ship, the *Hector*. It was about to sail for England, together with the *Solomon* and the *Thomas*. Hawkins and his wife embarked on the *Thomas*. On the voyage home, illness erupted and most of the crew died. The ship limped home but William Hawkins died off Ireland.

Hawkins's Armenian wife subsequently married Gabriel Towerson, the captain of the *Hector*. The couple went back to India. When Towerson returned to England, she remained behind with her family and friends at Agra.

It took a display of English naval force to finally open trade with Surat – not against the Indians, but against the Portuguese. Thomas Best, commander of the Company's tenth expedition, sailed from Gravesend in February 1612 – the same month that Middleton and Hawkins had left Surat. His ship was the 600-ton *Dragon* and was accompanied by three smaller ships. They reached Surat in September. The Mughals seemed to be willing to reopen negotiations with the English. Best, keen to make an impression, landed together with a hundred of his soldiers, accompanied by drummers and trumpeters. A temporary firman, an official permission, was issued that allowed the English to trade for forty days. The emperor, they were told, might make this permanent, and they were invited to send a delegation to the court at Agra. Envoys were despatched, carrying a message from King James and loaded with presents. These included paintings of Venus and musical instruments. Some musicians also went to give tuition. One of them, Robert Trully, who played the cornet, became very popular with Jahangir. He stayed in India and converted to Islam. All seemed to be set fair until a Portuguese fleet arrived off Surat.

Venture Capitalists and Adventurers

Four Portuguese galleons and twenty-six frigates descended on Best's anchored fleet. However, though the English ships were smaller, they were better armed. More importantly, they were very easily manoeuvrable. The Portuguese relied on getting in close to grapple with the enemy. The English made quick forays, fired their broadsides, retreated, and then attacked again. Three of the Portuguese galleons were destroyed. The English then attacked another four Portuguese galleons that lay off the coast and forced them to flee. Seeing that the Portuguese were no longer masters of the ocean, on 7 January 1613 Emperor Jahangir confirmed that the English could trade from Surat. Furthermore, he allowed them to fortify their factory. Thomas Best left and much of the credit for the successful establishment of the factory should go to Thomas Aldworth, who stayed behind at his own request and became the Company's first president.

The Portuguese, however, had not yet been vanquished. In 1615 they attacked the English fleet at Surat. The English fought from the shallows, where the Portuguese galleons were at a disadvantage. It was said that 500 Portuguese men were killed and only five English before the Portuguese fled.

Surat was not the Company's first trading post in India. Between 1608, when its first ship had arrived in Surat, and 1613, when it was given permission to establish a factory, there had been a success on the east coast. The Dutch had begun to trade there in 1606. Two disaffected Dutch traders approached the East India Company with a plan to establish an English presence there too. In 1611 the Company was granted permission for a factory at Masulipatam, a busy port on the Coromandel Coast in the

Sultanate of Golconda. It became an important source for the Company's trade in textiles.

In 1615, William Keeling, the amateur producer of Shakespeare's plays, led a Company expedition to India and the East. Invested with the title of commander-in-chief, he was keen to expand the activities of the Company. He sailed down the coast of India, periodically exchanging fire with Portuguese ships. In March 1616, while off Cranganore, he was intercepted by an emissary of the Zamorin of Calicut. The Zamorin, who was preparing to attack the Portuguese fort at Cranganore, offered to give the Company trading rights at Calicut in exchange for assistance and an agreement was concluded. Keeling left behind four men and a twelve-year-old boy to establish a factory. They had a stock of trade goods – tin, lead, cloth and half a ton of an aromatic gum captured from the Portuguese. They also had a stock of gunpowder. One of the men was a gunner and he would show the Indians how to operate the small cannon Keeling had given to the Zamorin.

The factory – the first English factory on the Malabar Coast – did not prosper. When Keeling sailed away, the Zamorin, disappointed with the amount of help he had received, failed to supply spices. A year later, when the fleet returned from the East, three of the men were taken away. A man and the boy were left behind to learn the language. The man soon died of dysentery; the boy, Edward Pearce, would, twenty-five years later, start the Company's trade at Basra.

While the English attacked the Portuguese at sea, other Portuguese were lobbying the Mughal emperor. He had provisionally agreed to ban trade with the English when an English ambassador who had travelled out with Keeling arrived at the Ajmer court.

Sir Thomas Roe had been sent out by James I, who had renewed the Company's charter on a more permanent basis in 1609, at the Company's expense to negotiate with Jahangir. Besides being active at court, Roe had business interests and was on the council of the Virginia Company. Both his grandfather and his uncle had been Lord Mayors of London. Roe arrived at the Mughal court at Ajmer in 1616. He had brought many presents, to the delight of the emperor. These included an English carriage, which Jahangir used and had copied. During Roe's three-year residence, the Company sent more gifts – including alcoholic beverages, which Jahangir was extremely fond of. Two English mastiffs became hugely popular with the emperor. One was extremely fierce and attracted Jahangir's admiration when it attacked an elephant. Jahangir gave each dog four servants – two to carry them around in palanquins; two to fan off flies. Meanwhile, the Portuguese offered more expensive gifts, including a ruby-like gemstone that weighed five ounces, to marginalize the English. Jahangir continued to allow the English to trade from Surat, but baulked at signing the formal treaty Roe desired. More depressing for Roe, the emperor also met a Dutch delegation and gave them equal rights to the English at Surat.

Despite his setbacks, Roe was a perceptive diplomat and was able to offer the Company much valuable advice. They should, he advised, only resort to force on the seas. He had seen the massive military strength of the Mughals as he accompanied Jahangir and 200,000 followers across India. He realized that the Company could not hope to challenge the Mughals on land. Roe pointed out that although the Portuguese had many soldiers and many forts, this had not resulted in their making large profits. Similarly, that the Dutch, who were bent on conquest, had found that the cost of their armed forces absorbed all their gains. Roe strongly advised 'that if you will profit, seek it at sea, and in quiet trade; for without controversy, it is an error to affect garrisons and land-wars in India'. The Company heeded his advice and followed it to their advantage for most of the following century.

Four

THE ENGLISH

SPLENDOUR AND DISEASE

The English East India Company esteem it necessary, as well for the honour of the English nation, as facilitating of their traffick, to maintain their principal servants in India, not only in decency, but splendour.

John Ovington
A Voyage to Surat in the Year 1689

In London the East India Company's establishment had, of course, grown from the original one-and-a-half employees. Nevertheless, it was kept very modest, much of the work still being done by the Company's directors. The Company finally moved out of Sir Thomas Smythe's house in 1621. It then moved to its own premises in Crosby House in Bishopsgate, part of which it had already been using as a warehouse. However, when in 1638 the lease expired, it moved back into the private house of its governor.

The employees, in London and abroad, were governed by very strict and comprehensive rules. Every person, from the treasurer to the beadle, had his duties exactly described in the 'Lawes and Standing Orders' of 1621. Apart from describing what accounts and reports were required, it laid down instructions for the searching of staff that handled stock, the locking of hatches during the dinner break and it even directed the surgeon general to make sure that he cut everybody's hair once every forty days.

Portuguese control of the Arabian Sea – the sea route that carried the trade between India and the markets of Arabia, Turkey and much of Europe – was finally destroyed at Ormuz, the fort at the mouth of the Persian Gulf that had been built by Albuquerque. The Company's factors at Surat had always been keen to open trade with Persia. In 1618 the first Persian silks exported from the Company's new trading posts in Shiraz and Isfahan reached Surat. In 1620 there was an inconclusive naval battle off the Persian coast between the English and the Portuguese. In 1621 the Shah of Persia, irritated by Portuguese attempts to gain a monopoly over his country's exports, sent an army to dislodge the Portuguese at Ormuz. However, since Ormuz was an island and the Persians had no proper navy, this failed.

A Company fleet of four ships, commanded by John Weddell, arrived off Ormuz at the end of 1621. Weddell had qualms about siding with a Muslim power against a Christian one, especially one that the English were supposed to be at peace with. Moreover, he had no authority to attack Ormuz. The Company in London was anxious to avoid expensive military adventures and had ordered its employees to confine their activities to profitable commerce. Not for the last time, their man on the spot ignored these strictures. Spurred on by promises of trading concessions for the Company and of booty for himself, Weddell 'resolved to invite our enymies to a banquet of fire flying bullits.'

First the English and Persians took Quism, a nearby island that the Portuguese used to obtain fresh water from. Weddell then ferried the Persians to Ormuz to besiege the fort. The English went into battle against the five Portuguese galleons, while the Persians mined the fort's walls. After two months of fighting and ravaged by disease, the Portuguese surrendered.

For a few more years there were sporadic battles between the English – sometimes in alliance with the Dutch – and the Portuguese. However, the capture of Ormuz combined with Dutch victories over the Portuguese in the East had effectively brought the years of Portuguese rule over the Indian Ocean to an end. In 1633 the English and the Portuguese declared a truce, which opened up Goa and the other Portuguese bases to English merchants.

———•———

There was, and still is, a perception in Europe that Mughal India was a land of plenty. The tales by travellers about the wealth of their rulers, about their chests of jewels and their marble palaces, obscured the reality that the vast majority of the population were poor people living in a badly managed economy. It was true that the Mughals had brought a measure of peace to their domains and that this had benefited the populace, but their system of governance was seriously flawed.

The land of India usually belonged to the cultivator. He was entitled to sustenance from it, but only for the bare necessities of life and nothing more. All 'surplus' produce was subject to seizure by the government. This was effected by either taking the produce itself or a cash equivalent. In theory, one-third of the crop might be demanded. In practice, as a result of corruption or greed, the amount taken usually varied between one half and two-thirds. Most foreign travellers in Mughal India who have left us a record were appalled. As the Dutch senior factor, Francisco Pelsaert, reported in 1626:

> The land would give a plentiful, or even an extraordinary yield, if the peasants were not so cruelly and pitilessly oppressed; for villages which, owing to some small shortage of produce, are unable to pay the full amount of the revenue-farm, are made prize, so to speak, by their masters or governors, and wives and children sold, on a pretext of a charge of rebellion. The rich in their great superfluity and absolute power, and the utter subjection and poverty of the common people – poverty so great and miserable that the life of the people can be depicted or accurately described only as the home of stark want and bitter woe.

The income from some land went directly to the emperor. The revenue from most land, however, was used to reward a small class of nobles, officers and administrators in return for providing troops and service, with the income from a number of villages. To stop these men from forming any close bonds with the villagers, which might possibly lead to a rebellion, the ownership of these villages was regularly changed every two, three or four years. As a result there was no incentive for the receiver of the revenue to make any improvements to his villages or the land. Even worse, often they farmed out by auction the right to the revenue, which led to an even greater oppression by those who had secured the rights by high bids. Moreover, there was no incentive for the

Mughal officials to invest their incomes in anything else that was productive since, when they died, their wealth could not be passed on to their families but it reverted to the emperor. With their money, the Mughals were great patrons of art and architecture, poetry and dance. However, except possibly under Akbar, they did virtually nothing to improve the economy of India or the life of its common people.

Probably the best account of life and work in the Company's service in India in the first half of the seventeenth century was written by Peter Mundy. Born in Cornwall, about 1596, he was the son of a pilchard merchant. He went to a local school; then when he was only twelve, his father sent him to France to learn the language. Three years later he became a 'cabin-boy', a type of apprentice, to a captain who travelled the Mediterranean visiting English factories. Subsequently, he spent four years in Spain as a factor and in learning the language. He then went for four years to Constantinople. He returned home overland in 1620 and began to write the observations and diaries he was to continue for the rest of his life. He was a competent draughtsman and made drawing of such people, animals, plants and buildings that took his fancy. In 1627:

> Desirous of imployment, as also to see forraigne Countries, I came to London againe, where I found entertainement of the honourable Company of English Merchants trading for East India, to proceed thither in their next shipps.

He had been engaged for five years at an annual salary of £25 and arrived at Surat in September 1628. Just before he landed, a collection was held in aid of the Company's alms house for the old and maimed recently established at Poplar in east London. Mundy, happy to have survived the journey, generously donated £3. For the next two years, he was employed as a 'writer' – a clerk. In 1630 it was decided to transfer him to the Company's factory at Agra to be the accountant and second in command. Together with his junior John Yard, he left Surat on 11 November. For protection, as the route was famously beset by bandits, they joined the caravan of '150 persons and about 15 or 20 carts with some cammells' of a Persian travelling to Burhanpur. This route took them due east to Burhanpur, before striking almost north to Agra.

It was a time of terrible drought and famine. Close to Surat, some women were selling their children for twelve old pence or less. On the way to Nandurbar a few miles further on 'all the high way was strowed with dead people, our noses never free of the stinck of them, especially about townes; for they dragg them out by the heeles starke naked, of all ages and sexes, till they are out of the gates, and there they are lefte, soe that the way is halfe barred upp'. When they reached Nandurbar, they 'were much troubled to finde a room convenient for our little tent, by reason of the number of dead bodyes that lay scattered in and about the towne. Att last wee tooke up our lodginge amonge the tombes'.

They stayed on in Nandurbar the next day, where they were assailed by a 'most noysome smell' that they eventually tracked down to a pit full or corpses. Mundy was shocked 'to see the poore people scrapeinge on the dunghills for food, yea in the very excrement of beasts, as horse, oxen, etts, belonginge to travellers, for grain that perchance might come undigested from them.'

When the caravan left the following day, it was joined along the way by many wanting to escape the famine – at least 1,700 people and 250 carts, together with oxen and buffaloes. When they reached Nimgul they found food for themselves and their horses, although the streets were full of the dead. On 27 November they reached Yaval, where there were fertile fields of sugar cane and fruit. Next day they were in Navi – 'Heere in the middle of the bazaree lay people new dead and others breathing their last with the food almost att their mouthes, yett dyed for want of it, they not haveinge wherewith to buy, nor the others so much pittie to spare them any without money'.

The caravan reached Burhanpur on 30 November. By then there was less sign of the famine. Mundy had been instructed to collect some money owed by the Raja of Bundi for a tapestry the Company had sold to him, but the raja was away. Mundy and Yard were now leaving the Persian's caravan behind. It took them several days to buy camels for their own journey onwards.

Mundy and his party left for Agra on 6 December. They had no trouble buying provisions and, despite having lost the Persian's protection, were not troubled by thieves. The fields were full of corn and they saw huge caravans of oxen, at least a mile-and-a-half long, taking provisions south to the Mughal armies.

On Christmas Day, a messenger arrived from the chief of the Company's factory at Agra with a letter inquiring about their welfare. For dinner – 'the cheifest dish boare the name of a peece of rostbeefe (because this day of all dayes it is most in request), but the trueth is, it was a peece of buffalo, both hard and tough, a sufficient tryall of our jawes and stomacks; but for our better digestion wee added a cupp of sack, of what was left us, and therewith remembering our friends'.

Next day they travelled on to Dongri. On the way, they met two Dutch merchants going to Surat with a caravan of 800 camels carrying saltpetre and indigo. Before the caravans passed in opposite directions, the Dutch gave them dinner. On 30 December Mundy reached Gwalior. He was greatly impressed with its massive fort and made a sketch. On 1 January 1631, the caravan crossed the Chambal River and safely navigated its famously bandit-ridden ravines – 'for there might lurke many thousand, and wee never the wiser'.

On 3 January 1631, Peter Mundy and his companions finally reached Agra. The chief of the Company's factory, William Fremlen, and his colleague went out to meet him. Soon afterwards they were joined by the chief of the Dutch factory and they all went together to the emperor's garden. Mundy relaxed at the English house for the next two or three days, where he met with various Dutch merchants and also with an Italian and a Frenchman.

Mundy calculated that on the eight-week journey he had covered 551 and a half miles. Having arrived safely, he wrote –'God's holy name be praised for our preservation to this place.'

We have no account of Mundy's first year in Agra. Towards the close of 1631 he went on a month-long expedition, north of Agra, to Koil and Shergarh to buy saltpetre, an ingredient of gunpowder and one of the Company's main exports, and indigo. At Koil, Mundy passed through a mango grove where the headless bodies of thieves hung upside down. The heads of the decapitated thieves were displayed in many small towers into which they had been cemented. Mundy made a sketch of these. Around the town there were also many bodies on stakes. He commented on the cruelties of the Mughal officials, who employ Hindus 'taking from them all they can gett by their labour, leavinge them nothinge but their badd mudd walled ill thatched howses, and a few cattle to till the ground, besides other misseries.'

Mundy took a short break from his business travels to see the River Ganges. As it was the dry season, it was only half a mile wide. He took a boat across but swam back. At Koil he weighed and packed up indigo. Then he proceeded to Shergarh to collect 400 bundles of saltpetre, before returning to Agra.

At Agra, Mundy witnessed the construction of the Taj Mahal – 'this Kinge is now building a sepulchre for his late deceased Queen Tage Moholl. He intends it shall excell all other.'

In August 1632, Peter Mundy made another foray from Agra. This was a seven-week journey east to Patna. The Company had a surplus of mercury and vermilion at Agra that it was keen to dispose of. Mundy was of the opinion, correctly as it turned out, that prices would not be better at Patna. He was also instructed to buy and sell cloth in the Patna region, but he doubted there would be sufficient time to do it profitably. Nevertheless, he welcomed the opportunity to see more of India.

From Agra, Mundy's eight ox carts followed a line just north of the River Jumna to Banaras. It was an area that had recently been plagued by bandits. These had been put down by a Mughal force of 20,000 foot soldiers and 12,000 horsemen. Many towns had been destroyed, their women and children enslaved and their men beheaded. Mundy saw another 200 towers into each of which had been cemented thirty or forty heads. At Ghatampur he was annoyed by the smoke from a fire being used to cook on by some of his Hindu carters. He took up a tent pin and threw it at their pot. Because his hand had indirectly defiled their food they gave the food to their oxen. Mundy had to hand them money to buy more. There were heavy rains and the poor road was pooled with water and badly pitted. Time after time the carts would get stuck. On the way they met with a caravan of 14,000 oxen carrying grain to Agra and then another of 20,000 oxen laden with sugar.

At Allahabad, where the River Jumna had joined the Ganges, Mundy's eight carts had to wait for boats to cross the now three-quarter-mile wide river. Once they had crossed, there was a thunderstorm, which left them struggling knee-deep in water. Twice they were stopped by bandits and Mundy had to make a small payment to proceed. At Banaras, Mughal officials threatened to commandeer Mundy's carts. These too had to be bought off. Mundy then went ahead of his carts to find accommodation at Patna. The caravan arrived three days later, forty-four days after leaving Agra.

Peter Mundy then set to business. As he had expected, he had little success. Finding the price of mercury and vermilion to be low he sent a messenger to Agra for instructions. Told to sell them at whatever he could get, he sold them at a loss. The cloth he acquired in the surrounding area was also sold at a loss. It eventually transpired that his superiors had sent him to the wrong place for the cloth and should have sent him to Samana, north of Agra. Mundy did, however, accumulate some information of future value to the Company. He made inquiries and compiled a list of ports on the Bengal coast. He also made a list of commodities at Patna that could be profitably exploited.

On the return journey he found Banaras ravaged by an epidemic that had resulted in nine out of ten 'dead or fledd'. Further on, the Mughals had been fighting rebels. The roads were guarded by soldiers and many towns had been destroyed. Mundy came across a mango orchard with fifty or sixty men's heads hung up by a string through their nostrils. The towers he had seen earlier had been augmented by another sixty with thirty-five or forty heads apiece. At Etawah he saw these towers being built from a 'great heape of heads lying by'. On 22 December, Mundy and his men reached Agra. It must have been a grave disappointment to him to find that the caravan he was supposed

Splendour and Disease

to command had already left for Surat. This meant he would not catch one of the ships returning to England at the beginning of 1632. He would have to wait for another year.

After two months in Agra, during which he saw the wedding festivities of two of the emperor's sons, Peter Mundy was placed in charge of the last caravan of the season to Surat. It consisted of 268 camels and 109 carts loaded with indigo and saltpetre and left on 25 February. The route was completely different to the one he had taken when coming — this time he was to go west to Marwar and then down south through Gujarat to Surat. It would be a three-month journey fraught with difficulties.

It began easily enough, for William Fremlen accompanied him for the first week. They joined together with the caravan of the arriving governor of Gujarat, which gave them protection but was difficult to keep pace with. Mundy was able to visit and marvel at the abandoned Mughal city of Fatehpur Sikri. By the side of the road near Bayana he saw the staked bodies of 300 rebels. Two of his carts then broke down, one in the river, and some of the indigo became damp. Fremlen returned to Agra, leaving Mundy on his own.

After Fremlen left, Mundy had an awful time. His carts continually broke down and he was unable to keep up with the governor's caravan. One of his men was killed by thieves. The drivers of the carts and the camel men started a feud – 'draweing their swords and wounding each other'. Mundy mistook some customs men for thieves and after one was 'misused', one of Mundy's men was killed. As a penalty, Mundy also had to pay double the normal transit duty. The roads, which were often lined with dead men on stakes, were very poor. On 28 April, two factors from the Company's factory at Ahmadabad rode out to meet Mundy's caravan, which arrived in the city the next day.

Mundy spent two weeks in Ahmadabad. He was impressed by the bazaars and streets – 'very large, faire and comfortable' – but they had been depopulated by the recent famine. He met with the Company's three other English merchants and also with a Lieutenant Smith and fifteen Englishmen who had transported money from Surat to the factory. He was also introduced to a number of Dutch merchants. When he went to pay his compliments to the newly installed governor, a large sum was extorted from him for the brief period of protection his caravan had received when it had left Agra.

Mundy left for Surat on 15 May. On the way to Baroda the caravan was stopped several times by armed bands and Mundy had to pay them off. At Broach he met two Company officials, one of whom was the John Yard, whom he had originally set out with. The area had been devastated by famine and disease. Barely one person in ten was still alive.

On 25 May 1633 Mundy entered Surat. What should have been a happy occasion for him must have been terrible. Of the twenty-one Englishmen he had left behind, only seven had survived. Of those seven, three more died soon afterwards. Business was almost at a standstill – 'there being scarce one man able to write or sett his hand to paper'.

Peter Mundy stayed at Surat until early the following year. As there was such a shortage of staff, he spent most of that time supervising the loading and unloading of the Company's ships. He sailed for England on 1 February 1634. Mundy would return the next year in very different employment.

The truce with the Portuguese that had been effected in 1633 should have heralded an expansion of the Company's trade in India, but the Company became fully occupied in fighting off a threat from another rival – an English one.

The Company's troubles had begun in 1630 when the rains and harvest in western India had failed. The next year there was an exceptionally violent monsoon and much of the crop was carried away by flood. Typhoid was rampant. In May 1631, when Peter Mundy was in Agra, a Dutch merchant returned from a visit to the interior:

> When we came to the city of Surat we could hardly see any living persons, where heretofore were thousands; and there is so great a stench of dead persons that the sound people that came into the town were with the smell infected, and at the corners of the street the dead lay twenty together, one upon another, nobody burying them. The mortality in this town is and hath been so great that there have died above 30,000 people.

These calamities brought trade to a standstill. The Surat factory went into serious deficit. The finances of the Company had also been affected by a dramatic fall in the price of pepper as the competing powers stepped up exports to the European markets. There was a feeling in London that the Company was not making the best of its monopoly. In 1635, Charles I reneged on the promises in the Company's royal charter. He licensed an associate of Sir William Courten to:

> Range the seas the all the world over to make prize of all such the treasures, merchandizes, goods, and commodities, which to his best abilities he shall be able to take of infidels, or any

other prince, potentate or state not in league with us beyond the line equinoctial.

This was clear encouragement to piracy – piracy that could jeopardize the East India Company's relationships in Asia. It was also authorization to compete in the Company's markets. The Company protested vigorously but to no avail. Not only had Courten advanced large sums of money to Charles I, but the king had also invested £10,000 of his own in the enterprise. The threat to the Company was particularly serious since Sir William Courten was an experienced shipowner who had made a vast fortune in Europe and the Americas.

Courten's first expedition justified all the Company's fears. Two ships were despatched to Aden. One was wrecked, but the other, captained by William Cobbe who flew Royal Navy colours, captured two Indian ships. One of these ships belonged to a prominent merchant in Surat. In order to find what money was on board, they took the captain:

> Bound both his hands and tied match to his fingers, which burnt them unto the bones; and then he confessed where the money laythen they burnt the nakhuda [captain], the boatswain, the merchants and the carpenters, until they were nearly dead, and confessed all they knew.

This had serious repercussions for the Company in Surat. Their president was arrested by the governor and thrown into jail. He finally bought his way out. A Company ship managed to capture the pirate ship in the Comoros Islands. Some stolen money and jewels were recovered and returned to their owners. William Cobbe escaped and returned to England with £40,000, which was never recovered. Nevertheless, the Company's actions convinced the Mughal authorities that it was not responsible for the misdeeds and its privileges were reinstated.

Courten then formed a new association, which received a royal warrant to trade in areas of the East controlled by Portugal. He recruited several able men who had been in the Company's service, but had become disaffected. The Courten Association bought four ships and two supply vessels and put them under the command of the hero of Ormuz, John Weddell. This fleet sailed for the East in April 1636. Sir William Courten died soon after and his son William took over as the head of the Association. The ships arrived in Goa in October.

One of Weddell's men was Peter Mundy. A year in England had been enough for him and he had joined the expedition less in the expectation of making money than for his love of travel. Mundy was somewhat obsessed with calculating the distances between the places he visited and usually recorded them in some detail. He later estimated that between 1611 and 1647 he had travelled 100,833 miles and 5 furlongs. Weddell and Mundy stayed in Goa for over three months 'finding nothing butt delaies, faire wordes and breach of promises'.

Mundy had plenty of time to look at Goa. He was impressed by its streets, churches, castles and forts built when they were 'drawing all trade from all parts into their owne handes to their incredible benefitt'. But he could see that times were changing – 'their prosperous estate much abated by the coming of the English and Dutch.' The Dutch were currently blockading Goa. They had the better of a naval battle just before Weddell's expedition sailed south.

In February 1637 Weddell landed at Bhatkal, between Goa and Mangalore, on the Malabar Coast. Peter Mundy and a colleague travelled inland for four days to Ikkeri to secure permission from the ruler to establish a factory at Bhatkal. With their mission accomplished, they returned to Bhatkal only to find that nearly eighty of their companions had died of fever. Surprisingly, fifteen men then volunteered to remain behind to establish the factory.

Weddell sailed east to Sumatra where he set up another factory. He then sailed for Macao and Canton, becoming the first Englishman to trade directly with the Chinese. In March 1638 he returned to Bhatkal to find the factory deserted. Of the original fifteen men, eight had succumbed to disease. The second in command had murdered the chief factor and two other men, and then fled to Goa with the Association's goods and money. Weddell re-established the Bhatkal factory. He sailed with two heavily laden ships from Cannanore for England in 1639. Both ships completely disappeared, presumed wrecked. Peter Mundy, with his usual luck, was on one of the other ships. He survived, returned safely to England, and twenty years later, made another voyage to India.

Later in 1639, the ruler of Bhatkal, under pressure from the Portuguese viceroy, withdrew his permission for the Association to trade. The factory, which had cost so many lives, had to be abandoned. The establishment was moved to a new site fifty miles south of Goa, at Karwar. The Association also began to trade a hundred miles north of Goa, at Rajapur. This last action particularly infuriated the East India Company's officials at Surat, for they had already started trading at Rajapur, and would now be in competition with the Association. They need not have worried, for the Courten Association was now in serious financial difficulties. The loss of Weddell's ships and their cargoes was a serious blow. Although some further expeditions were sent out to the East, the Association no longer had sufficient resources to trade effectively.

In 1641 William Courten began negotiations to relinquish the Association's privileges in return for compensation from the

East India Company. These negotiations dragged on for years without agreement. The Association's finances became even more precarious. It was rumoured the Association was minting counterfeit coins at a base in Madagascar. In 1649 – under a new management, for Courten had fled his creditors – the Association gave up the struggle and was amalgamated into the East India Company. It had been a disastrous enterprise, which had lost huge sums. Nevertheless, it had founded settlements on the west coast of India, settlements that could now be exploited by the East India Company.

There was a sequel to the closure at Bhatkal. Alexander Hamilton, who came out to India in 1688, and over the next thirty-five years commanded local ships and marines, wrote of an incident there. This story has never been satisfactorily corroborated but, as Hamilton is generally fairly reliable, it is difficult to imagine that it was entirely made up:

> The English Company had a factory there: but about the year 1670 an English ship coming there to lade, had a fine English bulldog, which the chief of the factory begged of the captain. After the ship was gone, the factory, which consisted of eighteen persons, were going a hunting, and carrying the bulldog with them; and, passing through the town, the dog seized a cow devoted to a pagod [temple] and killed her. Upon which the priests raised a mob, who murdered the whole factory; but some natives, who were friends to the English, made a large grave, with an inscription, that this is the burial place of John Best, with seventeen other English men, who were sacrificed to the fury of a mad priesthood, and an enraged mob.

Surat in the seventeenth century was a large town with perhaps 150,000 or 200,000 inhabitants. It lay on the banks of the River Tapi, ten miles from the sea. The lower reaches of the river, which rose 400 miles to the east, were heavily silted. At exceptionally high tides it was possible for large ships to sail up the river to the edge of the town. Normally, however, they had to anchor at a small port protected by a sandbar, which lay to the north of the Tapi's mouth – Swally Hole.

The dominant feature of the town was its fort. This had been built in 1540 to give protection against the Portuguese who had sacked Surat in 1530. It had high stone walls with a tower at each of its four corners. The river guarded one side and a ditch flooded with water from the river protected the other sides. There were streets of small shops, but most trade was carried out in the large open market situated close to the castle known as Castle Green.

Surat had many impressive mosques. There were also a number of Jain shrines. Many of the Hindu temples, however, had been defaced by Muslim invaders. Visitors were impressed by a number of large gardens and parks, and especially by the Gopi tank, an artificial lake intersected by stone walkways. There were a small number of large residences, occupied by the Muslim officials and the principal merchants from all communities. Many of the affluent non-Muslim merchants, however, lived in simple houses so as to avoid extortion. The mass of the population lived in shacks. These were located in separate neighbourhoods divided by religion and occupation. Sanitation was appalling. Everywhere smelled of 'want of privies, and their making every door a dunghill'.

There were many slaves, mostly from Mozambique and Madagascar. Most were employed by wealthy Muslims, but the Europeans also owned a few slaves, either as servants or bodyguards.

Splendour and Disease

There are a number of descriptions of Surat and of English life there in the seventeenth century. A German diplomat, Johann Albrecht von Mandelslo, visited Surat in 1638. Life inside the Company's factory, Mandelslo wrote, was very disciplined:

> The respect and deference which the other merchants have for the president was very remarkable, as also the order which was observed in all things, especially at Divine Service, which was said twice a day, in the morning at six, and at eight at night, and on Sundays thrice. No person in the house but had his particular function, and their certain hours, assigned them as well for work as recreation.

During the day, tea was drunk; in the evenings, wine. On Friday evenings, however, those that were married met to drink to their absent wives' health – 'Some made their advantage of this meeting to get more than they could well carry away, though every man was at liberty to drink what he pleased, and to mix the Sack as he thought fit, or to drink *Palepuntz*, which is a kind of drink consisting of *aqua vitae*, rose-water, juice of citrons and sugar.'

The day started with prayers in the chapel. The gates of the factory would then be opened for business. From noon to 4 p.m. there would be a break for the factors to eat together and to rest. Business would then resume until 8 p.m., when the factors would return to the chapel for evening prayers. The gates were closed by 11 p.m., after which the rule that no one was allowed in or out was strictly enforced.

It can be imagined what a scandal was caused in 1649 when a factor, Joshua Blackwell, following the Company's Sunday morning prayers, went to the governor of Agra 'before whome hee most wickedly and desperately renounced his Christian faith and professed himself a Moore, was immediately circomsised, and is irrecoverably lost'. He, of course, left the Company's service. A year later, however, Blackwell repented and begged for forgiveness. He made his way back to the Company at Surat where he was readmitted as a Christian. To avoid retribution by the Muslim population he was kept hidden and quickly sent back to England.

Surat was the focus of numerous caravan routes that brought goods from its hinterland. Vast numbers of oxen, camels, donkeys and humans carried merchandise from the interiors of India. Moreover, numerous small ships and boats ferried commodities from the other ports on the western coast.

Surat was also a conduit for goods coming from the East and from Arabia. Goods from China and other countries in the East arrived via Java and Sumatra – porcelain, tea, sugar, copper, mercury, gold and ivory. From Arabia and Persia came drugs and coffee. Some spices were transhipped from Malabar, but the main business from India was in textiles. Gujarat produced huge quantities of silks and embroideries. Fine cloths also came from Agra and other northern districts, as well as from south India. The Company exported at least 50,000 pieces a year. There was also a lively trade in indigo, precious stones and opium. The Company employed the services of a number of intermediaries. Some of these came from the trading communities of Armenians and Parsis who had long been important at Surat.

The Parsis had been in India for many centuries. They were descended from Zoroastrians who had left Persia after the rise of Islam. They are believed to have initially settled at Sanjan, about seventy miles south of Surat, in the eighth century. Later they migrated to other centres, including Broach and Surat. In the middle of the seventeenth century, they became prominent in commerce at Surat. A Parsi was the principal merchant of Broach and had ships trading along the coast and also to Basra. In 1650 the Company appointed his son, Hira Vora, as their broker at Surat. The Armenians had settled in India even earlier. Armenians had arrived with Alexander the Great. They reached the Malabar Coast in the eighth century from where they exported spices. In the seventeenth century the Mughal emperor had invited the Armenians to settle in Agra. They then spread to other Mughal towns and to Surat. The Company transacted major deals with them. Armenians were even placed in charge of the cargo on Company ships going to England.

Profits on international trade were enormous. Rather than ship goods directly back to Europe, it was much more profitable for the European companies to take merchandise, mainly textiles, to the Far East. They would sell them there and then buy goods to take either directly back to Europe, or to sell at Surat, where they would buy more stock to take on to Europe. It has been calculated that £100 worth of goods purchased at Surat might sell for £300 in the Far East, which might then be used to purchase merchandise that eventually sold for £900 in England.

The Dutch were the great rivals of the English at Surat. They maintained a factory of similar size and competed for trade. They had conquered much of the Indonesian archipelago and obtained a monopoly over their spices, which were much in demand at Surat. This gave them an advantage over the English throughout the seventeenth century and they made bigger profits. The French set up a factory in Surat in 1667. It never rivalled the English or the Dutch in size or profit. From the beginning it was wracked by internal disputes and extravagance, and it closed twenty-five years later.

There were Indian merchants at Surat who traded on an enormous scale. Some transacted more business in the seventeenth century than the European companies. Abdul Gafur was the most prominent of the Muslim merchants. In a single year he could send out twenty ships of 300 or 400 tons. As well as trading inside India, he conducted business in the Red Sea and the Far East.

The most important businessman the East India Company dealt with was an Indian from the Jain community, Virji Vora. From about 1619 to 1675 this merchant and financier bought and sold huge quantities of merchandise. He exchanged gold and silver imported by the Company into local currency; he established a monopoly to buy the Company's imports of coral; he sold the Company spices and textiles from Malabar. He also became the Company's banker. In England it was believed that if large quantities of gold or silver were exported to buy foreign goods, the currency would be devalued. As a consequence bullion exports were closely controlled. As the Company's trade expanded it began to rely on loans from Virji Vora to finance its purchases. By 1669 the Company owed him and his associates Rs 400,000. Without his support their business would have collapsed. In addition to this, Vora also made private loans to the Company's men. This indebtedness enabled Vora to negotiate very favourable terms in his dealings with the Company itself and to make vast profits.

The Company at Surat had set up a number of subsidiary trading posts – at Cambay, Broach, Baroda, Ahmadabad and Agra. From Agra the Company's men travelled as far as Lahore to make purchases. Normally, they used an Indian agent, a *gomasta*, as an intermediary. These were often wealthy moneylenders who advanced money to the weavers in return for their output. This, of course, gave them tremendous power to impose a monopoly and dictate the purchase price. As was to often happen in the future, the large purchases made for the European market did little to improve the standard of living of the artisans who manufactured the goods.

The Reverend John Ovington visited Surat in 1689 for two years and was the Company's chaplain. He left an informative and entertaining account of life in the Company's factory. The president and his factors lived in style. Their building – the latest in a series of tenancies – was leased from the emperor at a rent of £60 a year, but they were allowed to use most of this to improve the facilities. To avoid upsetting the Muslims, the chapel was kept plain and had no religious images. The factory had accommodation for forty warehouses, extensive cellars, a pool and even a Turkish bath. Sumptuous communal meals were provided at Company expense with choice meats and generous quantities of Shiraz wine and arrack punch. There were cooks from England, Portugal and India 'for the gratification of every stomach'. The diners could also purchase European wines and English beer – both very popular. All the plates and drinking goblets were of solid silver.

On Sundays and holidays, and when entertaining important Indian merchants or officials, the main meal was more elaborate, with as many as sixteen courses. There would be venison, peacock, hare and partridge; apricots, plums, cherries and pistachios. Toasts in European and Persian wines would be drunk to the king, the Company, the president, and then going around the table to everyone seated there. In the evening the factors would proceed to the gardens against the river to 'spend an hour or two with a bottle of wine, and cold collation'.

A similar, if simpler, collegiate life would have been observed at the Company's other factories. Originally, the Company insisted on its merchants being single. Over the years this rule was relaxed, especially for the senior ones. Nevertheless, many remained bachelors, such as Francis Breton, president of the

Company at Surat, 1644–49. There is a Latin inscription on his tomb that reads:

> Here lies Francis Breton, who, after he had discharged his duties with the greatest diligence and strictest integrity, went unmarried to the celestial nuptials, on July 21st, 1649.

Naturally, there were illicit liaisons with Indian women outside the factory. This was very much frowned upon in the early years. A chaplain, William Leske, had an affair with a sweeper woman in 1616. He also used a whip on some Indian brokers and was expelled. Later, however, it would become common for the Company's men, if not the clergy, to imitate their neighbours and maintain a zenana, a harem. Meanwhile, away from the watchful eyes of the Company's seniors in Surat, it was possible to taste prohibited pleasures. Johann Albrecht von Mandelslo went from Surat to Baroda. 'We went to the lodge belonging to the English where they made the greatest entertainment imaginable.' He was in German clothes rather than the local dress adopted by the English. The English sent for some local women, who wanted Mandelslo to take them off, 'but perceiving that I was unwilling to do it, and withal that I made some difficulty to accept of the profers they made to strip themselves naked, and to do anything I would expect from their sex and profession, they seemed to be very much troubled, and so went away'.

The first known 'marriage' of an Englishman in the Company's service to an Indian was uncovered in 1626. John Leachland had arrived in Surat in 1615 as a purser's mate and been taken on as a factor. He satisfactorily conducted business for the Company at various centres in Gujarat and further east. In 1626 the death of a child of his by a woman named Manya led to his liaison being discovered. The president and council of the Company at Surat entreated him to give the woman up. Leachland steadfastly refused, saying that he would prefer to be suspended rather than abandon her and left the Company's service.

In 1632, the Company, having lost many of its staff to disease, re-engaged Leachland. He was still with Manya and they had a daughter, Mary. Leachland commanded a caravan to Agra and returned safely to Surat, but died there in 1634. On his deathbed, he requested that his wages be given to his wife and daughter. He also asked the Company to ensure that the girl, who had been baptized, be brought up as a Christian. The Company at Surat wrote to London recommending that Leachland's dying requests be granted and, meanwhile, gave the mother and daughter an allowance. London did not approve and the allowance had to be withdrawn.

The Company's employees at Surat, however, continued to support the nine-year-old girl and her mother. An uncle in England tried to obtain custody of the child, but her mother refused to give her up. In 1643, when Mary was eighteen, her mother applied to the Company for permission for her to be married to William Appleton, a tailor at Surat. This ceremony was duly conducted by the Company's chaplain. Even after the marriage, the Company's employees at Surat continued to give charity. They also continued to plead with London for the release of John Leachland's unpaid wages.

———•———

There were penalties for those who broke the rules of the Company at Surat. Failure to return before the gates were shut incurred a fine of £2; absence from prayers on a Sunday five shillings, or half that on a weekday; swearing one shilling; being drunk two shillings and six pence; for striking or abusing persons not in the Company's service 'three days imprisonment in irons'. These were severe penalties to a young man coming out to India at a salary of £20 a year. Gambling was a dangerous occupation for it could result in being sent back to England and being dismissed. Nevertheless, there were cases when men lost several years' salary playing cards or dice. One man lost £1,000 in a single night.

The Company's president at Surat in the mid-seventeenth century received a generous salary of £500, plus an even more generous allowance for entertainment. His colleagues received much less – from £150 to the accountant down to £20 for the young 'writers'. These salaries were only half that of their counterparts in London. It was understood, however, that they could make extra money on their own account. The Company tried to limit this by giving each man a fixed amount of free cargo space on its ships – as much as they could stuff into a chest four feet by eighteen inches by eighteen inches. But there were other opportunities for the Company's men to enrich themselves. They could surreptitiously buy on their own account, using middlemen, and then sell on to the Company at an inflated price, or even sell to the Dutch or the Portuguese. The directors in London imposed fines on those it discovered who 'devour the Company's fruits'. Many of their men in India paid the fines and continued regardless.

The Company at Surat employed remarkably few Englishmen. In 1618 there were only six, and two of those were youths. By 1674 the total was still only twenty-eight. Nevertheless, every effort was made to give the impression that the Company was a rich and powerful agent of a rich and powerful nation. When, for instance, the president and his entourage went on a picnic, they went in formal procession. Two large flags, bearing the cross of St George, led the way. Following the standard-bearers would be a troop of cavalry, their horses decked in velvet and silver. Forty or fifty foot guards then accompanied the palanquin of the president and his wife. Behind them, the members of the council and their wives rode in open coaches, drawn by milk-white oxen and accompanied by men with silver-topped staves. And behind them the coaches or horses of the factors, all dressed in their finery.

The English, unlike the Portuguese, had no wish to become involved in military adventures. They wished merely to trade in peace. The Company deliberately employed men of the merchant class rather than aristocrats or gentry who might have been inclined to use arms. It was not, however, a peaceful time, for the power of the Mughals in western India was being challenged by an audacious Hindu raja, Shivaji. This brilliant commander captured his first Mughal fort in 1647 and by 1660 had captured forty more. In 1661 he plundered the Company's factory at Rajapur. In 1664 he attacked Surat and destroyed most of the town. In 1670 he attacked Surat once again. On both of these occasions, the Company managed to avoid being overrun, but their trade was seriously affected. Meanwhile, the Company had acquired land at both Madras and Bombay. It was to those places that the Company would look to expand its activities.

Five
THE ENGLISH

Religious Freedom and Peaceful Trade

My endevours at present beeing to draw hither as many merchants (Banians as well as Moores and Persians) as possibly as I cann from Suratt, Cambaya, Ahmadavad, Boroach, Diu, Tahtah, etc., other places; unto whom His Majesty will but graunt liberty to buyld their pagados and mesquitas to exercise theyr religion publiquely in, noe doubt then but this will bee made a very famous and opulent port.

Henry Gary, secretary of Bombay to
Charles II's Secretary of State, 1665

On the east coast of India, the Coromandel Coast, the Company had established itself in 1611 at Masulipatam. It had discovered, however, that the textiles most in demand were obtainable cheaper further south. In 1639 they received an invitation from the ruler of the area, Damarla Venkatappa Nayak, the Lord General of Carnatic, about Madraspatam village to trade from there. The ruler was to receive half the customs dues. Francis Day was able to conclude an agreement to not only build a factory, but to fortify it against possible attack by the Portuguese or the Dutch. He chose a strip of sand at a point between the mouth of a river and the sea. It was three miles long and one mile wide. This was the first significant piece of land to be owned outright by the Company in India – for at Surat and other places they were merely tenants. It was not sovereign territory for it was held as fief of the ruler. Nevertheless, the Company was able to impose many of its own laws within the enclave. In 1647 the area was captured by the Sultan of Golconda who allowed the Company to carry on its operations undisturbed. The fort was about a hundred square yards, with a bastion at each corner. The first bastion was constructed in 1640, but completion of the fort, named Fort St George, took some years. The factory was in the centre.

The new settlement was immediately successful. It was staffed with about thirty-five English and an equal number of Indians. The Company actively pursued a policy of religious tolerance. Catholic Portuguese from nearby San Thomé were persuaded to settle around the fort with offers of employment. Other Portuguese from along the coast were given loans to build houses for themselves. Most important of all, several hundred families of Indian weavers immigrated. Together, these groups established the township that would come to be known as Madras, now Chennai.

The Company had originally divided its operations into two presidencies: Surat and Bantam. Surat controlled activities north of Goa; Bantam controlled those in the Far East and the rest of India. In 1652, following the seizure of most of its Far Eastern business by the Dutch, the Eastern Presidency was transferred to Madras.

Madras grew apace. By 1670 there were 300 English, 3,000 Portuguese and perhaps 40,000 Indians. John Fryer, a surgeon with the Company, visited in 1673. He described an 'English Town' of clean streets lined with mansions, faced with Italian-style porticos and topped with battlements and terraces. The Indians lived outside, in the 'Heathen Town' with its long streets, bazaar and temple. The Company's governor lived in style. He had a personal guard of 300 or 400 Indians, with another 1,500 in reserve. 'He never goes abroad without fifes, drums, trumpets, and a flag with two balls in a red field; accompanied with his council and factors on horseback, with their ladies in palenkeens'. There were Company judges who were able to impose the death sentence, although not over the English. The Company had also established a mint for its own copper and gold coins.

Madras had a reputation for loose morals and drunkenness. There were the usual strict rules debarring those housed within the fort from leaving at night once the gates were closed. These did not stop the young Englishmen from exiting by the windows and scaling the walls. Charles Lockyer visited in 1704 and wrote of the soldiers in the New House – the 'scene of many a drunken frolick. Everyone keeps his boy; who, tho' not above ten years old, is procurer, and *vallet de chambre.*' In 1676 the Company's chaplain had written back to London:

> Your heads would be fountains of water, and eyes rivers of tears, did you really know how much God is dishonoured, his name blasphemed, religion reproached amongst the Gentiles, by the vicious life of many of your servants. Some come over under the notion of single persons and unmarried, who yet have their wives in England, and live here in adultery; and some on the other hand have come over as married of whom ther are strange suspicions they were never married.

Religious Freedom and Peaceful Trade

Others pride themselves in making others drink till they be insensible, and then strip them naked and in that posture cause them to be carried through the streets to their dwelling place.

The chaplain may have been slightly mollified when, four years later, the first English church to be completed in India was consecrated. Behaviour, however, seems not to have improved. The Company introduced a temperance rule:

No one person shall be allowed to drink above a half a pint of arrack or brandy and one quart of wine at one time, under a penalty of one pagoda upon the housekeeper that supplied it, and twelve fanams upon every guest that exceeded that modest allowance.

At the end of the seventeenth century, the 'English' civilian population of Madras and the rest of the Coromandel Coast was estimated as to be 119 men and seventy-one women. Of the forty-seven 'English' wives, twenty-six were indeed English, but there were also fourteen Portuguese, four of mixed Portuguese and Indian blood, two French and one Georgian. The rest of the women consisted of fourteen widows and ten 'single English young women'. Together with the soldiers the total 'English' population was still only about 400. The non-European population had, however, grown prodigiously. Lockyer estimated that by 1704 there were 300,000 in the 'Black Town'.

Slaves were commonplace in Madras. Not only were they kept by Company employees, but the Company itself purchased them for its own use. There was also a thriving export business. The accounts show that in the month of September 1687 no fewer than 665 slaves were exported.

In 1683 the Company wrote to Surat and Madras:

> His Majesty hath required of us to send to India to provide him one male and two female blacks, but they must be dwarfs, and of the least size you can procure; the male to be about 17 years of age and the female about 14. We would have you, next to their littleness, to choose such as may have the best features, and to send them home upon any of our ships, giving the commander great charge to take care of their accommodation, and in particular of the female, that she be in no way abused in the voyage by any of the seamen.

Following the death of Charles II in 1685, the Company countermanded the order, which had been intended for the king's mistress, the Duchess of Portsmouth. She had prudently departed for France.

The Company's main export business from Madras was in textiles. It imported lead and tin. It comes as no surprise to learn that there was also a good market for imports of wine, beer in casks and bottles, cider, spirits and cherry brandy.

Bombay was given to the English by the Portuguese. The Portuguese had first invaded the islands in 1509: 'Our men captured many cows and some blacks who were hiding among the bushes, and of whom the good were kept and the rest were killed'. Bombay was not, as it is now, the tip of a large island, but a group of seven islands. These would eventually be linked together by causeways. The spaces around and between the islands would be filled in so as to more than double the original area of land. The islands had been ceded to Portugal in 1534 by the ruler of Gujarat in exchange for help against the invading Mughals. The Portuguese did very little with their acquisition. They destroyed a few temples and built a few churches. Later in the sixteenth century, Garcia d'Orta, whose dead body would be tried by the Inquisition, was given a lease over the main island where he built a manor house.

Charles II married Catherine of Braganza, daughter of the king of Portugal, in May 1662. The treaty of marriage, drawn up the year before, provided for the transfer of the port and island of Bombay to the English king. The English had some previous knowledge of the island. In 1626 an Anglo-Dutch fleet, pursuing some Portuguese ships, had received information that they were refitting at 'a hole called Bombay'. They hurried there only to find that the Portuguese ships had already departed. In revenge they 'left the great house, which was both a warehouse, a friary, and a fort, all afire, burning with many other good houses'.

Charles II moved quickly. Two months before his marriage he sent out a fleet of five ships under the command of the Earl of Marlborough to gain possession. A farce then ensued. The Portuguese said that they would only deal with the commander of the English troops, Sir Abraham Shipman. Unfortunately, Marlborough had left Shipman behind in England. When he eventually arrived, the Portuguese found some defect in his commission. There was then a dispute as to which islands were a part of the dowry. Marlborough returned empty-handed and a diplomatic dispute ensued.

The Hindus of Bombay were anxious for the English to succeed. Tired of Portuguese oppression and confident that the English would give them religious freedom, they sent a Brahmin priest to Surat and offered their support should the English decide to take Bombay by force.

The viceroy at Goa, seeing the potential value of Bombay, was reluctant to hand it over and opened up a correspondence with the king of Portugal. Shipman moved his troops to Anjadip Island, just south of Goa, where 300 of them died of malnutrition and disease. Shipman also died. His commission was left in his will to his deputy, Humphrey Cooke. At first the Portuguese disputed the legality of this, but eventually agreed to deal with Cooke. There was a protracted wrangle over the islands near Bombay. Cooke finally secured six of these islands and the whole transfer was finally made on 18 February 1665.

Bombay was a disappointment. As Samuel Pepys wrote in his diary: '... but a poor place, and not really so as was described to our king'. There was a Government House that had some fortifications, a few defensive towers to repel pirates, some coconut plantations and a few houses and churches. There were some in the East India Company, however, who saw that Bombay had potential as a harbour. It was also a place, unlike Surat, where the Company would not be beholden to an Indian ruler. Charles II, seeing that Bombay had no revenue and was expensive to garrison, was happy to give it to the Company. He was further encouraged by a loan of £50,000. On 27 March 1668, Bombay was handed to the Company for an annual rent of £10.

The following year Gerald Aungier became the Company's president at Surat and also governor of Bombay. He immediately began to develop the islands and for three years from 1672 lived permanently at Surat. He set up law courts and established a mint. He improved the fortifications and established an effective navy.

Religious Freedom and Peaceful Trade

From the beginning, the Company was keen to persuade Indians and foreigners from Surat to move to Bombay. A senior Company official at Bombay had written to Charles II's Secretary of State urging a policy of religious tolerance:

> My endevours at present beeing to draw hither as many merchants (Banians as well as Moores and Persians) as possibly as I cann from Suratt, Cambaya, Ahmadavad, Boroach, Diu, Tahtah, etc., other places; unto whom His Majesty will but graunt liberty to buyld their pagados and mesquitas to exercise theyr religion publiquely in, noe doubt then but this will bee made a very famous and opulent port.

There were many Hindus, Jains, Parsis and Armenians inclined to leave Gujarat. Emperor Akbar had come to the Mughal throne in 1556. During his long reign many of the inequalities imposed on non-Muslims had been put right. He had brought religious tolerance and abolished the *jizya*, the hated poll tax on non-Muslims. His benign reforms had largely continued under his successor, Jahangir. Shah Jahan succeeded him in 1627. At first he seemed to have followed in his father and grandfather's footsteps, but he gradually became more zealously Muslim. In 1632 he ordered the destruction of newly built Hindu temples. Nevertheless, there was still a good deal of religious tolerance in Mughal India. More toleration than in many Muslim countries; more than in most of the countries of Europe.

Shah Jahan's son, Aurangzeb, was a religious zealot. Unfortunately for the Gujaratis, in 1645 his father had appointed him governor of Gujarat. He made life difficult for non-Muslims and desecrated Surat's main Jain temple, which was turned into a mosque. In 1658 Aurangzeb was proclaimed emperor. He imprisoned his father and eldest brother, and had another brother beheaded whom he regarded as an infidel. His forefathers had forged alliances with the Hindu princes of Rajasthan. Aurangzeb attacked them and set off a chain of wars that would last until the end of his long life. He ruled for nearly fifty years, until 1707, and left his empire ruined. Moreover, he undid years of religious tolerance and left a legacy of religious conflict that carries down to this day. He reimposed the hated jizya. Constant warfare and the high taxes to pay for them unsettled the majority Hindu population. In addition there was much oppression by Muslim local officials.

In 1667 the Company at Surat wrote to London that Aurangzeb's religious zeal 'hath greatly disturbed the whole kingdome'. He 'gives himselfe wholy upon the converting, or rather peverting, the Banians etc., and pulling down the places of their idolitrous worship, erecting muskeets [mosques] in their roome.' It added that if a Muslim were asked to repay a loan from a Hindu he would threaten to report him for insulting the Prophet and, if that happened, 'the poore man is forced to circumcission and made a Moore'. Naturally, this oppression by Aurangzeb encouraged non-Muslims to move to the sanctuary of Bombay.

The Company's attempts to draw people from Surat to Bombay enraged Aurangzeb. His governor at Surat wrote to the Company to protest and he threatened the expulsion of the English from the Mughal Empire. The merchants of Surat were summoned one by one, and made to sign a declaration that they had not been approached by the Company. The most senior Armenian, Kawaka Minas, demurred and upon being pressed, produced an invitation to settle in Bombay signed by the deputy governor. The Company pretended it had nothing to do with it and that the Armenian had probably 'invited himself first'. This had severe repercussions on the business enterprises of Kawaka Minas and his community. When he wrote to the emperor to complain, he was 'beaten with slippers and staves until they had almost killed him'.

Nevertheless, the stability that ensued from Aungier's wise rule, together with the Company's policy of religious toleration, enabled him to attract many merchants of all religions to Bombay. Armenians came, as did the Parsis who were given permission to build a fire temple inside the fort. Importantly, many weavers came too. These came not only from Gujarat but also from the country south of Bombay, which had a long tradition of fine weaving. The income they generated enabled Aungier to put Bombay's finances in good order.

Less successfully, Aungier arranged for some English women to be sent out. He was mainly concerned to prevent the English from forming relationships with women who had Portuguese blood and who would then convert their men or their children to Catholicism. Some of the women sent out from England soon found husbands for, as the Reverend John Ovington later noted, 'a modish garb and mien is all that is expected from any women that pass thither, who are many times match'd to the chief merchants upon the place, and advance thereby their condition to a very happy pitch'. However, as might have been expected, not all of these women were well behaved and they were instructed to 'apply themselves to a more sober and Christian conversation otherwise the sentence is this that they shall be confined totally of their liberty to goe abroad and fed with bread and water till they are embarked on board ship for England'. The experiment was soon terminated.

Most of the English had slaves. Some were Africans acquired from Arab traders and some were Indians. It was the fashion to own young slaves from Malabar – the women to have girls and the men to have boys.

The Company's courts administered justice in Bombay. The sentences were severe. Whipping was the usual punishment – either at the pillory or behind a cart. This might be augmented by time in prison or work on the sea defences. Even when the punishment was over, the stigma could remain for all to see, since the culprit's cheeks were often branded. Both men and women were whipped. Normally, mindful of the biblical injunction 'forty stripes he may give him and not exceed', the maximum number of lashes was thirty-nine. Those found guilty of witchcraft were also severely punished. A woman who was accused of using charmed rice to cure the sick was given eleven lashes. In 1671 a man was discovered with a teat on his arm and accused of being a wizard. Found guilty by a jury, he was handed over to the military to be hung. The soldiers felt he should experience a 'greater terror', and burnt him. They recorded their surprise 'that when he lay in the midst of so great a fire one of his arms quite burnt off yet notwithstanding his great knot of hair on his head, and his clout betwixt his legs was entire though they perfectly flamed above an hour together.'

As the population of Bombay expanded, Aungier oversaw a programme of reclaiming the marshes and building new houses. He planned and laid out his 'city, which by God's assistance, is intended to be built'. By the time of his death in 1677 the population of Bombay had expanded tremendously. Some estimates put it as high as 60,000.

The East India Company had its own army in India and this often made up much of the population of its settlements. Until it became more professional in the middle of the eighteenth century, it was not an impressive fighting force.

Religious Freedom and Peaceful Trade

From the beginning, the Company had maintained a guard at its factories, but these were in territories over which Indians had sovereignty, such as Surat, and where the Indians had their own armies. The first real Company army was probably at Madras, on the east coast. At that fort, from about 1642, the Company maintained a small garrison of English and Indian soldiers. These were principally for protection against attack by the Portuguese or Dutch.

On the west coast, a separate army developed from the troops Charles II had sent out to secure Bombay. When the king transferred the island to the Company, he stipulated that the Company should maintain at its own expense three companies of infantry. Initially, this force was composed of the remnants of the royal army but soon, as disease took its toll, it was filled with Portuguese, French and Indians. Many of these soldiers were Indian Christians with Portuguese blood, known as topas*ses*.

Life as a soldier was hard. Disease was rife. The First Bombay European Regiment of Foot lost 100 men – about half their strength – from October 1675 to February 1676. The Company supplied their soldiers with regular English army coats – not ideal for the climate. Soldiers had to pay for these, but the Company complained that soldiers' deaths often left it out of pocket. Discipline was harsh. The usual punishment for insubordination was thirty-nine lashes. Sometimes, men were made to 'run the gauntlet', which involved running naked between rows of fellow soldiers and being whipped or beaten. In one extraordinary case, Sergeant Thomas Cross and Corporal John Powle were made to throw dice on a drum under the gallows. The loser was to die. Powle lost, but two priests begged the Company's president to show mercy and he was exiled. Not surprisingly, it was difficult to find recruits, especially Europeans. The Company had to take on runaway sailors, deserters from foreign armies and prisoners of war. They did not make good soldiers.

Two years after Aungier's death, Bombay suffered a series of setbacks and the population plummeted. The Mughal emperor, Aurangzeb, was still at war with the Maratha king, Shivaji. The Marathas had developed a considerable navy and Aurangzeb had enlisted the help of the Siddis of Janjira – a small independent state with many warships. Both sides tried to obtain the help of the Company against the other. The Marathas took over Khanderi Island at the entrance to Bombay harbour. When the Company asked the Siddis to remove Shivaji's men, they used the opportunity to take the nearby island of Underi for themselves. They left Shivaji's troops in control of Khanderi but, as a consolation, they brought the Company a basket of Maratha heads. The capture of the islands and the continual warfare between the two navies made the seas unsafe for trade.

The Company had its own ships. It had leased a dock at Deptford from 1607. As it was too expensive to buy ships on the open market, it started to build ships in 1609. In 1614 it purchased a dock at Blackwall, which could take ships of a deeper draught and tonnage. It set up foundries to make chains, anchors and nails; a spinning house to make a cord for rigging. It prepared its own salted beef and pork for the voyages from animals that were killed in the Company's own slaughterhouse. Gunpowder was often in short supply and difficult to find on the open market. Accordingly, the Company set up a plant of its own to manufacture this essential commodity for its ships' cannon. Building and repairing the Company's ships and these ancillary activities employed a workforce of 500. The Company also employed up to 2,500 seamen. However, temporary financial difficulties led to Deptford being sold in 1644 and Blackwall being put up for sale in 1650. From 1639 onwards the Company chartered ships to carry its cargoes. Many ships were owned by members of the Company, but many were not. They were often built specially for trade with the East – continually rechartered, so that they spent their entire lives in the service of the Company. All of them operated under the strict control of the Company and utilized the privilege in its charter that they be armed.

The ships were generally much smaller than the lumbering Portuguese carracks of 1,500 tons or more. Nevertheless, they were some of the biggest ships operated by the English and bigger than most sent to the Caribbean or North America. They ranged in size from 100 to 1,000 tons – the size of the nineteenth century *Cutty Sark* now moored at Greenwich – but typically they were from 300 to 600 tons. A 100-ton ship might have a crew of only thirty; a 600 ton ship perhaps 150. These crews were bigger than strictly necessary for the efficient management of the ships, but it was considered prudent to allow extra men for the expected deaths by disease. Smaller ships might have ten cannons; larger ones forty. The journey to or from India should have taken about six months if the winds were favourable. There would also be six months in India waiting for the wind to turn. So if all went well a round voyage might take eighteen months. However, many voyages took much longer. Departing at the right time of year to make the best of the trade winds was absolutely crucial. As one Portuguese captain observed about leaving for the East from Lisbon: 'The last day of February is time enough, but the first day of March is late.'

Finding crews for the ships was not always easy. In the early days of the Company under Sir Thomas Smythe, his excellent reputation and the relatively infrequent voyages posed fewer problems. However, even under his stewardship things were often difficult. The Anglo-Dutch wars of 1618–19 in the Far East cost the Company many ships and their crews. England always had an advantage over Portugal in that its population was five million as against the one million of Portugal. Later in the century, however, with many sailors being needed for the Americas and the Caribbean, good men were hard to come by. The problem became bigger in times of war, when the Royal Navy was desperate to recruit. The Company complained bitterly when the navy's press gangs invaded Company premises and took away sailors waiting to enlist on its voyages.

A happy ship needed to be well fed. The ships were stocked for a round voyage of eighteen months. Some fresh produce might last a week or two out of England or India, but for the majority of the voyage foods that would keep well were required. The mainstays were salted or pickled beef and pork, dried fish, dried peas and beans, and ship's biscuits. The meat allowance was very generous, at a pound and a half a day. Biscuits were an important item too, with each man receiving about a pound of them each day. The ingredient varied slightly – those on Richard the Lionheart's fleet in 1190 were made with barley, rye and bean flour – but basically consisted of flour, water and salt, mixed into a stiff dough and baked for about thirty minutes. Contrary to popular myth, they kept well and weevil-free if properly stored. At the National Maritime Museum at Greenwich there is one dating from 1784.

For an eighteen-month voyage, the amount of food to be stocked was prodigious. For a Company crew of 150 in 1607 there were thirty-four tons of biscuits, six tons of salt beef, twelve tons of pickled beef and sixteen tons of pickled pork. They carried lemon juice to ward off scurvy. Alcohol was deemed essential too. There were thirty-eight tons of beer, forty tons of cider, 4,500 gallons of wine and 150 gallons of spirits. Understandably, the Company instructed its officers to keep to the daily quota of food and drink, which could well be desperately needed in the future, and not waste it in 'riot and feasting'.

The London insurance market for shipping in the seventeenth century was surprisingly sophisticated. From 1629 the Company regularly insured its ships and their cargoes against loss. It also became common to insure against the possibility of an expedition not returning with its cargo within a specified time, typically two years. A premium of 5 per cent of the sum insured was normal, but this increased in times of war. In 1653 the Company decided to no longer insure itself and leave its individual shareholders to make their own insurance arrangements. For about £5, a shareholder would protect his £100 stake.

A good idea of life on the Company's ships can be obtained from the journal of Edward Barlow. Born near Manchester in 1642, Barlow grew up in a deprived household. His father was a poorly paid worker on the land and had six children. Barlow did odd jobs as a boy, on the land and in the coal pits. This enabled him to buy clothes to replace the rags that had previously prevented him from attending church. He left school at thirteen, after a very rudimentary education, for an apprenticeship in the bleaching of textiles. This he found uncongenial. He then decided, 'I had as good to go seek my fortune abroad as live at home, always in want and working hard for very small gains.' Through a relative's friend, he managed to gain a new apprenticeship, this time to the chief master's mate of a Royal Navy ship, the *Naseby*. He was serving on the *Naseby* when it brought back Charles II at the Restoration. He worked on other warships until 1662 and then moved to the merchant navy. He travelled to Portugal, Spain and Brazil. For several years he swapped employment between royal and merchant ships.

In 1672, on his second voyage for the Company, Barlow went to Java and Taiwan. Unbeknown to him, war had been declared between England and the Dutch Republic. Barlow's ship, the *Experiment*, was intercepted by a Dutch fleet and he was taken to the Dutch stronghold of Batavia on Java. He was confined there for a year. To occupy his time, he began to draw and write up a journal of his earlier voyages. Thereafter he kept up this journal of his travels until the end of his career. He was an extremely good draftsman. There are 127 coloured drawings in his manuscript – now at the National Maritime Museum at Greenwich. They are beautiful miniatures with highly accurate depictions of the ships portrayed, together with details of their armaments, rigging and flags. There are convincing action scenes with added vignettes of topography, fish, birds and animals. In addition there are fifty-five pencilled outlines of ports and coastlines – again highly accurate. The manuscript, full of details of work and personal life, has 225,000 words. The story of his first voyage for the Company – when he travelled to Bombay, Surat, Goa and the Malabar Coast – is a graphic account of a seaman's life in the seventeenth century.

Barlow made his first visit to the East as an ordinary seaman aboard the same *Experiment*. It was a 250-ton ship, with a crew of sixty and armed with twenty-two cannons, bound for India. It left England, together with two other Company ships, in March 1670 and arrived at Bombay in September that year. There were some women on board who had come out to join their husbands in the Company's service. To their great distress, several discovered that their husbands were already dead.

The *Experiment* took a few days to offload some of its cargo. Barlow noted that most of the people inside the fort were Indian Muslims or Portuguese – the Portuguese being paid the same as the English. He also described the 'strangely attired' Indians (presumably Hindus or Jains) outside the fort. Although they 'worship all manner of images, and the sun and the moon, yet they live very peaceable under the English, enjoying all their old customs and privileges'.

A week later the *Experiment* discharged the rest of its cargo at Swally, near Surat. The shore was lined with the booths and tents of the local merchants. One of these merchants was engaged by each of the crew to purchase what they had brought to India and to sell them what they would carry home. He described them as wearing long white gowns, tied around the middle with a sash, and wearing turbans on their shaved heads. 'Very cunning and subtle people in all their dealings … There is none of them that marries out of his own sect, neither will they eat anything which hath had life in it, nor kill the least thing, that is, neither a louse or anything that lives. They will neither eat nor drink with any stranger or other but of their own religion or sect. They are all buyers and sellers, and many of them are very rich, and they are apt to learn any language. Their children of six and seven years of age can speak English.'

The *Experiment* then sailed south to Goa. Barlow noted that although it had few commodities of its own, Goa's position and deep harbour made it a convenient place for trade. But, he added, since the Dutch had captured many of the Portuguese bases, there was little business being transacted. A laden ship went back to Portugal only every two or three years.

After leaving Goa, the *Experiment* continued down the coast to the Company's factory at Karwar, where it dropped off money and letters from England. Three days further south, it went up an estuary to the recently established Company base of Valapattanam. Some lead was offloaded for the Company to use in exchange for spices. Barlow bought some coconuts to take home to England as curiosities. He also wrote that the local people would not sell them cows, but that for a small sum 'you may buy their children'. One of the ship's men jumped into the water and disappeared, presumed to have been taken by crocodiles.

From Valapattanam the *Experiment* went south to Tanur and Ponnani in Kerala to load the pepper that had been bought by the Company's factors. At first the Indians were wary of them, thinking they were Dutch – 'for there are few in all East India of the country people but are fearful of them and cannot abide or love any of them, having been so abused and their goods taken from them in so many places'. The *Experiment* was hit by an unseasonable storm. Barlow, being highly superstitious and distrustful of foreign religions, imagined this was the result of the inhabitants 'offering up as sacrifice one of their sons or daughters to their God, the Devil, and that Hellish Fiend, being offended at something, caused him to raise such a horrible tempest'.

Coming back north, the *Experiment* called in at Calicut 'a few scattering houses, being destroyed by wars'. Prostitutes were available cheaply. Barlow was more shocked to see both men and women, some of the women heavily pregnant, wearing only a loincloth. They collected a Company factor who wanted to go to Valapattanam. They also took on board three Dutchmen who were deserters from the Dutch East India Company at Cochin. At Valapattanam they dropped the factor off and took on board the man he was replacing to carry him up to Karwar.

At Bombay the *Experiment* stopped to let off some Indian traders from Surat who had travelled down the coast with them. They also put the Dutchmen ashore, since they were fearful of being taken to Surat where the Dutch East India Company might capture them.

It took five or six days, against the wind, to go from Bombay to Surat. The whole journey, from Surat almost to the tip of India and back, had taken two months. Some of the pepper was offloaded and replaced with other cargo for England. Barlow made a small investment in stock to sell in England on his own behalf. The *Experiment* went back to Bombay where it picked up some passengers before it finally departed for England. They bought some hens and pigs, unavailable at Surat, for their voyage home. On 15 January 1671, Barlow watched India disappear from sight.

Accompanied by two other Company ships, the *Experiment* reached Mauritius in February. Further south, they ran into very heavy weather, which almost capsized the ship. The hold was filled with water five feet deep. They had to cut away one mast and some of their sails to upright the ship. The hens and pigs were swept away. The winds eased and they rounded the Cape. They made for St Helena, where the Company had a small fort. They stopped for ten or twelve days to make some repairs and take on provisions. Eight days later they were at Ascension Island, where they stopped to capture turtles to eat. These came ashore at night to lay their eggs, when they could be turned on their backs to stop them escaping. Barlow recorded that they weighed three or four hundred pounds and could be kept alive for three or four weeks on board ship, before being eaten or turned into soup. They also killed some sea birds, 'so tame that you may kill as many as you please with a stick or stone'.

From Ascension they were delayed by poor winds. They spoke to a French ship and learnt that everyone in Europe was at peace with each other except with the Turks, and with an English ship going to Barbados from whom they learnt that an attempt had been made to steal the king's crown from the Tower of London. Eventually they sighted Cornwall. A few days later, after a six-month voyage, they went up the Thames to Blackwall.

The *Experiment* and her two accompanying ships had each been carrying two or three spotted deer. These were a present from the Company's president at Surat to Charles II. Some had died during the stormy voyage. When the flotilla reached Blackwall, the surviving animals were taken away by the Keeper of St James's Park.

Between 1670 and 1703 Edward Barlow made nine voyages to India and the East. He rose to be chief mate. He often recorded his disappointment at not being made captain. He was probably not an easy man to get along with. In 1683 he had a fight with the captain of his ship when at Sumatra. He was put ashore and had to work his passage back to England. In 1692, whilst in India, he had severely caned a seaman for insubordination. The man had subsequently died. On the ship's return to England, his widow engaged a lawyer. Some of the dead man's shipmates supported her and, to avoid going before the courts, Barlow had to give her the huge sum of £50.

Barlow showed his better side when writing of his family. He was married in 1678 to the maidservant of a friend in London. Both were poor but 'had I married another woman with a thousand pounds, I could never have met with one more deserving my love and respect'. Two days after the marriage, however, he sailed for Jamaica. While he was away, his wife was caught in a house fire and miscarried. In 1695 their youngest child died of consumption. 'She was about three-and-a-half old, and a fine hopeful child, our griefs being multiplied, one grief followed another. But blessed be the name of the Lord, who then out of six had left us two children for it has been a sickly time in and about London, and smallpox very rife, of which distemper my child had her first illness.'

In 1705, Barlow was finally made the captain of an East Indiaman. Under his command, the *Liampo* left Portsmouth for the Red Sea. Before Barlow left, 'it being a long voyage and many accidents and changes may happen and knowing all men are mortal and death certain', he made his will, leaving everything to his wife and children. Off the Mozambique coast his ship was lost. Fortunately, his journal was not on board.

Over the years, many animals and birds travelled from India to England on the Company's ships. Most were presents to the monarch. In 1619 Sir Thomas Roe brought home two antelopes for James II. In 1631 John Weddell presented Charles I with a leopard and the queen with a cage of birds. At the Restoration, Charles II laid out St James's Park as a sanctuary for deer and constructed aviaries on Birdcage Walk. The public were given access to it for the first time. In 1661 some antelopes, pelicans and parrots were despatched from Madras for the park. In 1671 a caracal, a species of lynx, was sent to London. In 1676 two sarus cranes were well received at court – their extraordinarily loud voice when alarmed had made them useful as sentinels. Some animals were brought privately to England. In 1684 a rhinoceros was sold by some East Indies merchants for over £2,000. In 1513 a rhinoceros had been sent from India to the king of Portugal. It was this animal, somewhat different to the African rhinoceros, which featured in the famous engraving by Dürer. In 1694 one of the ships accompanying Edward Barlow on his voyage back from Madras carried a tiger.

As well as East Indiamen, the Company also used locally built ships in India. At Surat they either bought, or had specially built, vessels 'of 100 or 200 tons with roomy holds' carrying eight or ten small cannons for use against the 'Malabar pirates'. There were good shipyards in Surat, Broach and several smaller places. From 1635, after the conclusion of peace with Portugal, the Company also bought ships from the Portuguese or had them made in their fine shipyards. By 1640 the Company had a fleet of ships to carry cargos from other Indian ports to Surat for onward transmission to England. When the Company acquired Bombay they ordered that an armed vessel be kept in the harbour to protect shipping. A shipbuilder was sent out from London to supervise the Company's shipyards. Its first ships in India had used local crews. Soon afterwards, however, the Company had asked London for seasoned sailors who, it argued, would be more effective in fighting pirates.

The seas around India were plagued by piracy. Pirates had operated off the western coast from time immemorial. Pliny, writing in the first century AD, observed that there was an annual voyage to India 'with cohorts of archers on board the ships; on account of the pirates who infest those seas'. Marco Polo wrote about them in the thirteenth century. Ibn Batuta described a meeting with a pirate chief on the Malabar Coast in 1342. The opening up of the western seas to Europeans gave piracy a major boost. There were pirates from Arabia and from India itself, but the most dangerous pirates were European. Charles I had licensed various ships to capture vessels and the goods of any nation not friendly to England. Captain Quail had captured a vessel from Malabar. Captain Cobbe had taken two ships in the Red Sea, which had resulted in the Mughals imprisoning the Company's servants. Sir William Courten's enterprises, often bordering on piracy, had caused similar difficulties for the Company.

The execution of Charles I brought this phase of English piracy to an end. After the restoration of the monarchy, the English were preoccupied with the riches they could seize from the Spanish in the New World. In the 1680s the European pirates returned to plunder the Indian trade. In 1687 an English pirate raided a Portuguese outpost in the Persian Gulf, and an English marauder took ships in the Red Sea. The *Charming Mary*, an Irish pirate ship, was seen off Tellicherry. By 1689 the Company reported that it was being 'pestered with pirates'. Two Armenian-owned ships carrying large sums of gold were then captured – one south of Goa and the other just off Bombay. In 1691 a ship with Rs 900,000 on board was taken at Surat. The Mughal authorities stopped all English trade until it was shown that the Danes were to blame.

The most successful of all the European pirates, however, were English. Henry Every, also known as John Avery, turned to piracy in 1694. Born near Plymouth, he had served as an officer in the Royal Navy before becoming master of a merchant ship. He then became first mate of a ship on hire to the Spanish government, which was supposed to intercept French smugglers off Peru. The crews' wages went into arrears and Every led a revolt. The captain was seized, together with those who would not join the rebels, and put ashore. Henry Every and his men then set sail for Africa on *Charles the Second*, which they renamed the *Fancy*. It had forty-six guns and 150 men. Off the coast of Africa, they plundered and burnt five ships – two Danish and three English.

Henry Every established a base in Madagascar, famously a haven for pirates, and conveniently situated between Africa and India. Off the Horn of Africa he captured the *Futteh Mahmood*, which belonged to a prominent merchant of Surat. Later he sailed down towards Bombay and took Emperor Aurangzeb's own ship, the *Gunj Suwaie*. It was an amazing feat, for the *Gunj Suwaie* had eighty guns and 400 men with muskets. She was returning from the Red Sea with some female pilgrims, together with gold and silver worth Rs 5,200,000. For a whole week Henry Every and his crew ransacked the ship as they searched for treasure. The women were assaulted. Several of them committed suicide by jumping into the sea or by knifing themselves. The plundered ship was then left to drift.

Emperor Aurangzeb, enraged by this insult, directed his anger towards the Company. The Siddi army marched on Bombay. The president of the Company at Surat and sixty-two of his men were arrested, put in irons, and kept as prisoners for nearly a year.

In a mere six months Henry Every made his fortune in Indian seas and decided to retire. He sailed for the Bahamas, where he paid off his crew. He was believed to have returned to England. There are, however, no authentic records of what became of him, only fantastic rumours. Six of his crew were tried at the Old Bailey and given long jail sentences. Henry Every completely disappeared. He was immortalized in ballads, and in a play – *The Successful Pyrate*.

Tales of Every's wealth drew many more Europeans into Indian piracy. Some baulked at attacking fellow Europeans, but saw little wrong in robbing Asians. Others were not so scrupulous – the Company estimated that its losses from piracy at Surat alone were a million pounds. Such was the temptation that even the Company's own crews were liable to turn pirates. A Company ship, the *Mocha*, which was going from Bombay to China was captured by mutineers. They killed the captain, renamed the ship the *Defence*, and for three years brought more terror to the Indian Ocean.

Captain Kidd was perhaps the most notorious of all the English pirates, as much for the political implications of his actions as for the scale of his operations. The Company had asked the head of the Admiralty, Lord Orford, to send a naval force to India to put down the pirates. This he refused to do but, together with the Lord Chancellor, Lord Sommers, and the governor of New York, Lord Bellomont, he formed a syndicate to send a privateer against the French and the pirates of the Americas. The *Adventure Galley* – a thirty-gunned sailing ship that also had about thirty oars – was fitted out and put under the command of Captain Kidd. He sailed for New York where he took on more men. Then, totally ignoring the rampant piracy in the Americas, he set sail for Africa and the Indian Ocean.

At Mocha, the *Adventure Galley* opened fire on an Indian merchant ship, but fled when an East India Company frigate, which had been sent to protect the Indian fleet, appeared. On 29 August 1697, just north of Bombay, Kidd captured a small merchant ship from Surat. He took the English master, Thomas Parker, prisoner and forced him to pilot the *Adventure Galley*. They sailed into Karwar for supplies, flying the English flag, but the people there had already been warned. John Harvey, chief of the Company's factory there, demanded the release of Parker, but Kidd denied all knowledge of him. Before he departed, some of Kidd's crew deserted and informed on him. He then sailed for Calicut, but received no assistance there. He did manage, however, to capture a small Dutch vessel.

Early in 1698, Kidd captured the *Quedah Merchant*, travelling from Surat to Bengal. It had an English captain, but was owned by local Armenian merchants. The loss of its valuable cargo resulted in a demand for compensation by the Mughal authorities, both for the *Quedah Merchant* and for the other piracies. Eventually, the demands were dropped, but the European companies had to agree to make good any future losses. The Europeans at Surat then took joint action to suppress piracy – the Dutch would guard the Red Sea and the pilgrims en route to Mecca; the French would guard the Persian Gulf; the English would guard the southern seas.

In England the actions of Captain Kidd caused a furore. His financiers were leading Whig politicians and, although Kidd had misled them, the opposition were in full cry. In India, meanwhile, Kidd was joined by others. He eventually had five ships wreaking havoc along the south-western coast.

Having made his fortune, Kidd abandoned the *Adventure Galley*, which had become unseaworthy, and made for New York in the *Quedah Merchant*. He thought that he could, with some judicious presents, smooth matters over with the governor, Lord Bellomont – one of his original backers. There was, however, too much at stake politically for Bellomont to be accommodating. Kidd was arrested and sent to London. He was tried at the Old Bailey and found guilty of murder and piracy. In 1701, Captain Kidd and six of his crew were hanged at Execution Dock. His assets were seized by the government and used to purchase the land for Greenwich Hospital.

Kidd's activities prompted Parliament to pass new laws against piracy. Previously, pirates had to be brought to England for trial; now they could be tried anywhere by a court of seven lay persons. One of these had to be someone senior, such as the chief of a Company factory. These courts could impose the death penalty on both pirates and on those who assisted them. Four Royal Navy warships were sent to the Indian Ocean. Free pardons were offered to pirates who surrendered. These measures gradually brought the activities of European pirates on Indian seas under some control.

The Company's difficulties were magnified by the appointment in 1682 of John Child as president of Surat and governor of Bombay. Child, under pressure from London, embarked on a programme of cost cutting. He drastically cut expenditure on the garrison at Bombay. He not only economized on stores and munitions, but he also cut military and naval pay. This prompted a revolt, which was joined and then led by the commandant of the Company's garrison and navy, Richard Keigwin, whose own salary had been drastically reduced. The rebels declared the island under the protection of Charles II, and elected Keigwin as governor. John Child came from Surat to Bombay to negotiate, but the rebels refused to yield. Meanwhile, independent English merchants took advantage of the Company's loss of authority to trade on their own account.

The rebellion was finally settled when Keigwin surrendered to the king's representative in return for a free pardon for himself and for the rebels. The highly popular Keigwin was given a public farewell dinner, accompanied by gun salutes to the king, the queen and to each member of the royal family.

Bombay was returned to the Company. Surat – twice devastated by Shivaji and no longer considered safe – was in decline. Moreover, the Company at Surat were at the mercy of their landlords, the Mughals, whereas Bombay was sovereign English territory. It was decided, therefore, to move the Company's headquarters from Surat to Bombay. Child relocated to Bombay where he continued to cut expenditure and clamp down on his employees' private trade. Meanwhile, he lived in luxury and was loathed.

Puffed up by being made captain general, admiral, commander-in-chief of all the Company's forces, director general of mercantile affairs and being made a baronet, Sir John Child then completely overreached himself. Angered by some private traders doing business, he presented a long list of grievances to the Mughal governor at Surat. Receiving no reply, Child threatened retaliation. The enraged governor seized the Company's goods in Surat, imprisoned the Company's factors and offered a reward for Sir John Child, dead or alive. Child then raised the stakes by seizing dozens of Mughal merchant ships. These were taken to Bombay where their cargoes were confiscated. Child wrote to London, where he had the backing of the governor: 'Wee think of nothing less now than goeing briskly to worke and letting the Mogull and all his hungry courtiers know and feel the force of your armes.'

Not only did Child launch an attack on the Mughals, but he also captured a fleet of ships carrying supplies to the Siddis of Janjira.

The Siddis of Janjira were Africans. They were usually described as being from Abyssinia or Ethiopia, but given their prowess as sailors, it seems more likely that they were from the coastal areas of the Horn of Africa, from what is now Somalia and Eritrea. Many from that part of Africa came to India, either as slaves or as mercenaries. Several rose to high ranks in the armies of the Muslim rulers. The name Siddis may be a corruption of the Muslim title of respect, Sayyid.

There are several stories as to how the Siddis came to Janjira. Most accounts place the event as occuring towards the close of the fifteenth century. Most accounts also agree that there was already a fort built by the native Kolis on the island and that the Siddis were in the service of the Sultan of Ahmadnagar. Some stories describe a long siege, but the most romantic story describes trickery. In this, one Perim Khan and other Siddis came to Janjira dressed as merchants. They received permission from the Koli captain of the island to unload a shipment of large boxes said to contain silk and wine. They then plied their hosts with the wine until they were incapable, opened the other boxes, which contained soldiers, and took the fort.

Whatever the truth, the Siddis had turned Janjira into a formidable fortress. They had also built up a powerful navy. When Ahmadnagar fell to the Mughals they put their services at the disposal of the new power, the Adil Shahs of Bijapur. They received little help from Bijapur when Shivaji attacked Janjira; so they then transferred their allegiance to the Mughal emperor, Aurangzeb. He gave them Rs 400,000 a year to maintain their fleet and gave their leader the high title of Yakoot Khan. He and his successors became the admirals of a Mughal navy. They had also built up a large army.

Urged to show restraint by one of his own captains, Sir John Child declared that if the Siddi came to Bombay he 'would blow him off again with the wind of his bum'.

In February 1689 the Siddis arrived. They landed just north of Bombay's town and castle with an army of 20,000 men. The English had only a tenth of that number and they were commanded by a Captain Pean, whom a Scottish observer described as 'a fellow as well made for running as any I ever saw'. The Siddis soon occupied the island and began to lay siege to the English in their castle. A number of the Company's soldiers, probably with grievances against Child, defected to the enemy. They advised the Siddis as to how the walls of the fort could be undermined. Although the Company's ships did manage to bring in some provisions, supplies began to run low. Meanwhile, the Siddis increased their army to 40,000.

The English bowed to the inevitable. Emissaries were sent to the emperor to ask for mercy. In February 1690 Aurangzeb relented:

> All the English having made a most humble submissive petition, that the crimes they have done may be pardoned, that they would present the Emperor with a fine of 150,000 rupees and out of his princely condescension agrees that the merchants' goods be returned, the town flourish, and they follow their trade as in former times, and Mr Child, who did the disgrace, be turned out and expelled.

Rather conveniently, before this message reached Bombay, Sir John Child died.

The restoration of the Company's privileges by the Mughals did not immediately result in the restoration of its fortunes. Bombay went into decline. The English population had dramatically decreased during the conflict – from 700 or 800 to only sixty – and it failed to recover for many years. There were two main reasons for this – the competition from English trading outside the Company's control and disease.

Bombay had a terrible reputation for disease and mortality. In all the Company's outposts, gluttony, excessive drinking and venereal disease took their toll, but Bombay seemed especially unhealthy. John Fryer, a doctor in the service of the East India Company, visited Bombay in 1673. He was impressed with the pomp that surrounded the Company's president:

> At meals he has his trumpets usher in his courses, and soft musick at the table: if he move out of his chamber the silver staves wait on him; if down stairs, the guard receive him; if he go abroad, the Bandarines and Moors under two standards march before him.

Fryer, however, had no wish to stay:

> But for all this gallantry, I reckon they walk but in charnel-houses, the climate being extremely unhealthy whence follows fluxes, dropsy, scurvy, barbiers (which is an enervating the whole body being neither able to use hands or feet) gout, stone, malignant and putrid fevers, which are endemial diseases: among the worst of these, fool rack [arrack]and foul women may be reckoned.

Similarly the Reverend John Ovington, who visited Bombay in 1690, declined an offer to become the minister, citing:

> My predecessors, one of whom was interred a fortnight before this time, and three or four more had been buried the preceding years: which common fatality has created a proverb among the English there that *two mussouns are the age of man.*

Ovington was wise to be nervous. Twenty-four Europeans had arrived on his ship in May; by the time he left in the September, twenty had died.

Despite the spectre of death, many of the English failed to make wills. When they died intestate the Company sold their effects.

The lists of contents make a fascinating read. Some of the effects of one Ambrose Thompson, presumably a doctor, give a glimpse into Bombay life and death in 1701:

> A box of medicines and instruments
> A pair of pistols
> 9 waistcoats
> A pallenqueen
> 3 wiggs
> 28 neck cloths
> 18 shirts
> A parcel of stockings
> 1 microscope
> A bible
> A slave boy
> A carboy of Portuguese wine
> 48 gallons of Clarrett

The slave boy sold for about the same amount as the parcel of stockings and somewhat less than the waistcoats.

Six
THE PORTUGUESE

Terror, Luxury and Decay

At the beginning of the sixteenth century, Gujarat was probably the most important trading centre in India. Broach, at the mouth of the great River Narmada, was its principal port and market. From there, goods were despatched to the Indian interior, southern and western India, Arabia, Central Asia, Europe and to the Far East. At the beginning of the century, much of the pepper and other spices of the Malabar Coast, and from the Far East, had been taken north to Gujarat for sale. When the Portuguese took control of the spice trade in Malabar and the East, and shipped directly to Europe, Gujarat's trade suffered. Nevertheless, with its access to the routes into northern India and Arabia, Gujarat was still a major business centre.

The Gujaratis were considerable shipowners. Moreover, the Gujarati merchants regularly travelled on business to Arabia and the Far East. In other parts of India where trade was mostly in the hands of Hindu merchants, these were inhibited by the Hindu prohibition on 'crossing the black sea'. Hindus who did travel were liable to be ruined by being expelled from their caste. In Gujarat, not only were there many Muslims who were, of course, free to travel, but also many well-off Hindus who had converted to Jainism. To become a Jain was perfectly acceptable to most Hindus since they regarded the Jains as a Hindu sect. Moreover, they were much admired for their belief in the sanctity of all life. Naturally, adhering to such a belief meant the Jains were unable to indulge in warfare, a common occupation of upper-caste Hindus. The Jains were free to focus their energies on moneylending, banking and trade. Moreover, their religion had no restrictions on travel, so they were able to conduct business abroad. Both the Jains and the Muslims established themselves as major overseas traders.

The Portuguese, having secured domination over Malabar, wanted to gain control over Gujarat too. Their first opportunity came in 1533, when the Mughals attacked Gujarat. In 1534 the ruler of Gujarat entered into a pact with the Portuguese to resist the Mughals. In return for their help, he gave them the district of Bassein and its dependencies, including the islands that would eventually become Bombay. The Portuguese greatly strengthened the existing fort at Bassein and built many more. Two years later, they managed to obtain the island fort of Diu. The Gujaratis tried to reclaim Diu in 1538 and again in 1546. The later siege was an epic battle. The governor of India (later viceroy), João de Castro, commanded the Portuguese relief. From Bassein, he sent one of his commanders on a preliminary foray to intercept any ships taking supplies to the enemy. This he did with great savagery. The mutilated bodies of the men he killed were cast into the mouths of the rivers so that they would drift up to the towns as a warning of Portuguese vengeance. When the commander returned to Bassein, the yardarms of his ships were decorated with the hanging bodies of sixty Muslims.

It needed all the naval and military resources of the Portuguese to raise this siege of Diu, which could well have terminated their attempts at domination, but they prevailed and massively extended the fortifications. The reprisals after the second siege of Diu were savage. The governor told the king of Portugal that he had sent a commander with twenty ships to:

> Burn and destroy the whole coast, in which he very well showed his diligence and gallantry, because he caused more destruction of the coast than was ever done before, or ever dreamt of, destroying every place from Daman up to Broach, so that there was no memory left of them, and he butchered everyone he captured without showing mercy to a living thing. He burnt twenty large ships and one hundred and fifty small ones and the town squares were covered in bodies, which caused great astonishment and fear in all Gujarat.

At Gogha, the Portuguese heaped up the bodies of those they had killed in the temples. They then cut the throats of cows and defiled the temples by sprinkling them with the blood.

In 1559, again as a result of a temporary alliance with a ruler of Gujarat, the Portuguese acquired the port of Daman. This they also heavily fortified. From these strongholds, the Portuguese set about the subjugation of Gujarat. The Portuguese were well aware that they could never actually conquer Gujarat. The population of Portugal was only about one million, which severely limited the number of troops that could be despatched. Moreover, Brazil had become a drain on manpower. Many soldiers that were despatched to India died on the seas of scurvy or in storms. Those that did survive were subsequently depleted by tropical diseases. Unable to capture and hold large swathes of Gujarat, the Portuguese mounted a war of terror.

The slaughter started in Portuguese territory, where many of the Muslim traders were put to the sword. The Portuguese then went to Magdala (a town largely populated by people from the Horn of Africa, of which there were many in Gujarat), close to Surat, and set it on fire. They killed all the inhabitants except one man. He was left to live, with his hands cut off, to tell others of the atrocity. Hansot, close to Broach, was set on fire too. In Diu, they attacked the city adjacent to their fort. Many coastal towns were destroyed, including Una, Mahua, Gogha and the major port of Gandhar. Somnath was attacked and many of its famous temples and mosques destroyed.

Finally, a Portuguese expedition was sent to Broach, whose soldiers were absent. The Portuguese arrived by ship in the night to begin the slaughter. Once they had killed all those who had come out on to the streets, they set fire to the houses and burnt those hiding within – 'the nobility and the people, the gardens and the houses, were reduced to ashes'.

These actions had the desired effect. The Gujarati merchants, the Vaniyas, were famously pragmatic. Their conciliatory behaviour, even when savagely provoked, was well illustrated by the Gujarati proverbs – 'the Vaniya is ready for compromise'; 'the Vaniya always changes allegiance according to circumstance'; 'the Vaniya will not commit himself to anything'. Accordingly, the Gujarati merchants meekly took a Portuguese cartaz for their voyages and meekly paid at Diu the Portuguese levy on all imports and exports into and from Gujarat. Diu became the biggest financial contributor, after Goa, to the exchequer of the Portuguese state in India.

The pragmatism of the Gujarati merchants eventually paid dividends. Portuguese officials and the commanders of Portuguese ships were keen to conduct business on their own account, even though this was frowned upon by their government. They were strictly forbidden to deal in spices, which were the preserve of the crown, but Gujarat had much else to tempt them with. Gujarati cloth, sold willingly by the Gujaratis to their oppressors, became the staple of this private Portuguese trade. Even more pragmatically, several Gujarati merchants set up business in Goa itself. They became wealthy. Gujarati goods found their way to Goa and from there to Portugal. The Gujaratis in Goa even loaned the Portuguese governor money when it was urgently needed.

The Portuguese also opened up trade into the Bay of Bengal. This, again, was mostly unofficial business, for the sea was lawless, outside Portuguese control and full of pirates. Despite these dangers, the lure of the fine textiles of Bengal proved irresistible. The captains of Portuguese ships and colluding officials bought large quantities of textile to sell to the Far East and Europe on their own account. They traded mainly at Chittagong and Hooghly. Hooghly grew into a substantial town, with monasteries and churches. The Muslim authorities were often affronted by Catholic places of worship – more so than by the austere Protestant Dutch and English – because of their statues and images. Nevertheless, nothing was done for a while. However, when the Portuguese decided to entrench further, a petition from the local authorities to Shah Jahan complained that they 'had mounted their fort with cannons, and had grown insolent and oppressive'. Retribution followed.

In 1632 the governor of Bengal barricaded the river below Hooghly with boats to cut off the Portuguese. He then had mines placed under their fort. When one of these was exploded, it caused massive damage to the fortifications and a great number of Portuguese soldiers were killed. Some Portuguese escaped but about 4,000 were taken captive, many of them women and children. They were marched to faraway Agra, a journey that took nearly a year. Shah Jahan then explained how much better their lot would be if they converted to Islam. Most did. They were found jobs or taken into harems. Those who refused to convert were whipped and imprisoned.

The Portuguese were expelled from all of Bengal. They had overreached themselves by challenging the Mughals. A few years before, the Portuguese might have exacted revenge. They might have mounted a blockage of the Bengal ports or bombarded the coastal towns. However, they were much weaker than at the turn of the nineteenth century. The arrival of the Dutch and the British had taken away much of their trade. The drain on their resources by having to maintain so many fortresses in a hostile environment was taking its toll. The Portuguese state in India was running a financial deficit.

The one great contribution the Portuguese made to India was to bring in the useful plants of the Americas. An extraordinary number of the fruits and vegetables that the Indians tend to regard as indigenous in fact came from South and Central America. Some of these arrived relatively recently – probably via other European countries – such as the tomatoes and potatoes. Others, however, arrived in the sixteenth and early seventeenth centuries and were almost certainly brought in by the Portuguese. These included pineapples, custard apples, papaya, prickly pears, guavas, passion fruit, cashew nuts and groundnuts, cassava and maize. Most surprisingly, chillies, such a feature of the present Indian diet, also came from South America. The first known reference to them as being in India was in 1604.

The Portuguese were keen horticulturists, and early travellers often remarked on their gardens. Garcia d'Orta not only grew Indian medicinal plants in Goa but also many other fruits and flowers. In 1563 he wrote of the mangosteen, from South-East Asia, that it was 'one of the most delicious fruit they have in those regions. I myself planted some of these in my own garden.' Grafting, although known in India in ancient times, was given impetus by the Portuguese. It enabled much faster development of new varieties. In particular, they developed new and famous varieties of mangoes, such as the alphonso, which soon spread across India.

On the debit side, the Portuguese brought in tobacco. Around 1604, one of Akbar's courtiers chanced upon some tobacco, which he bought and gave to the emperor and his nobles. From the court, its use spread. However, it suffered a temporary decline when Akbar's successor, Jahangir, issued an edict in 1617. 'As the smoking of tobacco has taken a very bad effect upon the health and mind of many persons, I order that no one should practice this habit.'

The most commonly cultivated flower in today's India is the marigold. It adorns almost every deity and ancestral photograph in temple, shop, home or office. This plant was native to Mexico. The Portuguese probably introduced it to India for their own religious ceremonies.

———•———

Three accounts of life in Portuguese India during the seventeenth century give a good idea of how all changed. They were by

French travellers – Francois Pyrard, Jean-Baptiste Tavernier and Abbé Carré. Pyrard was in Portuguese India from 1608 to 1610; Tavernier visited Goa in 1641 and again in 1648; Carré was in India from 1672 to 1674. Life for the Portuguese in India altered dramatically over those years.

Remarkably little is known about Francois Pyrard's early life. He came from Laval in northern France. Some businessmen from there and from Saint-Malo decided to set up a company to follow the Dutch and the English to the East. Two ships were commissioned and young Pyrard left with them from Saint-Malo in 1601, possibly as a purser. Storms delayed the expedition and it took over a year to reach the Maldives. As Pyrard's ship approached the islands, the captain was ill below decks, the first and second mate were drunk and the watch was asleep. The ship struck a reef. Forty of the crew managed to get ashore with some of the ship's silver. The Maldivians arrested them, beat them, confiscated their silver and refused them food so that they were reduced to eating grass and rats. Many of them died. Twelve men escaped and stole a ship, which they managed to sail to Quilon on the Malabar Coast. The Portuguese seized them and consigned them to the galleys after which they were never heard of again.

On the islands, Pyrard set about learning the local language. He then managed to ingratiate himself with the sultan and lived tolerably comfortably for five years. In 1607 the islands were invaded by some Bengalis, looking for Pyrard's ship's cannon. They rescued Pyrard and his three surviving companions and took them to Chittagong. From there the Frenchmen took a ship to Calicut, hoping to meet up with the Dutch. The Indians received them warmly since they were also enemies of the Portuguese. However, just outside Calicut, Pyrard and two of his companions were kidnapped by some Portuguese. They were taken as prisoners to Cochin where they were incarcerated in a prison so crowded that it was impossible to sleep lying down. They were then sent by ship to Goa. On board, a cable snapped and Pyrard was badly injured.

When Pyrard finally arrived in Goa in 1608, he was very ill and still shackled in irons. The chains were removed but Pyrard was too weak to walk. He was carried to the Royal Hospital. Pyrard was extremely impressed by the facilities. The hospital had been founded by Albuquerque and been generously supported by kings and viceroys. It was under the supervision of the Jesuits and was governed by elaborate rules. It only admitted European single men – mostly soldiers. There were 1,500 beds and Pyrard was soon tucked into one:

> Beautifully shaped, and lacquered with red varnish; some are chequered and some gilded; the sacking is of cotton, and the pillows of white calico filled with cotton; the mattresses and coverlets are of silk or cotton, adorned with different patterns and colours, the sheets, etc., are of very fine white cotton. Then came a barber, who shaved all our hair off; then an attendant brought water and washed us all over, and gave us drawers, a white shirt, a cap, and slippers, and also placed beside us a fan and an earthen ware bottle of water for drinking, and a chamber-pot, besides a towel and handkerchief, which were changed every three hours.

There were Indian servants always present and a Portuguese superintendent visited every hour. For supper that first day Pyrard had a 'large fowl roasted, with some dessert' served on Chinese porcelain. It was no wonder Pyrard thought himself in the finest hospital in the world.

In fact, despite the luxury of the accommodation and the solicitousness of the doctors, the Royal Hospital had a terrible reputation for mortality. There was something wrong with its management of disease and injury. A recent despatch to the king had reported that at least 300 or 400 men between the ages of eighteen and thirty died there every year. It has been calculated that 25,000 soldiers alone died there in the seventeenth century.

Nevertheless, three weeks later Pyrard was feeling better. He was persuaded, however, to remain in the hospital until his sick companion had also recovered. This was just as well since, unbeknown to him, he was to be rearrested when discharged.

On leaving the hospital, Pyrard was taken to the prison appropriately known as the *Salle*, which he described as, 'the most foul and filthy place in the world ... where all the galley slaves and other sorts of vile people are cast pell-mell in a stinking air, sometimes two or three hundred or more'. Fortunately for him, there was a private room kept for Christians. Fortunately for him also, a month later he was able to get a message to a French Jesuit who managed to have a plea made on Pyrard's behalf to the viceroy. At first the viceroy considered executing Pyrard and his companion, for they had disobeyed the law against the French travelling to the Portuguese East. After a month, however, they were released without charge. Having no money, Pyrard then managed to enlist as a soldier. Over the next two years he was mostly in Goa but he also travelled with his fellow soldiers to Gujarat, south India and Ceylon.

Pyrard was well positioned to write a full account of life in Goa. The soldiers were in the lower strata of European society, but they continually visited the houses of the upper-class Portuguese where, as was the custom, they were given free food and drink. He wrote:

> I have been often astonished how in so few years the Portuguese managed to construct so many superb buildings, churches, monasteries, palaces, forts and other edifices built in the European style; also at the good order regulation, and police they have established, and the power they have acquired, everything being as well maintained and observed as at Lisbon itself.

Pyrard wrote of the shops of the jewellers, goldsmiths, lapidaries, carpet weavers, silk merchants and money changers. He pointed out that, although the Portuguese had many enemies in India who refused to trade directly, merchandise often arrived at Goa through the conduit of friendly merchants. There were horses from Persia and Arabia. Also there were the auctions of 'numbers of slaves, whom they drive there as we do horses'. There were female slaves whose attraction was that they could play musical instruments, embroider or make sweets and preserves. And others that were virgins, for they 'deem it no sin to have intercourse with their slaves'.

The Portuguese gentry travelled on horses caparisoned with silk embroidery, enriched with gold, silver and pearls. Stirrups were of silver gilt and the bridles set with precious stones. The Portuguese women travelled in palanquins hooded in silk or leather, carried by four slaves and followed by pages and female slaves all dressed in silk. When they went to church they dressed in all their finery – gowns of silk embroidered with gold and silver; crepe veils from head to foot. On their feet they wore slip-on pattens, the upper parts covered with pearls and gems. The cork soles were six inches high and so unstable that the women had to be assisted into church by the men. It could take them a quarter of an hour to cover the forty or fifty paces to their pews.

For entertainment there was horse riding and martial arts, picnics and music, but no dancing. There were authorized gambling houses where men played cards and dice, drank, ate and slept. Others played chess and draughts, skittles and bowls.

The soldiers were a rough lot. Some had been exiled from Portugal's prisons for serious crimes and could not return to Portugal until they had served their time. For others, a passage back and an allowance was only granted after eight years' service in the army. Most of those who came out were under no obligation to join the army, but would receive no pay until they took up soldierly employment. In theory, they were free to return to Portugal whenever they wished. Since, however, it was the custom to give them full rations on the passage out but only water on the return voyage, this resulted in many of them never leaving India. These unemployed, unpaid soldiers caused much trouble. It was dangerous to walk in the town after 9 p.m. since bands of them would rob and, if necessary, murder their victims. In the evenings there would be an illegal market for stolen goods, sometimes with as many as 500 vendors. The government of Goa tried to mitigate this disorder by offering a small allowance to those soldiers who were prepared to decamp to other fort towns, but with no great success. Pyrard estimated that there were sometimes as many as 5,000 Portuguese soldiers in Goa.

Pyrard's fellow soldiers either lived with a woman or shared a lodging with a few colleagues. Those who shared were often supported by married women or widows. They dined freely at the aristocrats' mansions. Despite their often dubious origins, the soldiers put on a great show of being gentlemen. 'All the poor Indians they despise, as though they would trample them under their feet. So the Indians were all amazed when we told them these fellows were sons of porters, cobblers, drawers of water and other vile craftsmen.' Often they did not have enough fine clothes to promenade in, so they would go out to make a show and then return to hand over their clothes so that the next person could leave the house.

Pyrard gave very little personal information about his own actions in his accounts on Goa. Nevertheless, he seemed inordinately interested in the habits of the women whose dress and behaviour he described at length – taking 'their ease in their smocks or bajus, which are more transparent and fine than the most delicate crape of these parts; so that their skin shows beneath as clearly as if they had nothing on; more than that, they expose the bosom to such an extent that one can see quite down to the waist'. He wrote that 'the women at Goa are exceedingly lewd, so amorous and so addicted to fleshy pleasures, that when they find the smallest opportunity, they fail not to use it'. He described how they used their servants and slaves to make assignations, even drugging their husbands so as to take their pleasure without risk. The viceroys would take any pretty woman they wanted, if necessary first sending their husbands away on official expeditions.

As the office of the viceroy was used as a way of rewarding the king's friends, viceroys were frequently changed. This gave them only two or three years to make their fortunes. They did this with great rapacity. Much was given to them by the captains and governors who only held office at the viceroy's pleasure. Jobs and permits were sold to the highest bidders. In their final year the viceroys would make a tour of their forts with many ships, seizing all they could to take with them back to Portugal.

Even in that first decade of the seventeenth century – the first decade of the Dutch and English challenge – Pyrard noted that things were beginning to change. Not only were the Portuguese no longer the masters of the sea, but their monopoly was also disappearing. The competition from the Dutch and English was driving up the buying price of commodities in Asia to four or five times their previous level. Moreover, the competition was driving the selling price in Europe of these commodities down. Nevertheless, several huge ships left Goa every year for Portugal. All were the king's ships – for trade with the East was still in the hands of the Crown. These were massive ships – several times the size of those of the Dutch and English – of up to 2,000 tons, with 1,000 or more a board. However, many of these ships were lost, either to the Dutch or in storms. This was due to both the unwieldiness of the ships and to the lack of professionalism among the officers. Many of these had given bribes to secure their appointment; others had been appointed purely as a reward.

In 1609 an edict arrived from the king to the viceroy commanding him to expel any Dutch, English or French, in case they were spies. Pyrard managed to get a free passage on a carrack going to Brazil. He must have been well regarded because he received farewell sums of money from the viceroy, the archbishop and other men of substance. Unfortunately, his pocket was then picked and his purse stolen. His companions helped him out and he eventually sailed in February 1610. From Brazil he took a Flemish ship to Spain, landed near Vigo, and then made the pilgrimage to Santiago de Compostela, which he had vowed to do if he ever safely returned to Europe. Finally, he took a ship from Corunna to La Rochelle. Francois Pyrard arrived back at his hometown of Lavel, nearly ten years after his departure, in February 1611. It is said he took to drink.

Jean-Baptiste Tavernier was born in Paris in 1605, where his father was a merchant. He travelled widely in Europe as a very young man and learnt several languages. In 1631 he went off to the Levant and Persia. Tavernier's main business was in precious stones and pearls. He presented himself as a gentleman trader rather than as a common merchant. This opened many doors for him and on later voyages he was able to sell jewels to both the Shah of Persia and Emperor Aurangzeb. In 1638 he went off to Persia again and from there carried on to India, visiting Surat and Agra. He was in Goa in 1641. In 1643 he left Paris again on another expedition to Persia and India. In 1648 he reached Goa once more.

Tavernier was much struck with the changes for the worse that had occurred in the seven years since he had last been in Goa: 'The Portuguese were then all rich, the nobles on account of the governments and other offices, the merchants by the trade which they enjoyed before the English and Dutch came to cut the ground from under their feet.' He described the condition in the Royal Hospital, the one that Francois Pyrard had so fulsomely praised, as deplorable. It was impossible to even obtain a drink of water without bribing the staff. 'Many Europeans who enter it,' he wrote, 'do not leave it save to be carried to the tomb.'

It seems, however, that there might have been some advantages in the decline of the Portuguese for Tavernier:

> On my first visit to Goa I saw people who had property yielding up to 2,000 écus of income, who on my second visit came secretly in the evening to ask alms of me without abating anything of their pride, especially the women, who came in palanquins, and remained at the door of the house, whilst a boy, who attended them, came to present their compliments. You sent them then what you wished, or took it yourself when you were curious to see their faces; this happened rarely, because they cover all the head with a veil. Otherwise when one goes in person to give them charity at the door, the visitor

generally offers a letter from some religious person who recommends them, and speaks of the wealth she formerly possessed, and the poverty into which she has now fallen. Thus you generally enter into a conversation with the fair one, and in honour bound invite her to partake of refreshment, which lasts sometimes till the following day.

As the century progressed and Portuguese finances became ever more parlous, their soldiers in India became even less likely to be paid on time. Many deserted to join the armies of Indian rulers. Another favourite escape route for disaffected soldiers was to join one of the religious orders – not an obvious calling for 'scoundrels from the prisons of Portugal'. The church was the one sector not in decline. The Jesuits, the Dominicans and the Augustinians, with the vast endowments they had acquired in more prosperous times, had built numerous monasteries, convents, colleges and schools. Parish churches had sprung up everywhere until there were nearly seventy. Work on the great Se Cathedral had been started in 1562. It proceeded very slowly until the end of the sixteenth century and then began in earnest. The cathedral was finally completed in 1652. It was 250 feet long and 165 feet wide – the largest church in all Asia.

———•———

The onslaught of the Dutch in the middle of the seventeenth century dramatically affected Portuguese India. A blockade of Goa brought trade between Portugal and India almost to a halt. In 1659 the Portuguese queen-regent told the French ambassador that no news had been received from Portuguese India for three whole years. It was only after the marriage of Charles II to a Portuguese princess that things improved, but only slightly. The

English and the French put pressure on the Dutch to make peace. The Portuguese were then able to resume sending ships to India, but they only managed to despatch one or two a year.

In 1670, the Portuguese suffered another humiliating blow. Their fort at Diu, which had successfully withstood the great sieges of the previous century, was attacked by a small band of Arabs from Muscat. The Portuguese were unable to fend off this raid. The Arabs sacked Diu, took away much booty and destroyed it as a centre of trade.

Abbé Carré was sent out to India by a minister at the court of Louis XIV to assist the head of a fledgling French East India Company, which would establish itself at Pondicherry. He travelled widely in India and made many interesting observations. After he departed from Surat, his Muslim-owned and -crewed ship was becalmed for weeks. He wrote of the superstitious rituals employed to summon the wind – throwing great basins of food from the ship into the surrounding sea; bathing in the sea so as to 'wash away the dirty impurities they commit with their young slaves'. At Goa, he noted that, since the trade in gems was a government monopoly in Portuguese India, it was usual for the merchants to do covert deals with the visiting English.

When Abbé Carré arrived in Goa in 1672, he noted that he could 'hardly find any shadow or vestige of its former splendour'. The principal palace, apart from the viceroy's quarters, was derelict. The great arsenal, which had formerly housed the armaments that supplied the Portuguese war machine across the East, was being used to store ships' cables and rigging. There were insufficient new arrivals from Portugal to maintain the population. The Portuguese nobles, who used to come out to

India in droves, had disappeared. Such new arrivals as there were had been sent out from the jails and the scaffold.

Thus it seems that this grand town, once so rich and called the Treasury and Queen of the East, is now at its last gasp. Everything changed very suddenly. First the great trade and commerce, which so enriched this town, ceased: and then all the treasure and immense wealth, which they had collected, vanished like smoke.

Seven

THE DUTCH, THE ENGLISH AND THE DANES

THE TRIUMPH OF PEACEFUL TRADE

For it was but an unwise undertaking for our East India Company, with a handful of men and money, to go make wars with one of the greatest monarchs in the world who, although not so well versed in war and manage of guns, yet had men enough to have eaten up all the Company's servants for a breakfast.

Edward Barlow, *Barlow's Journal*, 1692

In 1594 a group of Dutch merchants had sent four ships to the Far East, which successfully brought pepper back from Java. Other, often competing, companies soon followed suit. In 1602 these Dutch companies amalgamated their interests into the Vereenigde Oostindische Compagnie (United East India Company), known as the VOC.

In 1604 the VOC sent a fleet of thirteen ships to western India. Its commander met with the Zamorin of Calicut and made a treaty, both to trade and to join forces to drive out the Portuguese. The Dutch then sent annual fleets to Calicut to buy spices. The Portuguese, however, were too powerful to be dislodged and they continued to dominate the Malabar trade. The Dutch, therefore, decided to concentrate their energies on setting up trading posts in other parts of the Indian Ocean. They set up factories on the east coast of India, in Surat, in Ceylon and, most importantly, in the Far East. They built up an eastern fleet of heavily armed and outstandingly manoeuvrable ships – a fleet larger than those of the Portuguese, Spanish and English combined. It was only when they had sufficiently weakened the Portuguese by taking away much of their trade that they returned to attack them on the Malabar Coast.

Cochin was the most important Portuguese base in Malabar. The Dutch realized that if they could capture that superb port, they could capture the spice trade of Malabar. The Portuguese might still hold on to Goa, but it would be of little value.

Royal politics in Cochin played into Dutch hands. The senior branch of the royal family had fallen out with the Portuguese and had been supplanted by a pliant junior branch. When the raja died in 1658, the Portuguese again bypassed the senior members of the royal family. These disgruntled aristocrats then sent an emissary to the Dutch in Ceylon to ask for assistance. The Dutch, under Rykloff van Goens, saw their opportunity. Van Goens had no sympathy with the VOC's current guidelines, which urged peaceful trade: 'There is nobody in Asia who wishes us well but on the contrary we are hated by all nations, so that in my opinion sooner or later war will be the arbiter.' He gathered forces from Ceylon, eastern India and Java, until he had a fleet of two dozen ships and 4,000 soldiers.

The Dutch first attacked the tiny Portuguese fort of Pallippuram, opposite Cochin. This was soon overcome and they then took Quilon and Cranganore. The battle for Cochin was protracted and claimed 360 Dutch and 900 Portuguese lives before the Portuguese surrendered to van Goens on 6 January 1663. A week later the Dutch took Cannanore, the last remaining Portuguese fort on the south-west coast.

The Dutch then installed the prince whom the Portuguese had sidelined as Raja of Cochin. He was merely a puppet of the Dutch. Van Goens himself put the crown on his head, a crown that bore the insignia of the Dutch East India Company. The raja then gave the Dutch a monopoly over his kingdom's spice trade. The Portuguese had built a huge fort with five miles of perimeter wall. This the Dutch much reduced in size. They also demolished many fine buildings or converted them into warehouses. They renamed Cochin 'New Orange'.

The Dutch, although overwhelmingly Protestant, were tolerant of Catholic wives and mistresses. Respectable Dutch women were loath to come to India. Women did travel to try and make a rich marriage, but the majority were described as 'filthy strumpets and street-walkers'. Initially, the Dutch authorities tried to get their men married off to higher caste Hindus or Muslims, but there were few takers as this would have cut the women off from their families and communities. The majority of the men ended up making alliances with Indo-Portuguese women. In general they were anxious to retain their Catholic religion which, together with Portuguese as a first language, they passed down to their children.

Most of the Dutch in Malabar were servants of the Dutch East India Company. The lower levels were staffed by men who, for the most part, had only left the Dutch Republic as a last resort. Those who had a good job in Europe were not likely to exchange it for a journey of hardship followed probably by death from tropical disease. In general, the VOC's men were 'poor, ignorant, slavish-minded Netherlanders or debauched foreigners'. There were some independent adventurers who became smiths, carpenters or who ran taverns. They often married local women. These unions were not well regarded by the Dutch officials. As one remarked, 'The scum of our land are marrying the scum of the East Indies.'

Dutch life in the East was governed by strict protocol. An act covered the order of precedence and the precise details of how each level of society should behave and dress. Rules governed the value of the jewellery that wives and their servants could wear. They specified who could use silver cloth or who could sport a gold hatpin. Even the use of parasols and the decoration of the children's chairs were regulated.

The non-Dutch were treated with contempt. Although probably most of the Europeans in India thought themselves superior to the Indians; the Dutch Calvinists were the most extreme. They habitually described themselves as the 'Elect of God', and the Indians as 'black dogs'.

The vast majority of the inhabitants in the Dutch forts were slaves – a single Dutch household might employ fifty or sixty. Such was the poverty in parts of India that people sold their families into slavery in order to survive. Some even sold themselves. The Dutch fort at Pulicat, which had been built a little to the north of Madras in 1609, was the main centre for the export of slaves. Each year the Dutch in India sent at least 500 slaves to their establishments in the Far East. Not that slavery was new to India. In Malabar, particularly in Travancore, there had been large numbers of slaves from time immemorial. Their owners had power of life and death over them. They were forced to speak in a special inferior way – not referring to themselves as 'I', but as 'your slave'; not to refer to their food as rice, but as 'dirty gruel'. Not only were they 'untouchable' to upper-caste Hindus, but they were also 'unapproachable'. They were not allowed within sixty-four feet of a member of a Nair, warrior caste, or within ninety feet of a Brahmin.

The Dutch attacked Goa twice, but without success. However, their blockades severely affected Portuguese exports. Moreover, with much of the trade of the Far East and Malabar in Dutch hands, Goa dramatically declined in importance. It became a well-fortified backwater, which the Dutch could afford to ignore. For Goa the 'Golden Years' were over.

For the Dutch, Malabar and their other Dutch bases in India were never as important as were Java and the Far East. Nevertheless, following their victories over the Portuguese, the Dutch had expected to make large profits from the Indian spice trade. However, the Zamorin of Calicut soon fell out with his recent ally. He wanted to have his old primacy over the Cochin rajas reinstated. The Dutch turned a deaf ear to his pleas. The Zamorin then took to trading with the English, the Danes and various independent merchants. In places where the Dutch were paramount, they tried to impose a monopoly and buy commodities cheap. Nevertheless, local merchants often managed to bypass the Dutch and sell at a higher price to others – principally to the English.

The Dutch ran into trouble at Cochin when they interfered with the succession in the royal family. This sparked a rebellion of the Nair warriors. This rebellion – together with the failure to establish a monopoly in pepper as the English expanded their operations – severely affected the VOC's finances. In 1697 the company scaled back its operations in Malabar. It both reduced the size of its forts and reduced their garrisons. Cochin was left with only 300 soldiers, while Quilon, Cannanore, Cranganore and the five smaller outposts were each left with less than 100. The English were poised to take over much of their Malabar trade.

The English East India Company had found it hard to establish itself on the south-west coast. The most important spice-growing areas of India lay in the hills behind that coast. The Portuguese and later the Dutch had secured bases in many of the better ports and estuaries, and then used their influence to undermine the English. The English had been at a disadvantage since they were loath to use military might. The Portuguese and Dutch had shown no compunction about using force to obtain and hold their Malabar bases – force, which in the long term, proved too expensive to produce a profit.

A Company factory was established at Valapattanam, just north of Cannanore, in 1669. There were conflicts with local traders and it closed in 1675. That same year, the Company reopened a factory at Calicut. The Zamorins, however, were suspicious of Europeans – understandably so, given the behaviour of the Portuguese and the Dutch. Any attempt to fortify the factory was forbidden and for many years the Company was not even allowed to tile the factory roof. The Company decided, therefore, to look for new bases in Malabar.

An opportunity came in 1682 when the French abandoned a small factory with mud walls they had at Tellicherry. A regent of the royal family at Cannanore, which controlled the area, agreed to the Company occupying it. The French later complained that they had intended to return, but the English refused to budge. Tellicherry, which the Company later fortified, was built on a rocky cliff projecting into the sea. It had neither access to a major river nor a major harbour. It had, however, the great advantage of being close to hills that produced pepper in abundance and the finest cardamom in the world.

The other opportunity for the Company to establish itself came at Anjengo. The Rani of Attingal, in whose territory it lay, had invited the Company to set up factories in her domains in 1678. Two small trading posts were established. Alexander Hamilton, who visited Malabar in 1703, described how the rani was given a yearly present from these factories:

> In anno 1685, when the present was sent, a young beautiful English gentleman had the honour to present it to her black majesty; and as soon as the queen saw him, she fell in love with him, and next day made a proposal of marriage to him, but he modestly refused so great an honour: however, to please her majesty, he staid at court a month or two, and it is reported, treated her with the same civility as Solomon did the Queen of Ethiopia, or Alexander the Great did the Amazonian Queen, and satisfied her so well, that when he left her court, she made him some presents.

Whatever the truth of this, the rani was certainly well disposed towards the English. She gave the sandy spit of Anjengo to the Company for it to build a factory and a fort. Soon after work commenced, following protests by the Dutch, the rani cancelled this permission and tried to cut off supplies. The English, however, continued to receive necessities by sea. There was a skirmish, which the English won, and a treaty was concluded in the Company's favour. The fort at Anjengo was completed in 1695. A row of houses ran from the fort to the Portuguese church at the other end of the spit. Although small, the fort's location on the narrow spit gave its guns command over the sea on the one side and over the river on the other. In other respects, however, it was not an ideal site. Fresh water was often scarce. It was not a good anchorage for heavy surf made it impossible to bring ships in closer than a mile and small boats had to ferry their cargoes to the shore. Nevertheless, Anjengo became a major conduit for the Company's purchases of spices and textiles. Business increased because financial difficulties had forced the Dutch East India Company to reduce operations at its Malabar factories. Anjengo became second only to Bombay in the western presidency.

The last great trading region to be opened up by the Company in the seventeenth century was that of Bengal. Some trade into Bengal had already been done from the Company factories further south, but this had not amounted to much. In 1651 a factory was established on the bank of the River Ganges at Hooghly. Mindful of the expulsion of the Portuguese by the Mughals when they had attempted to fortify their base at Hooghly, the English arrived in a humble fashion. They left their ship off the coast and merely requested permission to bring small boats up the river. They were under instructions to make secret enquiries into the business methods of the Dutch and to see how they could be superseded. The English had a useful advantage. A few years before, they had judiciously lent one of their surgeons to the Mughal viceroy of Bengal. He had granted a licence for the English to trade freely. It was not clear whether this document contained permission to trade in the interior as well as at the seaports, since it had been mysteriously lost. Nevertheless, the English took it as authority to trade both on the coast and in the interior. After some initial difficulties, Hooghly became the chief agency of the Company in Bengal, together with several subsidiary factories.

Over the course of the seventeenth century there had been an extraordinary transformation in the Company's trade. Initially, textiles had been bought, not for export to Europe, but to take to the Far East in exchange for the spices that the English desired. There was almost no market for Indian decorative textiles in England. Plain and cheap calico and quilts were all that London wanted. When, in 1615, Sir Thomas Roe had come as ambassador to India, he had been bitterly disappointed with the goods on offer. He had imagined he would be able to find the highly decorated 'oriental' textiles and objets d'art he had seen on sale in the 'China shops' of London. 'I had thought all India a China shop,' he complained, 'and that I should furnish all my friends with rarities.' The Mughals too were not impressed by Indian artistic endeavours. They were taking steps to import craftsmen and techniques from Persia and Turkey, but these had yet to spread across India. The first textiles sent to England by the Company found few buyers.

The main attraction of Indian painted textiles – called 'painted' because the dye was applied with a brush – was that their dyes were fast and their colours lasting. In Europe, patterns were applied to cloth and then, when washed, soon disappeared. The Indians had long since discovered that mordants could make their colours bright and permanent. Seeing the superiority of the Indian techniques but doubtful of their artistic ability, the Company in London wrote to Surat in 1643, suggesting modifications – flowers and branches as the painter pleased, but on a white rather than on a dull red background. In the 1660s detailed patterns were sent from England for the artisans to copy. Later, the Company even sent out the seeds of weld, a plant used to make yellow dye in England, suggesting that it could be used to advantage by the Indian dyers. What finally emerged was a synthesis of European and Indian taste. This sold well.

The Indians had used painted textiles principally for clothing. Initially, the Europeans used these cloths mostly for wall hangings (which had gained popularity as homes acquired smoke-free chimneys), cushions and bedspreads. As the century progressed, however, English taste in clothing changed. Instead of heavy broadcloth, light silks and cottons, readily obtainable from India, became the fashion for both men and women. In 1661 Samuel Pepys recorded in his diary that he had 'bought an Indian gown for myself'. Two years later, he bought his wife 'a very noble particoloured Indian gown'. When imports from France into England were prohibited in 1678, imports from India gained further impetus.

As the price of spices in Europe fell over the years due to oversupply in a limited market, Indian muslins and chintzes became the height of fashion and a more important source of income for the Company. In 1694 the Company wrote to Madras observing that the greatest ladies in England were wearing chintzes for both their upper garments and petticoats – and that the Indians could 'never make, nor you send us, too many of them'. Muslins, so fine that they were almost transparent, were also in demand as were bales of silk. Coarser Indian calicoes were cheap enough to be purchased by the poor. At first only lengths of cloth were exported, but later ready-made clothes became important too. The East India Company was in the enviable position of being suppliers to an insatiable market. Indian textiles, as Daniel Defoe wrote 'crept into our houses, our closets, and bed chambers, curtains, cushions, chairs and at last beds themselves were nothing but calico or Indian stuffs. In short, everything that used to be made of wool or silk, relating either to the dress of women or the furniture of our houses, was supplied by the Indian trade.' In addition to this vast market, the Company was also re-exporting to mainland Europe on a huge scale. By 1700, textiles comprised three quarters of all the Company's exports to England. The share with the greatest value came from Bengal.

Despite periodic changes of viceroy, the Company was able to renew its early privileges in Bengal, although it had to pay heavily. In 1685 the Company's agent asked the viceroy for permission to fortify a landing place for goods. This was indignantly refused, the Company's trade brought to a halt and one of its factories besieged. The Company in London then initiated an important change in policy. Up until then they had always insisted that war and trade were incompatible. Occasionally, their men in India had ignored this directive, but London had always continued to urge peace. This time, however, they decided on confrontation. Asserting that the local authorities had taken to 'trampling upon us, and extorting what they please from our estate from us, by the besieging of our factorys and stopping of our boats upon the Ganges, they will never forbare doing so till we have made them as sensible of our power, as we have of our truth and justice'.

An expedition of ten ships with six companies of infantry was despatched to Bengal. It was under instructions from London to rescue the Company's employees in Bengal, capture the ships of the Mughals, go to Dacca and extract a treaty from the Mughal viceroy there by force. There was no chance whatsoever of these objectives being achieved against a viceroy with an army of 100,000. The river below Hooghly was impassable to the Company's large ships, so 300 soldiers were sent up the river in small boats. To counter this, the Mughals surrounded the Hooghly factory with several thousand soldiers and several hundred cavalry. They then closed the bazaar to the English, which left them without food.

The Company's chief agent at Hooghly was Job Charnock. Charnock had been in Bengal for thirty years. He had married an Indian widow, with whom he had at least four children, was fluent in several Indian languages and dressed as an Indian merchant. It was said that his wife was a widow whom he had rescued from committing sati on her husband's pyre and that after her death Charnock made a yearly sacrifice of a cock on her tomb. It was also said of him, probably truly, that 'when any poor ignorant native transgressed his laws, they were sure to undergo a severe whipping for a penalty'. Charnock had a deep knowledge of the Bengal trade, but his manners were rough. This led to a prickly relationship with some of his superiors – who often knew less than Charnock – and he was continually denied promotion. It was only as a result of his superior's death that he had assumed command.

In October 1686 there was a skirmish between the English and the Mughals. The English had the better of it but, realizing that their long-term prospects of holding out were poor, they left Hooghly in small boats. Twenty-seven miles downstream, they landed on a bank with three villages, one of which was called Kalikata. It seemed to be a good defensive position – on one side there was a deep pool in the river, suitable for the heavily armed Company ships; on the other sides there were swamps.

Charnock built a few huts for his men and opened up negotiations with the local governor. However, as the dry season progressed the swamps diminished and the viceroy attacked. Charnock and his men had to take to their boats again. As they went downstream they attacked several Mughal forts and burnt a town. One boat was captured, some of its crew beheaded and their heads displayed at Hooghly. The rest of the men took refuge seventy miles further downstream at Hijli.

Hijli was a famously unhealthy place about which there was a local proverb: 'It is quite one thing to go to Hijli, but another to come back alive.' And so it proved. The viceroy's army cut off supplies. It began to pound the encampment and the ships on the river with cannons. Disease took its toll. Within three months, 200 English soldiers died and another 100 were either sick or wounded. The 100 that remained active were racked with fever. Out of forty officers, only five and Charnock himself were alive and fit. The Company's largest ship had been holed and the others had severely depleted crews.

All looked lost, when a new ship came into view carrying seventy soldiers. Charnock put on a great display of welcome: with cheers, banners, trumpets and drums. He then duplicated this welcome with the same troops, so that the enemy were deceived into thinking a great relief force had arrived. Charnock was allowed to march out under truce with drums and flags. Once again, he departed downstream.

Later, Charnock meekly accepted a rebuke from the Mughal viceroy. He then somehow managed to obtain permission to return to Hooghly or anywhere else of his choosing. Because of its defensive possibilities and trading location, he chose to return upstream to Kalikata. He built more huts and some minor defences. Then a Captain William Heath arrived there with a fleet and instructions from the Company that Charnock and his men should come aboard and sail away to capture Chittagong. It seems that the Company were under the impression that Chittagong lay up the River Ganges whereas, of course, it was actually on the north-eastern coast of the Bay of Bengal. Charnock remonstrated, but he had to leave. As they departed, Heath burnt and pillaged Kalikata. This led to the arrest of the remaining Company factors in Bengal. Chittagong, as might have been expected, turned out to be heavily defended by the Mughals. After a month of fruitless negotiations, Heath's fleet was forced to return to the sanctuary of Madras.

Charnock had to remain in Madras until 1690. The Mughal occupation of Bombay precipitated by the foolish aggression of Sir John Child had made the Company realize that it was much weaker than it had imagined. Any idea of challenging the Mughal supremacy was jettisoned. The Company apologized, paid an indemnity and was authorized to continue its trade throughout the Emperor's dominions. Charnock waited at Madras, however, until he had obtained a specific promise from the viceroy of Bengal. He managed to secure an agreement that, in return for an annual payment of a derisory Rs 3,000 a year, the Company could trade free of local duties. On receipt of this, he and his men returned to Kalikata or, as it would soon be called, Calcutta, and now Kolkata.

At Calcutta, Charnock found that the buildings painstakingly constructed the year before had been burnt. Through the monsoon of 1690 he and his men were forced to live in boats. Nevertheless, work proceeded and by the summer of 1692 there was a small settlement. The adjacent deep water attracted ships and trade. Indian merchants began to settle. A large number of Portuguese and Armenian merchants moved to the safety of the town and were given plots for their churches.

Job Charnock died in 1693. He was buried at Calcutta. Within a decade, the Company would have acquired the two adjacent villages, begun work on the massively strong Fort William and put Calcutta well on the way to becoming its most important base in India.

Until the last decade of the seventeenth century, the East India Company had invariably been able to pay handsome dividends of 20 per cent or more. In the 1690s the Company suffered heavy losses due to the war against France and in 1696 the French seized the Company's returning fleet of five fully laden ships. As the century came to an end the Company was also locked in a struggle for survival against a new company. This led to producers in India raising their prices and profit margins narrowing. Facing all these difficulties, the Company stopped paying dividends.

The gravest threat to the Company, however, came from events in England. The Company's very success had provoked envy. There was an abortive attempt to resuscitate a Scottish company that had been given royal authority, afterwards rescinded, to trade with the East. This prompted the English Company to ask Parliament to confirm its own privileges. This had disastrous consequences. The government of the day was short of money and decided instead to auction the monopoly. The 'Old Company' lost out to a 'New Company', which was incorporated in 1698. The Old Company was, however, to be permitted to trade until 1701. Moreover, as the Old Company took the precaution of subscribing to a loan made to the New Company, it could legally continue to trade to the amount of this loan each year. It was a recipe for bitter conflict.

The ill feeling between the two companies in India was further inflamed by the New Company appointing all its senior officials from the staff of the Old Company. The Mughals initially sided with the Old Company. When, for example, the New Company's president at Surat, Sir Nicholas Waite, despatched his men to haul down the Old Company's flag, the Mughal governor sent his own troops to replace it. Waite retaliated by telling the Mughals that the Old Company was in league with pirates that were attacking Mughal ships. The Mughals then arrested the governor of Bombay, Sir John Gayer, and his wife. The unfortunate Sir John Gayer languished in prison for seven years and was not released by the Mughals until 1710. The following year he sailed for England. The French intercepted his ship off the tip of India and he was killed. There were similar disputes between the two companies in southern and eastern India. It became clear to the shareholders in London that the companies would have to be amalgamated. An agreement was made in 1702 to phase this in over seven years.

All these difficulties, however, were only temporary – the war with France came to an end; the New Company was absorbed. As the United Company of Merchants of England Trading to the East Indies – generally known just as the East India Company – entered the new century, it was in an excellent position to expand its trade and profits. It had raised over £3 million by share issues to 3,000 investors. Short-term bonds supplied a further £6 million of capital. It was importing over half a million pounds worth of goods a year into England. It had set up a network of trading posts all over India. In general, it had been true to the counsel of Sir Thomas Roe to avoid wars or the establishment of large forts with many soldiers. Its many bases had all been acquired with the permission of Indian rulers; none had been acquired by force. There had been a few spats caused by overzealous Company or Indian officials, but generally these had been satisfactorily resolved. The fact was that both parties wanted to make money. The Indians were as keen as the English to expand trade, customs duties and mutual profit. There was no advantage to be gained by aggression.

The Company was also benefiting from its policy of religious tolerance. In contrast to the Portuguese, the Company had gone to considerable lengths to achieve religious harmony. At Surat they had prohibited the display of any images in their chapel that might offend the Muslims. At Bombay they had encouraged the settlement of Hindu merchants and weavers. At Madras and Bengal they had attracted Catholic Portuguese and Orthodox Armenian merchants. All these communities had been allowed to worship freely. The Company, in spite of the strict enforcement of Protestant observance on its own senior employees, was happy to coexist with the followers of any religion that boosted its profits.

All seemed fair as the Company entered the new century. By avoiding the expensive aggression of the Portuguese and the Dutch, the Company had secured the largest share of trade between India and Europe. The strictures of the Company's founders and of the king's ambassador, Sir Thomas Roe, that they confine their activities to peaceful trade had produced great rewards. It was difficult at that time to imagine that the Company might jettison this advice.

At the beginning of the eighteenth century, embezzlement by its own employees was probably the biggest problem the Company had to face. The Company was happy for its men to conduct private trade to supplement their meagre salaries. They were not, however, supposed to compete with the Company in those commodities the Company itself traded in. Moreover, they were not, of course, supposed to use the Company's money to trade on their own account. Many ignored these strictures; William Gyfford was a classic example.

In 1717 William Gifford was appointed to be the chief factor at Anjengo. Gyfford devoted his energies to making a fortune for himself. Using the Company's money, he bought and sold pepper, a Company monopoly, on his own account. Furthermore, he alienated local merchants by making false entries in account books and by using counterfeit weights. There was also an altercation when his interpreter's mistress threw coloured powder, which was used by Hindus during the festival of Holi, over some Muslim traders. When one of the traders wounded the woman with his sword, Gyfford had the traders arrested and expelled from the fort. He also insulted them by breaking their swords. This incident provoked a series of skirmishes. Eventually calm was restored, but the resentment against Gyfford simmered on.

The custom of giving annual gifts to the Rani of Attingal had been neglected for several years. Gyfford decided to make amends. On 11 April 1721, bearing seven years' presents, he set off on the four-mile journey up the river to Attingal. It was a large expedition comprising about 120 merchants and soldiers together and 120 porters. A large, seemingly friendly, crowd met them. Gyfford and his men were herded into an enclosure. They found themselves separated from their porters who had foolishly been allowed to carry the ammunition. Gyfford managed to send a note to Anjengo:

> Captain Sewell,
> We are treacherously dealt with here, therefore keep a very good look-out of any designs on you. Have a good look to your two trankers [palisades]. We hope to be with you tonight. Take care and don't frighten the women; we are in no great danger.

Shortly afterwards, the crowd overwhelmed them. Most of the soldiers were killed. The Company's merchants were tortured to death. Gyfford's interpreter died in great agony as he was slowly cut to pieces. Gyfford's tongue was cut out. He was then nailed to a log and floated down the river towards Anjengo.

Gyfford's note reached Anjengo and some wounded soldiers followed. There were only three British officers and a gunner in the fort. One of the officers was ill and died soon afterwards. The other two set about plundering the warehouse and treasury. Then spirited their booty away in small boats. Only an artillery officer, Gunner Ince, remained steadfast. Fortuitously, a boat loaded with cowrie shells from the Maldives had arrived. Ince commandeered it and was able to evacuate the British women, including Gyfford's widow. He then set about preparing the fort for a siege. He moved all of the Company's servants from the outside houses into the fort. They were mainly boys and old men of whom there were 'not twenty fit to hold a firelock'. The warehouse was also outside and Ince moved the food and the contents of the treasury – such as had not been plundered – to within the fort.

When the mob from Attingal arrived, they laid waste to the small town and killed many of its male inhabitants. The women and children were subsequently taken into the fort and were eventually given refuge by the Raja of Quilon. The attackers shot fire arrows into the fort. All its roofs were thatched with palm and these had to be hurriedly stripped to prevent a conflagration. This exposed all inside to the sun at the hottest time of the year. A fortnight into the siege, two small British ships from Cochin delivered some supplies and seven soldiers. A week later, another fifty-two men from Calicut and Tellicherry were shipped in.

On 24 June the attack on the fort was launched. There was a large house set against the factory's wall, which the attackers occupied and then used as a base. Some of the Company's men made forays to dislodge them. At first they were unsuccessful, but finally they managed to hurl grenades through the windows with devastating effects. This completely demoralized the enemy. There were a few more small raids and the blockade was maintained, but there were no more serious attacks.

The arrival of the monsoon made it impossible for the Company to send a major relief expedition for several months. In their roofless fort, the defenders of Anjengo were exposed to the torrential rain. Finally, on 17 October, 300 men from Karwar and Surat arrived to lift the siege. Their commander, Mr Midford, immediately set about emulating Gyfford to make his own fortune – using the Company's money to trade pepper on his own account. However, he died within a year. It was left to his successor to conclude a formal treaty with the Rani of Attingal. This was highly favourable to the Company – the attackers were to be punished and their estates confiscated; the rani would compensate the Company for the affair and the Company would have the exclusive right to the pepper trade in the rani's dominions.

Perhaps the most interesting person of all those associated with the debacle at Anjengo was William Gyfford's wife, Catherine. Her life, both before and after her escape, was extraordinary.

Born Catherine Cooke, she first landed in India at Karwar on 8 October 1709 when she was only thirteen or fourteen years old. She was with her father, a captain in the Company's Bengal army, her mother, brother and two younger sisters. They had sailed on the *Loyall Bliss* from England in March and had a difficult voyage. This tough journey had so delayed them that they had missed the south-west monsoon that would have carried them directly to Bengal. Being unable to round the tip of India, and anxious to evade the French who were rumoured to be harassing the British along the west coast, they had sought shelter at the Company factory at Karwar.

The Company's chief, John Harvey, offered hospitality to them and to the ship's officers. He was glad to receive the latest news from England. He was also delighted by the highly unusual arrival of a young unmarried and 'most beautiful' girl. John Harvey had been on the coast for many years. He was old – old enough to be Catherine Cooke's grandfather – and deformed. He was, however, rich. Captain Cooke was poor and he allowed himself to be cajoled into approving of a marriage by the promise of a lavish settlement. He and his wife then persuaded their daughter to comply. Since the captain of the Company's ship was keen to depart, the marriage was rushed through. On 22 October the *Loyall Bliss* sailed away and Catherine was left behind with her aged husband.

The following year, John Harvey began the long process of settling his affairs in India. It was a complicated matter for he had, as was then usual, traded on his own account as well as the Company's and the two accounts were intertwined. Perhaps Catherine assisted her husband with the accounts. Harvey's successor was appointed and in August 1711 the couple went to Bombay.

The new chief at Karwar died after only three months in post, long enough for him to embezzle a considerable amount of the Company's money – and another chief was appointed. The Harveys took the opportunity to travel down with him from Bombay to Karwar to sort out some of their accounts. Four months after their arrival, John Harvey died.

The Company then impounded Harvey's assets. This was normal procedure since virtually all their employees were mixing Company trade with their own. It would have been necessary for John Harvey to obtain clearance from the Company to leave India, and the same would be true for his widow. Catherine began to work on the accounts. She also laid claim to John Harvey's estate.

Two months after Harvey's death, Thomas Chown was sent from Bombay to be a factor at Karwar. Chown had come out on a ship that had been wrecked off Bombay the year before. When the ship went down he had lost all his possessions. At Bombay he had already met Catherine Harvey. Some weeks after his arrival at Karwar he married her.

On 3 November 1712, Thomas and Catherine Chown sailed from Karwar for Bombay on the *Anne*, which carried a cargo of pepper and wax, to pursue their claim to Harvey's estate. Catherine was expecting a baby. Because of the danger from 'pirates', they were given an escort of an armed yacht and a frigate. Next day, four ships of the Maratha admiral, Kanhoji Angre, attacked them. The yacht had its masts shot away. Two ships took the *Anne* alongside and, running out of ammunition, it surrendered. During the battle, Thomas Chown's arm was ripped off by a cannon ball. He died in his pregnant wife's arms.

The captured ships were sequestered. Their crews were taken to Angre's fort at Gheriah. The Europeans, including Catherine Chown, were taken to the Maratha island fortress of Colaba. The Company at Bombay sent a letter to Kanhoji Angre asking for everyone to be repatriated. A month later all the prisoners were returned, except for the ships' officers and Catherine Chown. They were all held for ransom.

Complicated negotiations then ensued. Angre wanted money and a promise of no retaliatory action against him by the British. Eventually, he got what he wanted. A lieutenant was sent with Rs 30,000, and he returned with all the remaining prisoners on 22 February 1713 – sixteen weeks after their capture. It was reported that Catherine was so poorly clothed that the lieutenant had to 'wrap his clothes around her to cover her nakedness'. She was, however, unbowed. Shortly afterwards she gave birth to a son.

There was much sympathy in Bombay for Catherine's plight. The Company advanced her Rs 1,000 and a small monthly living allowance. Her long-term prospects, however, were not good. She had a child and her claim against her first husband's estate was looking weak. It had seemed at first that he had died without making a will – in which case she would have received one-third of his assets. Later, however, it had been reported that he had made a will the year before they had met. This might leave her destitute.

On her previous visit to Bombay, Catherine had met a young Company factor, William Gyfford. He now appeared to be a favourite of the governor and had been put in charge of Bombay Market. Catherine married him. She must have been well regarded by the governor too, for his consent was necessary for the marriage. The union had benefits both for Catherine and for William. Catherine's claim on her first husband's estate proceeded apace. John Harvey's will seemed to disappear. It was officially recorded that both of her previous husbands had died intestate. In October she received one-third of Harvey's estate – Rs 70,492. She and her new husband were now well off.

The following year William Gyfford was made supercargo of a Company ship trading to the Arabian port of Mocha. This gave him plenty of opportunities to make money on his own account in private trade, especially as he now had capital to invest. Three years later he was promoted chief at Anjengo. Four years after that he reaped the folly of his behaviour at Anjengo and was dead. Catherine, still only in her mid-twenties, was a widow for the third time.

The boat that evacuated Catherine from the siege of Anjengo made for Madras – a voyage around the tip of India and up the east coast of at least 500 miles. The journey, at the hottest time of the year, took over a month. She was with the two other British women and six children who had lived at Anjengo. The little boat had been carrying cowry shells that were used in India as small currency. It would have smelled dreadfully and would have been swarming with flies and insects. It must also have been overcrowded and unsanitary. But Catherine had been through worse before and she would have been comforted by the knowledge that she had the foresight to take the Company's account books with her.

Catherine reached Madras on 17 May 1721. She then fended off the Company's repeated demands for the return of the Anjengo accounts. Meanwhile, she received a letter from Lieutenant Lapthorne at Anjengo whom she had appointed as her agent:

> Upon examining the Company's treasure, we found in gold & silver not above 2,100£, but Capt. Sewell says he saw an account by invoice that your husband had received by the Bombay fleet ten chests of treasure of the Company's.

Catherine decamped to Calcutta to stay with her family. She eventually agreed that some money was owed to the Company and paid them Rs 7,312. Her agent at Madras eventually handed over the Anjengo account books to the Company. They were incomplete. Perhaps some papers had been genuinely lost; perhaps they had been deliberately removed. Whatever the truth, when the Company claimed Rs 50,000 from her, Catherine was able to reply:

> I was favoured with yours, which unhappily informed me of advice from the Honble President and Council of Bombay, in relation to a debt which the said Council did suppose to be due from my deceased husband to the amount of fifty thousand

rupees. In which I cannot but think they have used me a little hard in consideration that he met with his fate in performing his duty to his Masters, as his death was sudden and unexpected and all the Company's servants (belonging to the settlement) destroyed in that fatal expedition, so it occasioned a general confusion of affairs, attended with the loss of several papers, which might perhaps been very instrumental in clearing the deceased from this demand.

I have now gentlemen nothing to add, but to beg the favour of your Honble &ct to consider a little the vast complication of misfortune I have laboured under, and I cannot but hope from your candour and equity, that the hard circumstances of an unfortunate widow, and orphan, will draw from you a just and favourable representation of this affair to the Honble company in behalf of

Your humble servant
Cath^n Gyfford
Calcutta, 26 April 1722

However much Catherine protested, she was still at the mercy of the Company, for there was the law that she needed their permission to leave the country. Once again, however, Catherine would show her mettle.

Commodore Thomas Mathews had come to India in command of a Royal Navy squadron charged with suppressing piracy. In fact, he was more interested in making money for himself and for this he traded aggressively. This was probably illegal and certainly against the interests of the Company. With his own warships, however, Mathews could do as he pleased. He and the Company had become bitter enemies. The fiasco at Colaba had increased this enmity. The Company's employees also railed against Mathews, for he was damaging their own, officially approved, private trade.

Commodore Mathews arrived off Calcutta aboard his flagship, *Lyon*, in September 1722. Catherine Gyfford immediately became friendly. Mathews was appalled that a young British woman, thrice widowed by Company men – two of them killed while defending the Company's interests – should be so persecuted by the Company. He informed them that he was putting Catherine under the protection of the Crown and that they should cease their harassment.

The Bengal authorities tried to take money from Catherine in another way. Her brother commanded a trading boat, the *Thomas*, in which Catherine had a major share. The Company commenced legal proceedings to seize the boat. They soon received a letter from Mathews advising them that Catherine had sold her share in the boat to him.

Ignoring the Company's plaintive appeals, Commodore Mathews sailed for Bombay with Catherine Gyfford. There they shared a house, which caused much scandal. At Bombay, the Company's demands on Catherine increased for they now had more precise details of William Gyfford's business activities. It seemed that all the goods at Anjengo – pepper, cloth, opium and rice – that supposedly belonged to him had actually been purchased with the Company's money. Once again the Company wrote to Catherine demanding that she not leave India before they were reimbursed. To forestall any attempt by the Company to arrest or confine her, she moved from the town house to Mathews's ship.

At the end of 1723, Mathews sailed from Bombay with Catherine aboard. He wanted to do some final business transactions before leaving for England. The two of them stopped off in Karwar and Tellicherry. They also went to Anjengo – which must have caused a stir — so that Catherine could try and reclaim some of her possessions. Her agent, Peter Lapthorne, had written 'I have in my possession nothing more than 2 wiggs & the bolster & bed on which you used to lay.' She plainly did not believe him.

In July 1724 the *Lyon* reached England. Catherine's dispute with the Company rumbled on. She took the initiative by claiming against them. Whether this was a ploy or whether she really believed she had been ill-used is unclear. She backed out of arbitration. The Company were the first to go to court, but she then counter-sued. Patient research might find out if any final judgment was made, or whether, as often happened in those times, the litigation went on for years without resolution. We do know that at some stage she returned to Madras, where she was given a pension by the Company prior to her death in 1745.

After Portugal, the Dutch Republic and England, Denmark – or more correctly Denmark-Norway as their crowns were united – was the next European country to establish a base in India. The Danish East India Company was incorporated in 1616 at the instigation of some Dutch merchants doing business in Denmark. King Christian IV was the largest investor. Two ships left Copenhagen for the East in 1618, escorted by a tender and two of the king's warships. They first went to Ceylon where they started negotiations with the king of Kandy. These negotiations would eventually prove fruitless, but meanwhile an expedition to the south-eastern coast of India was more successful. In November 1620, the provincial governor of Tanjore granted the Danes a permit to trade duty-free on his territory and build a factory and fort at Tranquebar. Moreover, he barred the Dutch and the English from trade in his domains. Those two countries were too occupied with fighting each other in the Far East to intervene.

Roland Grappe, a merchant who had considerable experience with the Dutch East India Company, was left in charge of the Tranquebar factory. A large fort was built, named Dansborg. In 1623 a ship was despatched from Denmark to Tranquebar. It returned in 1625 with valuable cargo. As a company from a neutral country the Danish company was able to take advantage of the competition between the English and Dutch companies. In addition to this, they were able to undercut the prices offered by those companies as the Danish company received free protection from its king's navy, whereas the Dutch and the English had to finance their own warships. The Danes established factories at Masulipatam and Pondicherry on the south-east coast and at Pipli in Bengal. They also set up bases in the Indonesian archipelago. Not having yet shown a profit, however, the company needed more capital to finance its promising trade. Since Denmark was entering the Thirty Years War against Germany, capital was not available. Nevertheless, the company's Indian bases were able to survive by conducting local trade.

Prospects began to look a bit brighter in the 1630s. However, when the able Roland Grappe departed in 1637 trouble followed. A new leader, Willem Leyel, was not despatched from Denmark until 1639. His ship, the *Christianshavn*, was detained in the Canary Islands and did not arrive in India until September 1643. Meanwhile, the settlement was led by a Dutch merchant, Barrent Pessart. His speculations severely depleted the company's finances. Attempts then followed to sell Tranquebar to the Dutch, but these were unsuccessful. Events in Europe had severely damaged the Danish economy and Dutch merchants managed to increase their shareholding in the Danish East India

Company. They marginalized it relative to the Dutch East India Company.

When Willem Leyel eventually arrived at Tranquebar, he was briefly shown around the seriously dilapidated fort by Pessart, who told him there was no business to be had locally and suggested they both take their ships north to make up a cargo for the *Christianshavn* to take to Denmark. Pessart put off their departure for two weeks while Leyel remained aboard the *Christianshavn* fretting at the delay. Pessart had time to secretly remove all the fort's removable assets – including the best guns, the account books and the money – and secrete them aboard his own ship.

Leyel and Pessart finally departed north in their own ships. They went to Madras and Masulipatam. Leyel was shocked to discover that Pessart had run up such huge debts in Masulipatam that the company was no longer considered creditworthy. A few days later, some of Pessart's men came secretly in the night to Leyel and told him that Pessart intended to sail off on his own. Leyel decided to arrest Pessart. He was too late, however, for Pessart had already disappeared. Moreover, with the onset of the northeast monsoon it would be months before the *Christianshavn* could return Leyel to Tranquebar. He reached Madras in April 1644 and Tranquebar in June of that year.

The arrival of the *Christianshavn* at Tranquebar was greeted by a strange silence – no guns fired a salute, and no one came to the beach. A message was then sent to the fort addressed to Jacob van Stackenborg, an old and infirm merchant whom Leyel had met previously, asking for information as to the state of the fort and also for provisions. There was no reply. Another similar letter was then sent, this time addressed to one of the two chaplains. At first there was no reply, but later that day a reply came signed by both van Stackenborg and the chaplain. It stated that they were unaware of any royal decree that allowed the removal of Pessart as leader. No provisions were sent.

The *Christianshavn* remained anchored off Tranquebar for four days and then sailed a few miles down the coast to Karikal to take on much-needed provisions. Leyel returned the following week with seventy armed men. The inhabitants of the town outside the fort, whose livelihoods had been damaged by the lack of trade, welcomed him. Together they blockaded the fort. This eventually resulted in the head of the guard emerging to negotiate. Leyel granted a pardon to those inside the fort who had resisted him and was allowed to enter and assume command.

The fort was a sorry sight. Pessart had removed all the serviceable guns as well as all the company's cash, believed to have comprised 20,000 of the silver Spanish dollars known as 'pieces of eight'. Closer examination of doors and window frames revealed them to have been hollowed out by white ants. The moat no longer functioned properly as it was filled with bricks and rubbish.

Leyel was an energetic man with years of experience in the service of the Dutch VOC. He immediately set about importing good wood from further up the coast to renovate the fort. Within a short time the buildings were put into good condition, the moat was cleared of debris and Fort Dansborg was restored to its former glory.

Unfortunately for Leyel, as a consequence of the wars in Europe that Denmark had become embroiled in, the Danes had no spare ships to despatch to India. From 1639 to 1669 no Danish ships left Denmark for Tranquebar. Its inhabitants were left to fend for themselves. Following an incident in Bengal in which some Danish ships had been stranded on the coast and subsequently had their cargoes seized, a few residents of Tranquebar had taken to attacking and plundering Bengal ships.

This privateering had become a steady source of income, much to the annoyance of the English and Dutch whom the Mughal authorities lumped together with the Danes.

Leyel tried to restrict privateering. In 1648 this provoked a mutiny amongst Leyel's officers. Using the pretext that he was misappropriating the company's money, they imprisoned him and seized the treasury. Leyel's papers were despatched to Denmark together with an indictment against him. When Leyel was released he was put aboard a ship going to Java and given enough money for an onward passage to Denmark. In Copenhagen he was cleared of any wrongdoing and in 1654 the king gave 'our well-beloved Willem Leyel' an annual grant of foodstuffs. Unfortunately, later that year he died, probably of the plague.

Poul Hansen Kosør became the new leader at Tranquebar. Other Danes also departed. When Kosør died in 1655 the small remaining population of Danes chose Eskild Andersen Kongsbakke to succeed him. Shortly afterwards he became the sole Dane left at Tranquebar.

Kongsbakke, an almost illiterate commoner, managed with the help of the local Indians to defend Tranquebar for the next fourteen years. The ruler of Tanjore, incensed that tribute had not been paid, besieged the town several times, but Kongsbakke managed to survive. To better protect the town and its inner fort a wall was built around the whole. Privateering was accelerated and a large cash reserve was amassed from the proceeds. Progress reports were regularly despatched to Copenhagen. These were viewed with some scepticism in Denmark, but when augmented by a verbal report sent via a Dutch emissary, the Danish government decided to send a frigate to relieve the settlement. In 1669, after a gap of twenty-nine years, this Danish ship finally arrived at Tranquebar. It carried a notice from the king that formally appointed Kongsbakke as governor.

In 1670 the Danish government reorganized and refinanced the Danish East India Company. Towards the end of the century, the Danes were able to take advantage of the damage to the Dutch and the English economies wrought by the nine years war (1688–1697) to increase their profitability in India and the East.

Moving into the eighteenth century, the Dutch and the British once again became the dominant European merchants in India and the East. The Danish company went into decline and was dissolved in 1729 to be reborn as the Asiatic Company in 1732. This company was given a forty-year monopoly on all Danish trade east of the Cape of Good Hope. In 1755, following various payments to the Nawab of Bengal and his local official, the company acquired land a few miles north of Calcutta at Serampore. It was governed by a regent of the Danish Crown, answerable to the company's governor of Tranquebar, and was renamed Frederiksnagore. A considerable trade was developed in textiles and saltpetre.

In 1763, Balasore, on the coast just south of Bengal, became a Danish possession governed from Tranquebar. Its bay was too shallow from which to conduct much trade and it only ever had a small Danish community.

The Asiatic Company also decided to colonize the Nicobar Islands, which were 800 miles east of the tip of India, with a view to plant spices and other crops. They were declared Danish in 1756, named Frederiksøerne and administered from Tranquebar. The colony had perished miserably by 1759. The Danes then invited the Moravian (Herrnhuter) Mission to establish a new colony. This lasted from 1768 to 1787, but did not flourish. The Asiatic Company, dismayed by another failure, withdrew its protection in 1773 and left the missionaries to a miserable fate.

When the charter of the Asiatic Company came up for renewal in 1772, its monopoly was removed and trade with India opened up to all Danes. The company limped on. In 1777 it was decided that administration of the company's sovereign territories in India – Tranquebar, Serampore and Balasore – would be removed from the company and that they would henceforth be ruled directly by the Danish Crown.

Eight
THE FRENCH AND THE BRITISH

Towards Conquest

From his first visit to India dates the renown of the English arms in the East. Till he appeared, his countrymen were despised as mere pedlars, while the French were revered as a people formed for victory and command. His courage and capacity dissolved the charm.

Thomas Babington Macaulay, *Lord Clive*, 1840

The Portuguese, the Dutch, the English and the Danes were finally followed into India by the French. It was the French who would precipitate the European conquest of India. When Emperor Aurangzeb died in 1707 there was a battle among his sons for the succession. The Mughal Empire started to disintegrate. Mughal nobles who had been held in check by the central administration became largely autonomous. They fought each other and also had to fight the Marathas and southern Hindus who saw their opportunity. These were ideal conditions for the Europeans to play one side off against the other. The French became very accomplished in these diplomatic manoeuvres.

After the disastrous expedition of 1601, when Francois Pyrard was shipwrecked, a company was set up in 1604, which was granted a monopoly of trade between the East and France for fifteen years. Nothing was achieved. In 1615 it was amalgamated with a newly established company and its privileges confirmed. This company did make two expeditions to the Far East, but then lapsed into inaction. In 1642 Cardinal Richelieu sponsored a new company. This company became bogged down in conflict at Madagascar, where the native people strongly resisted attempts at colonization, and lost its capital.

In 1664 the French at last established a company that could trade seriously with India. Jean-Baptiste Colbert, finance minister to Louis XIV, sponsored the establishment of a Compagnie des Indes. It was given exclusive right to trade with the East for fifty years. Moreover, any losses incurred during the first ten years of operations would be reimbursed by the government. The state bought 20 per cent of its initial share offering, which made the launch a success. The company initially concentrated its efforts on Madagascar, where another debacle would ensue. There were enough resources, however, to also investigate possibilities in India.

In 1666 six ships set sail for Madagascar. From Madagascar two of these ships made for Cochin. Afterwards they went north to Surat, where in 1668 was established the first French trading post in India. The enterprise was commanded by the director general of French commerce in India, Francis Caron. He was an experienced trader who had run the Dutch East India Company's agency in Japan. Valuable cargoes were soon being exported from the Surat factory.

Caron was assisted by an Armenian from Persia, Marcara Avanchinz. He knew India and was despatched to the independent kingdom of Golconda, on the west coast of the country, where he obtained a permit to trade. He also secured permission to construct a trading post at Masulipatam, where the English and Dutch were already established. Perversely, Caron became jealous of this success and denounced Marcara to Colbert. Marcara was fully exonerated, but the incident led to enmity between the two. Destructive conflicts between the leading personalities would become a feature of the French enterprises in India.

Caron then embarked on a more ambitious project. He persuaded Colbert to back an expedition to Ceylon with the objective of securing a base to enter the spice trade. It was also envisioned that such a base would be fortified, so giving the French a permanent settlement where they would not be at the mercy of a local ruler. A French fleet was put at Caron's disposal. The king of Kandy intimated that he would support any ousting of the Dutch. In 1672 the French attacked Point de Galle, but were unable to capture it. They had more success at Trincomali, which they captured and began to strengthen. Soon, however, a Dutch fleet arrived. The French ships fled, leaving the garrison unprotected. It was quickly overcome. The French fleet then abandoned Ceylon and made for St Thomé on the east coast of India. St Thomé had a formidable Portuguese fort that, a few years previously, had been taken by the Dutch. The French managed to capture it with only a few casualties.

The directors of the Compagnie des Indes were not pleased when they learnt of the meagre success achieved by such vast expenditure. They recalled Caron. Together with the fortune he had accumulated, Caron sailed for Marseilles. As his ship entered the Mediterranean, Caron learnt that the authorities wanted to investigate his finances. He had the ship turn about and make for Lisbon. As it entered the harbour, it hit a rock and sank. The only survivor was one of Caron's sons.

In India, the French feared an attempt by the Dutch to recapture St Thomé. They sent François Martin, who had distinguished himself in the engagements at Ceylon, to plead with an official of the Ruler of Bijapur for the grant of some land. The company was allocated a plot on the coast, about 100 miles south of Madras. Martin returned to St Thomé to learn that the Dutch intended to attack. The Dutch had also persuaded the ruler of Golconda to aid them by convincing him that the French were in a dangerously expansionist phase. These allies were able to blockade the fort and force a French capitulation. The French were, however, allowed to leave for a destination of their choosing. Most, including the company's chief officers, went to Surat. François Martin, together with sixty men, marched south to the plot he had recently acquired. He arrived in April 1674 and began to construct a settlement. This became known as Pondicherry.

By shrewd bargaining with native officials and rulers, François Martin was able to obtain revenue rights to the villages near Pondicherry and was given permission to fortify the town. Martin's soldiers were given land on which to build houses. The colony prospered until 1689, when war broke out again between France and the Dutch Republic. The Dutch were determined to exterminate the settlement at Pondicherry. In 1693 they arrived with a fleet of nineteen ships carrying over 2,000 soldiers. After a twelve-day siege, Martin capitulated. Once again, the French were allowed to march out in honour. This time, however, they had to undertake return to Europe. It seemed that French ambitions on the Coromandel Coast had been permanently extinguished. However, as was to happen so frequently in the eighteenth century, it was events in Europe that would determine what would happen in India.

Peace came to Europe with the Treaty of Ryswick in 1697. This stipulated that all captured places should be returned. Moreover, in the case of Pondicherry, it stated that the additional fortifications made by the Dutch should be handed over intact. François Martin was accordingly sent back to Pondicherry to assume command again. He was sent 200 regular French troops and some artillery. He was also instructed to further improve the fortifications.

Martin drew up an ambitious plan for the development of Pondicherry. Hundreds of new houses were quickly built. In 1701 it was decided to close the unprofitable factory at Surat (leaving behind large debts) and move the company's Indian administration to Pondicherry. Martin was appointed director general of French affairs in India. He built up excellent relations with local rulers and attracted many Indians to take up residence there. He came from a family with long connections of the French trade with the East. His father owned a spice shop in Paris. Although François Martin was born illegitimate, his father had seen that he was given good business training. François Martin was primarily a businessman, but he had scruples. In 1687 he wrote a note about the slave trade:

> The English and the Danes derive considerable profit from the sale of slaves at Atjeh [Achin in Sumatra]. It was very easy now to obtain slaves on the Coromandel Coast as people were willing to sell themselves or their children into bondage for food. It was estimated that in two years as many as fifteen or

twenty thousand had been brought in this way to Atjeh. I was approached by some parties to participate in this trade, but I refused as I felt this to be too demeaning an activity for the Company.

By the time of François Martin's death in 1706, Pondicherry was a prosperous and well-ordered city with a population of 40,000.

———•———

Although Pondicherry prospered – mostly by trading with its neighbours in India and the East – the finances of the parent company were precarious. Military escapades had consumed much of its capital. It was unable to find sufficient resources to equip expeditions to trade with India and was reduced to assigning its rights to other French merchants. Nevertheless, when its fifty-year privileges lapsed in 1714, it was able to renew them to 1725. It had, however, no money. For several years no ships went out to India. Pondicherry was left to fend for itself.

Towards the end of the financial chaos that followed the death of Louis XIV in 1715, and the speculative bubble and collapse that ensued, the company was generously refinanced. Moreover, it had managed to renew its privileges again without any time limit. From 1720 it therefore became known as the Perpetual Company of the Indies. In 1723 it resumed operations, sending out ships laden with merchandise to Pondicherry. By 1730 Pondicherry was sending home annual cargoes worth over Rs 2 million.

The French were also anxious to expand their sphere of operations. They wanted a share of the important spice trade on the south-west coast. A few miles to the south of the British base at Tellicherry, there was a small town called Maihi, later named

Mahé, near the mouth of a river. Rocks made it very difficult to enter this river and the town was thought impregnable. However, a French naval captain, Mahé de La Bourdonnais, devised and led a successful French invasion on a large raft. The French then took control of the estuary and set up a trading post for their Perpetual Company of the Indies in 1725. Naturally, this infuriated the British at Tellicherry, and there were clashes between the militia of the two settlements as they disputed their boundary. Since Britain and France were supposed to be at peace, this alarmed the two governments and instructions were sent out for them to behave amicably. Friendly visits resulted, and 'much gunpowder was spent in salutes'.

Significant developments also took place at Chandernagore in Bengal. Chandernagore, on the Hooghly River, had been occupied by some French settlers since 1676. In 1688 the Mughals had officially transferred the settlement to them. It had then been fortified. In 1701 the French government put it under the control of the governor of Pondicherry. Its trade was insignificant until the arrival of Joseph François Dupleix.

Dupleix was the son of a director of the Compagnie des Indes. He went to sea when only seventeen and when only twenty-three his father secured for him the position of first councillor and military commissioner at Pondicherry. This post, the second most important in Pondicherry, he assumed in 1720. He took the lead in expanding trade and traded vigorously and very profitably on his own account. In 1726, however, he had a misunderstanding with the directors and was suspended. He was offered a free passage back home, but chose to stay in Pondicherry while awaiting the outcome of an appeal. Four years later he was cleared of any wrongdoing. In recompense he was sent to Chandernagore as director. He arrived there in 1731.

Dupleix put the wealth he had accumulated at Pondicherry to work. He purchased ships, opened up inland trade and induced Indian traders to settle. He did this for the company and, with the approval of the company, on his own account. He made money for the company and added to his own fortune. From being semi-derelict, Chandernagore became a commercial hub. Some ships were loaded directly for France; others for Pondicherry and then to France. Dozens of other ships carried merchandise to Indian ports, and beyond to Arabia and China. There was a large trade from the interior in saltpetre, which was used in making gunpowder. This was sent on to Europe and many other destinations. Large quantities of cowrie shells were imported into Bengal where they were used as small currency – several thousand making one rupee. Pepper was brought from the Malabar Coast. Coral from the Mediterranean was also in demand. Dupleix also ran a brisk trade in slaves from the interior. Many of these were sent on to Mauritius.

While Dupleix at Chandernagore was expanding French trade, a new Governor General at Pondicherry was expanding French political influence. Pierre Benoît Dumas had been a successful governor of the Isle de France and Bourbon – renamed Mauritius and Réunion – until in 1735 when he became director general of French affairs in India. He built on the good relations the French had already established with the rulers adjacent to Pondicherry. In particular he developed a close friendship with Dost Ali Khan, the Nawab of the Carnatic. Dost Ali, probably anticipating that French power might be useful in the future, obtained permission from the Mughal emperor for the French to produce Mughal coins with the Pondicherry stamp on them. The

French took care to mint coins of high quality. These became popular and gave Pondicherry a considerable profit.

In 1739 the Carnatic was invaded by large army of Marathas. Dost Ali met them in battle but was killed. Five days after the battle, Dost Ali's widow arrived outside Pondicherry, together with an escort of cavalry, a large entourage of relatives and her valuable jewellery. She asked Dumas for sanctuary. Knowing full well that the Marathas might attack Pondicherry if he acceded to her request, Dumas decided that the dishonour of not doing so would affect French interests even more and the gates of the city were thrown open. The widow and her entourage – which included 1,500 cavalry, 300 camels, 200 bullock carts and eight elephants – were welcomed by gun salutes. Some days later the wife and son of Chanda Sahib, Dost Ali's son-in-law, were also given protection.

The Marathas moved a considerable force into the vicinity of Pondicherry. An emissary went to Pondicherry to demand Rs 6 million and an annual tribute. He also demanded the surrender of Chanda Sahib's family and jewels. Dumas politely refused. The envoy was then taken on a tour of Pondicherry's now impressive fortifications. He was also given a gift for the Maratha commander of ten bottles of liqueurs. The commander's wife sampled these and found them very agreeable. Dumas sent another thirty bottles. The Marathas, impressed by Pondicherry's defences and Dumas's hospitality, withdrew.

In recognition of this French assistance against the Marathas, the Mughal emperor in Delhi gave Dumas the title of nawab with the rights over 4,500 local horsemen to be provided free of any charge. Before he resigned, so as to return to France, Dumas managed to have this title made transferrable to his successor.

Dumas was succeeded by the successful director of Chandernagore, Dupleix. On his arrival at Pondicherry in 1741, Dupleix made sure he was confirmed as a nawab of the Mughal Empire. As a mark of favour, the Mughal Emperor sent a flag and kettledrum from Delhi. Dupleix also had himself installed as a nawab at Chandernagore. He accepted tribute from local nobles of lower rank and generally insisted on the respect due to an imperial officer. He then married the widow of a councillor, Joanna Vincens. Of mixed Portuguese and Indian blood, she had been born and brought up in India and was fluent in several Indian languages. She also had a good knowledge of Indian politics. She and Dupleix made a formidable couple.

The directorate in France wrote of the probability of there being a war with Britain. They intended to reduce the number of ships coming to India. Perversely, they commanded Dupleix to cut expenditure, especially on fortifications. Dupleix ignored these instructions and proceeded apace with strengthening the walls around Pondicherry. The directors made no objection since Dupleix paid for the work out of his own vast fortune.

Dupleix was also instructed to approach the English East India Company at Madras to suggest, should Britain and France go to war in Europe, that the two nations' settlements in India should remain neutral. The Company at Madras rejected this overture. They had already been told that a British fleet, which had been intercepting French ships going to China, was coming to India to exterminate French trade. Dupleix, who only had one warship at his disposal, decided to appeal to the Nawab of the Carnatic. Mindful of the assistance the French had given to his predecessors and anxious to avoid any disruption of trade, the nawab told the Company in Madras that he would not tolerate any attack by the British on the French in his dominions.

Equally, he would not countenance any attack by the French on the British. Reluctantly, the Company at Madras acquiesced.

The British fleet confined itself to attacking the French on the open seas. In 1746 the French sent a fleet of their own into Indian waters. The two fleets met off the south-east coast of India. There was an indecisive encounter. The British, with one of their ships leaking, decided to abandon the fight and left for Ceylon. The French fleet then anchored off Pondicherry. It was commanded by Mahé de La Bourdonnais, the man who had captured Mahé, and followed Dumas as governor of the Isle de France and Bourbon. Dupleix and La Bourdonnais immediately began to plan an attack on the British at Madras.

There were arguments between Dupleix and La Bourdonnais, who wanted to wait for reinforcements, over the timing of an assault on Madras. Eventually, La Bourdonnais was persuaded to set sail. He was given a contingent of 500 men from Pondicherry. On 14 May he landed these men together with cannons on the coast twelve miles south of Madras. Next day he landed another 2000 troops, mostly Europeans.

Madras was thrown into panic. It had never occurred to the Company that the town might be attacked by a powerful European force – a force with modern weapons. The governor, Nicholas Morse, was the very same man who had rejected Dupleix's offer of neutrality. He now remembered the Nawab of the Carnatic's injunction against European wars on his territory. Accordingly, he sent a messenger to the nawab seeking protection. Foolishly, he omitted to send the customary gifts that were normally sent when seeking a favour. The nawab prevaricated. The French began the siege and bombardment of Madras. On 20 May the British made an attempt to buy off the French. This overture was rejected. The town was heavily bombarded throughout the night, both from land and sea. The next day the British capitulated.

There were protracted negotiations to fix the terms of surrender. La Bourdonnais was inclined to ransom the town and then return it. The British encouraged this magnanimity by giving him a personal gift of £40,000. Dupleix, who wanted complete French domination of that coast, was outraged. Meanwhile, the Nawab of the Carnatic had learnt of the French assault and was also angry. Dupleix, determined that the British should be permanently ousted from Madras, accordingly informed the Nawab that the French had taken over the city on his behalf and would hand it over once the surrender had been finalized.

Dupleix and La Bourdonnais continued their wrangling. It was perfectly clear that Dupleix had the final authority over French affairs in India, but La Bourdonnais continued to argue that his fleet was independent and under his own control. When Dupleix sent a deputation to implore La Bourdonnais to fall in with his plans to expel the British from Madras, and to insist on his right of command, La Bourdonnais arrested them.

Dupleix realized it would take a year or more to obtain confirmation of his position from France. It looked as though La Bourdonnais might get his way when the weather struck. A huge storm hit his fleet. Of eight ships, four were lost, two so damaged as to be unseaworthy and two were seriously incapacitated. Over 1,200 men were lost. La Bourdonnais decided he must leave Madras for Goa, a neutral port where his ships could be repaired and where he could buy new ones. He left Madras under the control of Dupleix's deputies, with the signed capitulation and the troops from Pondicherry. La Bourdonnais sailed to Pondicherry. He tried to obtain money, guns, men and provisions from Dupleix. As he might have expected, Dupleix refused. La Bourdonnais then limped off to Mauritius to repair his ships. When he finally returned to France, he was arrested for disobeying orders and imprisoned in the Bastille.

Dupleix was now faced with a serious dilemma. He had promised to hand over Madras, after it had surrendered, to the Nawab of the Carnatic. It may be that Dupleix made this offer in good faith. However, if so, he had probably intended to destroy its fortifications first, so as to avoid giving the nawab another powerful base close to Pondicherry. This destruction had been held back by La Bourdonnais's plans for a ransom. The Nawab knew of the capture of Madras. He became agitated when, over a month later, it had still not been handed over to him.

The nawab sent 10,000 men – a small proportion of his army – under the command of his son, Mahfuz Khan, to make clear his determination to secure Madras. On the day La Bourdonnais left, they camped outside the city walls. Dupleix realized that to commence the destruction of the fortifications now would only further enrage the nawab. Furthermore, he feared that if the nawab obtained control of the city he might ransom it back to the British. Dupleix sent instructions from Pondicherry that his men must hold on to Madras at all costs, but should not initiate any hostilities towards Mahfuz Khan's army. This was prudent since the French had less than 1,200 troops. The French commander was forced to commence hostilities when Mahfuz Khan cut off Madras's only supply of fresh water. He decided to send a force to recapture the spring.

Four hundred men, with two cannon hidden behind them, made towards the spring. Some Mughal cavalry charged towards them. When these came within point-blank range, the French troops parted to reveal their cannon. Their first shots ripped into the Mughal horses. Before the cavalry could regroup, the French fired their cannon again. For the Mughals, such rapid reloading of artillery was a new and unpleasant experience. Several other cannonades followed in quick succession. There were many casualties and the survivors fled.

Meanwhile, Dupleix had decided to despatch some of his soldiers at Pondicherry to the aid of those besieged at Madras. About 1,000 troops marched north. They were under the command of an engineer, not a regular officer, whom Dupleix had chosen for his ability and decisiveness – Louis Paradis. Mahfuz Khan learnt of their approach and moved his huge army a little to the south of Madras on to the bank of a river that it would be necessary for Paradis to cross. Paradis had no artillery. It must have been a daunting sight for him to see the massive force awaiting him on the other side of the river. The river was fordable, however, and Paradis did not hesitate. He led his men across the river and straight into the middle of Mahfuz Khan's army. They fired their muskets and then charged. The startled Mughals fled. They made for the nearby town of St Thomé. The French followed them. They were able to fire repeated volleys into the troops confined by the narrow streets. The French soldiers at nearby Madras soon joined the action. Mahfuz Khan fled. His army followed in great confusion.

This extraordinary French victory transformed the relationship between the Indians and the Europeans. Previously, it had never occurred to the Europeans that they might challenge the supremacy of the huge Indian armies. Dupleix and his predecessors had always taken every precaution to placate the Mughals. Now, an extraordinary series of chance circumstances had shown how a relatively small European army, modernly equipped and trained, could defeat a vastly bigger Indian one.

———•———

Dupleix was now master of Madras. He made Paradis its military governor. The final terms of surrender for the British were made more stringent than those proposed by La Bourdonnais, but they were still generous. Nicholas Morse and his council were taken as prisoners to Pondicherry. The rest of the British were, on undertaking not to fight against the French, allowed to leave. Some refused to give this assurance and escaped.

Fort St David, twelve miles south of Pondicherry, was well fortified. It had now become the East India Company's main base on the eastern coast. A little to the south was the smaller Company fort at Cuddalore. Dupleix decided to take this fort and completely destroy the British on the Coromandel Coast. He summoned Paradis from Madras to take command of a military expedition from Pondicherry. Paradis set off for Pondicherry with 300 soldiers and numerous porters carrying booty. Despite being harassed by the Mughals, he reached Pondicherry with his force intact. Dupleix now had a considerable army at his disposal.

The British at Fort St David had 200 Europeans and 100 local troops. Dupleix had 900 Europeans, 600 locals and 100 African soldiers. In spite of this overwhelming superiority, however, Duplex had a problem. He wanted Paradis to command the expedition against Fort St David. The military establishment at Pondicherry opposed this. Louis Paradis was merely an engineer and the French army in India was under the command of General du Bury. Du Bury was old and indecisive, but he insisted on his right to lead the expedition. Reluctantly, Dupleix gave way. On 19 December 1746, du Bury marched his troops towards Fort St David.

The British at Fort St David were determined to resist the French. They had recruited another 1,000 local troops. Moreover, they had mended relations with the Nawab of the Carnatic who was becoming seriously alarmed by the rise of French power. It had been agreed that when the French attacked the British, the nawab would attack the French rear.

Du Bury's men set up camp in a garden a mile or so from Fort St David. They set about cooking a meal and du Bury neglected to post any sentries. Six thousand cavalry and 3,000 soldiers of the nawab descended on them. The French fled, with the Mughals in pursuit. Fortunately for the French, they managed to cross a river and their artillery were then able to inflict heavy damage on the Mughals. The nawab lost 2,000 men. Both sides then withdrew.

Dupleix did not abandon his ambitions. He instructed his troops to harass the Mughal forces around the nawab's base at Arcot. He also managed to summon a small flotilla of warships from the Far East. He then reopened negotiations with the nawab, pointing out how much stronger the French were than the British. The nawab succumbed. He signed a treaty confirming French control over Madras and abandoning his support for the British. Furthermore, Dupleix managed to persuade his own officers that they be led by Paradis.

Paradis marched on Fort St David. In the same garden that Du Bury had abandoned, he set up camp and prepared an attack for the next morning. This was a crucial moment in French history. If the French could overcome the much weaker British, they would end the British presence on the Coromandel Coast and lay the foundations of a French Indian empire. When morning came, however, it brought a nasty surprise. A squadron of British warships from Bengal had arrived. There were ten ships, all heavily armed. They had brought soldiers too.

Paradis immediately realized that he would have to abandon his plans to attack Fort St David. Moreover, a fleet this size would be a threat to Pondicherry too. He hurried back there to offer protection.

The British now temporally had the upper hand. They shipped in troops from the western coast to reinforce the garrison at Fort St David. Meanwhile, Dupleix summoned up a French naval squadron from Mauritius. This managed to land soldiers and supplies for the French at Madras. It then, unbeknown to the British, returned to Mauritius. The British squadron went off in search of the French ships. This enabled Dupleix to make yet another attempt to capture Fort St David. The French plan was to attack the nearby fort at Cuddalore and from there move against Fort St David. The British pretended to evacuate Cuddalore and the French tried to occupy it by night. They were unnerved by formidable resistance and fled in disarray to Pondicherry.

At Pondicherry, information had been received that the British were sending a fleet to India. Dupleix put Paradis's engineering abilities to good use in strengthening the fortifications. Just beyond the city he erected impressive earthworks.

In Britain the loss of Madras had enraged both the Company and the government. The government decided to send a Royal Navy fleet together with British soldiers to the aid of the Company. Admiral Boscawen set sail in November 1747. He arrived on the Coromandel Coast the following August where he was joined by the squadron from Bengal. In all, the British had amassed thirty warships – the most powerful force ever seen on Indian waters. It landed troops at Fort St David. This brought the garrison there up to 6,000 men, over half of them European.

Seven hundred men were sent to attack the outworks at Pondicherry. The British were unaware of the great improvements made by Paradis. They had no scaling ladders. When they were only forty yards away, the French mowed them down. The French then rode out and the British were routed. However, soon afterwards, the French gunpowder store exploded, killing many of their men. The outworks had to be abandoned and the survivors retreated into Pondicherry.

When the main attack on Pondicherry began on 6 September 1748, it was by the largest European force that had ever set foot in India. Admiral Boscawen had command of about 4,000 European and 2,000 Indian soldiers, complete with artillery. A few days into the siege, Paradis made a sortie out to attack a British detachment and was killed. He was an outstanding officer, almost impossible to replace. Dupleix himself, not of course a soldier, took over the command of the military. He proved to be as efficient a soldier as he had been an administrator. The British admiral, in contrast, knew little of land warfare. Under constant fire his men managed, over many days, to push forward to within half a mile of the fort. They then found that a marsh made it impossible to advance further. Boscawen's ships endeavoured to bombard the town, but could not get in close enough to cause serious damage. More disastrously, the rains had arrived, accompanied by fevers and dysentery. On 17 October, after six weeks of fighting that left over 1,000 British dead, Boscawen withdrew his army to Fort St David.

Two months after the raising of the siege of Pondicherry, news arrived of impending peace in Europe. In May 1749, details arrived of the Treaty of Aix-la-Chapelle. This forbade any further hostilities between the French and the British in India. It also stipulated that Madras be returned to the British. The war between the British and the French in India had been a complete waste of money and lives.

———•———

It had become clear during the years of conflict that Indian armies, although they had huge numbers of troops, were no match for the new European military. A few years previously the soldiers of the British and French had still been using pikes; now they all had modern muskets and bayonets. They had earlier been using artillery that took several minutes to reload, now in one minute they could fire a dozen times. Now with the advent of peace, both the British and the French companies had considerable armies that they could not use against each other and that were expensive to maintain. It was inevitable that some way would be found to employ them. Perhaps they could be loaned out to Indian rulers or pretenders, to mutual advantage.

The British were the first to try this post-war device. They decided to interfere in the affairs of the princely state of Tanjore. In 1749, Raja Sahuji had been deposed and replaced by Pratab Singh. Sahuji offered to pay all the expenses of an expedition to put himself back on the throne – which, he assured the British, was the desire of a people oppressed by Pratab Singh. He would also give the British the coastal town and adjacent land of Devikota, which lay 120 miles south of Madras. It seemed a generous offer and the British despatched 1,500 troops. When, however, they reached Tanjore territory they found there was no support for Sahuji. Moreover, a formidable army lay in wait. The British decided to abandon any immediate attempt to restore Sahuji but, nevertheless, capture Devikota for themselves. To do this they needed naval support. This was disrupted by a huge storm that sank several ships. Finding Devikota too strong to attack unaided, the expedition returned to Fort St David. A second, much stronger, expedition was then assembled. This was taken south by ship and Devikota was captured. Pratab Singh then agreed to it being controlled by the British. In return, the British promised to abandon and restrain Sahuji.

While the British were preoccupied with Tanjore, the French had more ambitious plans. The Mughal Empire in the south, the

Deccan, was nominally under the control of the Nizam. When the Nizam died in 1748, there were two claimants to his throne – his son, Nasir Jang, and his grandson, Muzaffar Jang. In the far south there was the Nawab of the Carnatic, nominally a vassal of the Nizam but actually largely independent, who had a smaller territory around Arcot. The current nawab, Anwar-ud-din, an impostor, was opposed by a member of the legitimate family, Chanda Sahib. However, Chanda Sahib was in no position to take action. He had been captured by the Marathas and was being held at Satara in western India for ransom. Muzaffar Jang met him there and the two agreed to work together against Nasir Jang and the illegitimate Nawab of the Carnatic. Nothing could be done, however, until Chanda Sahib was released.

Chanda Sahib's family had long been on excellent terms with the French. In difficult times, they had received shelter at Pondicherry. Much of their jewellery and other wealth was at Pondicherry. Dupleix decided to stand guarantor for Chanda Sahib's ransom, so as to allow his release from captivity. He also loaned him 2,000 Indian and 400 European troops. These would join Chanda Sahib, who had mustered an army of 6,000 and Muzaffar Jang who had another 30,000 men in the Carnatic. In return, the French would receive more land at Pondicherry.

On 3 August 1749 the Nawab of the Carnatic, Anwar-ud-din waited for the advancing army at Ambur, fifty miles west of his capital of Arcot. He had an army of 20,000 supported by artillery operated by sixty European adventurers. They were in a well-chosen and fortified position. The French led the assault. Twice they were beaten back. Their commander was killed and his place taken by Charles de Bussy. A third assault broke through the enemy lines. A rout ensued. Anwar-ud-din was killed.

Next day, the allies entered Arcot. Chanda Sahib was proclaimed the new Nawab of the Carnatic. He and Muzaffar Jang then proceeded to Pondicherry to thank the French for their support. Dupleix arranged a sumptuous reception. Full of gratitude, Chanda Sahib more than fulfilled his own promises. In addition to the villages around Pondicherry that he had undertaken to give to the French, he gave them the port of Masulipatam. He also gave them the district of Bahur, which surrounded Fort St David. The British feared that this might signal a French plan to cut them off from trade with the interior.

The British decided to pursue their late war against the French by proxy. They would support the son of Anwar-ud-din, Mohammed Ali, against Chanda Sahib; they would support Nasir Jang, the Nizam of the Deccan, against Muzaffar Jang.

In 1750 Nasir Jang was taking his army north to Delhi to help repel an invasion from Afghanistan. When he received the news of the victory of Muzaffar Jang and Chanda Sahib at Ambur, he turned back to confront them. Aided by Marathas and Pathans, he had a massive army of 60,000 soldiers, 45,000 cavalry, 700 elephants and a lot artillery. Fearing defeat, Muzaffar Jang opened negotiations with his uncle and was promised confirmation of his titles. However, when he surrendered he was imprisoned. Nasir Jang then made for Jinji, midway between Chanda Sahib's capital at Arcot and the French at Pondicherry. His army was then bogged down for two months by the monsoon.

The nearby French used this lull to open up negotiations with Nasir Jang. Under cover of these, they also opened up secret negotiations with some discontented Pathan officers in his court. These officers agreed to stand aside if the French attacked. They would signal when the time was favourable. At the very moment Dupleix had agreed terms with Nasir Jang, the signal was given. The French military, unaware that their instructions were being countermanded, stormed Nasir Jang's camp. As promised, there was no resistance. One of the rebels shot Nasir Jang. Muzaffar

Jang was released and instantly proclaimed as the new Nizam of the Deccan.

Muzaffar Jang immediately went to Pondicherry to thank Dupleix. The French organized another elaborate reception. Muzaffar took along Nasir Jang's captured treasure – eighteen chests of jewels and Rs 10 million. With some of this, he generously rewarded the French. He confirmed Chanda Sahib as the Nawab of the Carnatic. He also made Duplex his own deputy for all of southern India south of the River Krishna, including the Carnatic.

Early in 1751, Muzaffar Jang went north to consolidate his position in the Deccan and to ascend the throne at Aurangabad. He asked Dupleix for a French escort. Charles de Bussy, together with 300 European and 2,000 Indian soldiers, was despatched. En route the allies were attacked and Muzaffar Jang was killed. This could have been a serious setback for the French. De Bussy, however, consulted with the Mughal officers and it was agreed to put Nasir Jang's brother, Salabat Jang, on the throne. Salabat was accordingly released from captivity. He was extremely grateful to the French for this sudden change of fortune and immediately awarded them several more parcels of land and townships. At the end of June, Salabat Jang and de Bussy made a triumphant entry into Aurangabad. The French were now at the height of their power. In effect, Dupleix was the master of all of southern India. Except, that was, for the tiny enclaves of the British and the beleaguered Mohammed Ali.

Mohammed Ali was still holed up in the west of the Carnatic, at the fort of Trichinopoly. Late in 1749 the British had sent a few troops to him as a gesture of their support. In 1751 a larger force was sent to intercept an army of Chanda Sahib together with some French soldiers who were making for Trichinopoly. The British were forced into disarray and had to retreat to

Trichinopoly. There, Mohammed Ali suggested to Robert Clive that the forces of Chanda Sahib might be diverted by an attack on Arcot.

Robert Clive had arrived in Madras in 1744 to work as a 'writer', a clerk, in the East India Company. He was eighteen years old. His journey from England had taken nearly fifteen months. His ship had been blown towards Brazil – a common occurrence – and had also been damaged. The wait for repairs and a fair wind enabled Clive to learn some Portuguese. This would prove useful, since a debased Portuguese was the lingua franca – a language used to make communication possible between those who did not know each other's own language – of much of coastal India. He arrived in India with debts, no useful connections and was prone to depression. As a boy he had been adventurous, famously climbing the outside of the church tower in his hometown of Market Drayton, so he must have found writing up ledgers very dull. Eight months after his arrival, he wrote to his cousin: 'I have not enjoyed one happy day since I left my native country.' A year later, the humdrum routine of an accounts clerk was suddenly interrupted by the arrival of the French army.

After the surrender of Madras, the British had been allowed to leave provided they gave an undertaking not to fight against the French. Some of the Company's men refused to do this. One was Robert Clive. He and some companions disguised themselves as Indians by darkening their faces and wearing black stockings on their legs. They managed to travel south, beyond Pondicherry, to the Company fort of St David.

At Fort St David, Clive had volunteered for military service. This did not bar him from doing the private trading that was the normal and authorized way for the underpaid Company m... make their fortunes. He invested in handkerchiefs and ruffles. In the military he did well enough in the repelling of the two attacks by the French to be given a commission as an ensign. He was under the command of Major Stringer Lawrence. This highly professional soldier, a veteran of Fontenoy and Culloden, was not like the usual Company officers who were famously incompetent. He took Clive under his wing and taught him much.

In the post-war expeditions that followed the peace with the French, Clive had seen action at Tanjore and Devikota. He impressed Stringer Lawrence with the courage he displayed when leading his men into battle. When Madras had been returned to the Company, Clive had applied for a promotion as captain in the Company's army. When this failed, he decided to return to civilian post. He became a steward at Madras, responsible for provisioning the settlement and its garrison. This was a highly lucrative appointment with plenty of commission. It also taught him how to provision an army.

In 1751 Clive was in charge of supplies at the Trichinopoly debacle. He had returned to Fort St David and volunteered to rejoin the military without extra pay, provided he was made a captain. This offer had been gratefully received. Shortly afterwards, Clive was given command of the expedition to attack Arcot. This town was Chanda Sahib's capital and had been left with only a skeleton garrison. Severely reducing their garrisons at Fort St David and Madras, the Company assembled a force of 300 sepoys – 'sepoy', a word of Persian origin was used to describe an Indian soldier drilled and dressed in the European manner – and 210 European soldiers. Captain Robert Clive was given command.

Clive and his expedition left Madras on 22 August 1751. Arcot was about sixty-five miles away. This was not a modern professional fighting force. Most of the officers were civilians; the European soldiers of the time would later be described by Clive as British 'scum and refuse'; the Indian soldiers had hardly been trained. There were three small cannons. Halfway to Arcot, Clive learnt that Chanda Sahib's garrison at Arcot was somewhat stronger than he had been led to believe. He sent a message to Madras to request more cannon, but continued to march. His detachment was hit by a huge thunderstorm, but Clive continued marching towards Arcot. He arrived at the gates of Arcot fort on the morning of 1 September. To everybody's amazement, they encountered no resistance. Chanda Sahib's men had learnt from their spies that Clive had been undaunted by the heavens opening and continued his march. To them, this indicated some supernatural force. The garrison of over 1,000 men had fled. The British took over the town.

A spy sent details back to Pondicherry of the British success. He noted that they had arrived with two chests of liquor. Eighteenth-century soldiers were not noted for their restraints when fuelled with alcohol. However, the governor of Madras, Thomas Saunders, had given instructions that they were 'not in any shape to molest or distress the inhabitants'. This injunction was strictly enforced by Clive. He noted the way it calmed opposition from the town's population of 100,000, opposition that would have made life difficult for the invaders, and he would adopt this same policy in the future. He also took care to hoist the flags of the Mughals, so as to maintain the pretence that the British were solely acting on their behalf – another fiction that he would find useful in the future.

Clive then prepared to resist an inevitable siege. The former garrison of Arcot moved their camp closer and closer to the fort. After a couple of failed attempts to harry them, Clive decided on an attack in the dead of night. Most of them were asleep when the British arrived. Before anyone could flee, Clive and his men opened fire. They wrought great damage before retiring back to the fort without losing a single soldier. In the days before the siege began, the two larger cannon that Clive had requested arrived, together with 300 cattle for sustenance.

Chanda Sahib's 4,000-strong army, together with 150 French soldiers, finally arrived to begin the siege. Supplemented with the former garrison and some other nearby troops, the besiegers had more than 10,000 men. Clive had 120 European soldiers and 200 sepoys. The very size of the fort at Arcot made it difficult to defend. The walls, which had to be constantly patrolled, were a mile in circumference. These walls were surrounded by the houses of the town outside, which made it easy for the enemy to get close enough to keep up constant musket fire. Three times during the siege the sergeant who accompanied Clive on his rounds was shot dead.

At Madras and Fort St David desperate efforts were made to assemble a relief force, but it was the end of October before 130 European soldiers and 100 sepoys left Madras for Arcot. This detachment was intercepted and had to take refuge. Meanwhile, artillery sent from Pondicherry had started to pound the fort and damage its walls. The outlook was grim until help arrived from an unlikely source. A Maratha army was camped in the hills away to the west. These 6,000 soldiers had been engaged to help Mohammed Ali, but were waiting to finalize details of their remuneration. Clive sent messages to them asking them to come to his rescue. Negotiations dragged on, but finally the Marathas moved towards Arcot. A detachment of Company troops was also marching towards Arcot. News of these relief columns spurred the besiegers into action. They delivered an ultimatum to Clive, offering him honourable terms to surrender. Otherwise, they would storm the fort and put all to death.

The attack began on 14 November. A spy had given Clive the timing and he was well prepared. Elephants charged towards the fort gates. Well-directed musket fire made them turn in panic and trample the men they were leading. Prolonged musket fire decimated the sepoys who tried to enter the fort through a breach in the wall. It was said that in one hour Clive's men fired 12,000 shots. Nevertheless, the sepoys managed to advance and their commander was able to plant a flag in the breach. Soon afterwards, he was shot and killed. His death demoralized his men. The French troops were badly led and ineffectual. Gradually, it became clear that the attack had failed. There was a truce to collect the dead. In the night the attacking army departed, leaving behind most of their artillery. The siege had come to an end. This was the first significant British success against the French and their allies.

Later that morning the relief column from Madras arrived. Seeing that they were no longer needed, most of the Marathas went to join Mohammed Ali in Trichinopoly, but 1,000 cavalry remained with Clive for further action against the forces of the French and Chanda Sahib. There were victories at Arni and Conjeeveram. The governor of Madras wrote to congratulate Clive – 'I am informed the Mullahs are writing a history of the wars of Arcot wherein you will be delivered down to future ages.'

The Marathas left to join the main body of their army at Trichinopoly. There was little more that Clive could do with his small force so he returned to Madras. He recruited another 500 sepoys. Another 100 European soldiers came from Bengal. Clive was ready to march into action again, when Stringer Lawrence arrived back from England to take command. This was a blessing for Clive. He had excited much jealousy among the Company's senior officers. These may well have refused to serve under him.

With Lawrence in command – an officer who had already shown confidence in Clive – these problems were deflected.

Lawrence and Clive arrived close to Trichinopoly at the end of March 1752. Mohammed Ali had been joined in the fort by the Marathas and other allies. The army of Chanda Sahib and the French was camped to the east. They failed to stop many of the Company's soldiers inside the fort from slipping out to join their approaching colleagues. Using a building for cover, Clive managed to move close to the enemy and rake them with his artillery. Chanda Sahib's cavalry commander's head was blown off by a cannon ball and his men retreated in disarray. Lawrence and Clive then entered Trichinopoly.

To the north of Trichinopoly, the River Cauvery divided into two with the island of Srirangam in between. The French, together with most of Chanda Sahib's men, crossed the river to Srirangam. A temple on the island was surrounded by a series of strong walls. The French thought it highly defensible and took it over. The British decided to mount a blockade of the island. They sealed access from the south and then sent Clive over the river to stop any supplies reaching the island from Pondicherry and the north. Clive was nearly killed when a French detachment, led by British deserters, surprised his camp one night, but they were beaten off. A French relief column was sent from Pondicherry, but Clive destroyed it. He was then able to defeat the last of Chanda Sahib's troops north of the river and train artillery across the river on to those camped on the island. The constant barrage demoralized Chanda Sahib's men. Many deserted and a large number transferred their allegiance to Clive. The French troops surrendered. Chanda Sahib was captured by one of Mohammed Ali's allies and beheaded.

The battle of Trichinopoly seemed to have made Mohammed Ali the undisputed master of the Deccan with the British as his ally. The French appeared to have been marginalized. In the Carnatic they still held Pondicherry and some minor outposts, but they had lost most of their army. It was true that they were still in a powerful position with the Nizam further north, but that was a relatively poor region without the ports essential for overseas trade.

Dupleix, however, was not yet finished. He received some reinforcements from France. He was able to bribe the Marathas to switch sides and support the French. He used his extraordinary diplomatic skills to persuade the powers at Mysore to pay the French for the use of the French army in a joint effort to take back Trichinopoly. This ended in failure with the French losing 400 men. At the beginning of 1754, Dupleix initiated peace talks. Meanwhile, however, Dupleix was being undermined in Europe. The directors of the company in France were alarmed by the cost of the continual warfare. They were not convinced by the fiction that the battles with the British were merely in support of the Mughals. Moreover, the company was running out of money. The French company sent a deputation to discuss affairs with the East India Company in London. The French ambassador had talks with the British government. It was decided to dismiss Dupleix.

On 1 August 1754 Charles Godeheu arrived off Pondicherry. He delivered three documents to Dupleix. One was a letter from himself hoping that matters could be resolved as amicably as possible; one asking for a full report on French affairs in India; one from the king to recall Dupleix to France. Next day, Godeheu came ashore, went to the council chamber and read out his own commission to replace Dupleix. In the silence that followed, Dupleix shouted out – 'Vive le Roi!'

Godeheu entered into negotiations with the East India Company. A provisional treaty was drawn up in which the two companies agreed to a policy of equal possessions. In theory this would have meant the French giving up most of the territory that Dupleix had acquired. However, the treaty had to be ratified in Europe before this actually happened. Progress towards this came to a halt when the two countries went to war once again in 1756.

Before Dupleix left Pondicherry, the French government had reconsidered its action. A message had been sent to Dupleix suggesting that perhaps Dupleix might continue as governor, but with Godeheu as emissary to make peace with the British. Unfortunately for Dupleix, he sailed before this arrived. When he reached France, he was initially well received. However, once the provisional treaty was finalized it was decided that Dupleix was of no further use. He had advanced large sums of his own money to the company to further his ambitions. He had also obtained credit for supplies. When his creditors demanded payment, the company refused to help him. The bailiffs were sent in. Fighting off efforts to imprison him for debt, he died in poverty in 1764.

One concession was made by the French company before the treaty was ratified – they returned to the British a company of Swiss mercenaries captured on the sea off Pondicherry. The Swiss were the mercenaries par excellence in eighteenth-century battles between European forces. Out of 1,800 troops that the Company had recently landed at Madras, 500 were Swiss. Often, however, the 'Swiss' were adventurers from other European nations.

European military adventurers had long been coming to India where they were particularly prized for their expertise, real or supposed, with artillery. Many Indian rulers, especially those who had originated from Persia, had an ambivalent attitude to artillery. It was considered necessary, but unchivalrous. It was not an occupation for a gentleman. The Portuguese had similar reservations and, although they manufactured good artillery pieces, the accuracy they achieved in using them was notoriously poor. From almost the beginning of their time in India they had recruited German gunners. They also imported experts from other European nations to manufacture cannon. In 1503, two of their gun-founders from Milan defected to the Zamorin at Calicut, where they cast much artillery and trained many gunners. The Indians were making artillery from before the arrival of the Europeans, but it was mostly of an inferior quality. Moreover, they lacked the expertise in its effective use.

Many Europeans entered the service of the Mughals. In the first half of the sixteenth century, Rumi Khan from Turkey modernized the artillery of Bahadur Shah of Gujarat. This led to the victories over the Rajasthani Rajputs. He was aided by European mercenaries, principally Portuguese. In the middle of the seventeenth century, there were enough Portuguese in the service of the Mughals at Narwar, 100 miles south of Agra, to warrant a Jesuit priest. The Venetian, Niccolao Manucci, was an artillery officer for both Aurangzeb and his brother. Gemelli Careri observed of Aurangzeb's vast armies: 'All this artillery, especially the heavy, is under the direction of Franks or Christian gunners, who have extraordinary pay; especially the Portuguese, English, Dutch, German and French.' A few decades later, the senior artillery officer of Nasir Jang was an Irishman. Many other hopefuls followed, often having very little military experience. After it had been shown that a small force of soldiers with muskets trained in the European manner could defeat much larger traditional armies, Indian rulers also took on a great many European military officers for their infantry. By the end of the eighteenth century, European artillery and infantry officers were attached to most Indian armies.

After the victory at Trichinopoly, Robert Clive fought in a couple of minor battles and then resumed his post at the commissariat in Madras. He was ill for a while with stomach problems, possibly from gallstones, that would recur in the future. He recovered and began to look forward to soon returning to England. A friend wrote of 'the pleasure I propose myself in ******* in company with you in Covent Garden'. However, this was not to be because, shortly before his departure, Clive married. Margaret Maskelyne had come out to visit her brother who was one of those who had escaped in disguise with Clive from Madras. It was an impulsive gesture. Only three days before the ceremony Clive had booked a single passage back home. The couple sailed from Madras in March 1753 and arrived in England in the October. Clive had been in India for ten years. He was now wealthy, having made £40,000 in the commissariat and some extra by his private trading.

Clive was in England for eighteen months. He stood for Parliament, was elected and then unseated by political machinations. He paid off most of the mortgage on the family home. The Company presented him with a sword – the hilt of gold set with diamonds – and made much of him. He entered into a five-year contract to return to India as the deputy governor of Fort St David with the right to eventually become the governor of Madras. He was also promoted to lieutenant colonel.

Nine

THE BRITISH

THE SEIZURE OF BENGAL

Robert Clive returned to India in 1755. His convoy reached Bombay during October, carrying three companies of artillery and several hundred British soldiers. It had been intended that he would move against the French in the Deccan. However, the authorities in Bombay (who were still independent of Madras) were reluctant to join this operation. They were busy trying to destroy the 'pirates' of the coast – something they had been trying to do for many decades.

In 1674, Shivaji had been made king of the Marathas at Raigad. He was the first Hindu king in that area since the rise of Muslim power four centuries before. The East India Company saw that there was a new authority to placate and they had sent a senior official bearing gifts who had successfully negotiated a treaty to facilitate trade.

Only six years later Shivaji died and his eldest son, Sambhaji, became king. Sambhaji had few military gifts and many vices. He drank to excess, participated in sexual orgies and could not control his temper. Nevertheless, he had military ambitions. He concentrated his efforts on trying to defeat the Siddis, the Mughal's allies on the coast south of Bombay. He had insufficient resources to do so. Various attempts to take the Siddi's island fort at Janjira came to nothing and Sambhaji's navy was largely destroyed in a foolish attack. Meanwhile, the Mughals, directed by Emperor Aurangzeb, had defeated the Adil Shahs of Bijapur – the former rulers of Goa. Now they were moving to attack the Marathas from the east. They, not the Siddis, should have been commanding Sambhaji's attention.

In 1689 a small column of Mughal soldiers had made a foray deep into Maratha territory. They made for the lakeside palace of Sangameshwar. Unlike the strong Maratha hill forts, it was a soft target. It was easy to capture the palace and easy to capture the king of the Marathas for Sambhaji was drunk.

The Mughals took Sambhaji to Aurangzeb's camp in Tulapur. A red-hot iron was pushed into his eyes and his tongue was cut out. Later, he was beheaded, dismembered, and thrown to the dogs.

During Sambhaji's disastrous reign there had been few consolations for the Marathas. In his battle with the Siddis, however, there had been one memorable event. The year before Sambhaji was captured, the Siddis had decided to besiege the Maratha fort of Suvarnadurg. This island fort, 100 miles south of Bombay, was a mile offshore, had freshwater wells and was enclosed by thick fifty-foot high walls. The Siddis blocked any replenishment of supplies by putting a large fleet into the surrounding waters and an army on the nearby shore. They waited a while, and then opened secret negotiations with the Maratha commander. It was a tactic that they had often used successfully.

A young Maratha officer, Kanhoji Angre, whose father had once been deputy commander of Suvarnadurg, learnt of the proposed surrender. With some fellow officers, he arrested the fort commander and took control himself. He announced that they would resist the Siddis till the end. He led an attack against the Siddi army on shore. Many of his men were killed and he was taken prisoner. However, Kanhoji Angre managed to escape and swam back to the fort.

The Siddis maintained the siege for a while. However, the monsoon was approaching, when it would become impossible to keep a fleet at sea and difficult to supply an army on land. The Siddis withdrew and a grateful Sambhaji confirmed Kanhoji Angre as commander of Suvarnadurg. When the new regent restructured the administration, he appointed an admiral with two deputies – one for southern Konkan and one for northern Konkan. The northern commander would take over the remnant of the fleets operating from the forts of Gheria and Suvarnadurg. The huge navy left by Shivaji – perhaps 200 warships – had been reduced by the follies of his son to a pitiful number. The northern commander inherited only eight or ten ships. He was Kanhoji Angre.

Kanhoji began to rebuild his fleet. The commander of southern Konkan led a sedentary life and was happy for Kanhoji to operate within his territory. The southern seas – sometimes far south of Konkan and away from the powerful Siddi and English fleets – were easier places to capture stray shipping.

The Portuguese in their heyday had introduced a system of selling permits, their cartaz, to give safe passage. Anyone found by a Portuguese warship without one, or breaking its conditions regarding cargo, was liable to forfeiture. Kanhoji began to implement a similar system with his own permit, the *dastak*. In 1702 he seized a merchant ship without a dastak off Calicut.

Although not an English ship, it had Englishmen aboard and the East India Company demanded the ship and passengers be released. Kanhoji defied them.

The next year, the Company again became agitated when Kanhoji captured a Dutch warship of thirty guns. When a ship from Konkan that carried one of Kanhoji's dastaks came to Bombay, the Company seized it. A year later, Kanhoji arrived with seven warships and parked them off Bombay. He made no threats, merely leaving them in a position where they could have cut off the island. A week later he sailed off. The Company rushed to be conciliatory, but Kanhoji refused to compromise on his demand that all ships travelling along the coast would need his dastak. The Company made it clear that they had no intention of carrying the dastaks.

The Company described Kanhoji Angre as a pirate. 'Angria, a Sevagee pirate independent of that Rajah, came into the bay,' they reported back to London. This would continue to be the Company's appellation, even though Kanhoji always took care to sign himself as admiral of the Marathas. For some of Kanhoji's time, because the succession to Sambhaji was disputed, the Company could perhaps claim that he was backing a usurper to the Maratha throne. Even when the succession had been settled, however, and Sambhaji's son, Shahu, had been confirmed as king of the Marathas, the Company continued to describe Kanhoji as a pirate. Even when King Shahu made Kanhoji his chief admiral and the commander of the whole of Konkan, he was still a pirate to the English.

As the activities of the European pirates decreased, the seizure of ships by Kanhoji Angre began to increase. In 1706 his ships captured the Company's *Monsoon* at Karwar. In 1707 he attacked the Company's frigate *Bombay*, which sank. In 1710 there was an inconclusive battle with the Company's ship *Godolphin* – an engagement that lasted all day and was witnessed from Bombay. In 1712, off Karwar, Kanhoji Angre took the governor's armed yacht and the *Anne*. That same year he also attacked the annual armada of Portuguese ships that took the profits from Goa back to Lisbon. One warship of thirty-four guns guarding the armada was captured and the other forced to withdraw. The East India Company wrote to London that Kanhoji Angre's fleet could 'take any ship except the largest European ships'.

All this was despite the expansion of the British navies – Company's and Royal. The Company's navy had one ship of thirty-two guns, four ships of twenty or more guns, and twenty smaller ships carrying from five to twelve guns. In addition to this, the Royal Navy had an Arabian Sea fleet of one ship with seventy-four guns, one with fifty, eighteen with twelve to thirty-two guns each and some smaller boats with four to eight guns.

How did Kanhoji Angre manage to defy what had become one of the most powerful naval powers in the world? Year after year he had gradually built up the small navy which he had inherited. He had also recruited well – not only from among the Marathas, but also from among the Europeans. There were numerous renegade Europeans in India, some of them once pirates, who were only too willing to take a share of the Maratha spoils. Kanhoji was always on the lookout for good gunners and good shipbuilders. It was said that many of his best captains were Dutch. Kanhoji's main asset, however, was his grasp of tactics. He operated like the guerrilla commander he had so successfully been on land. He avoided confronting the European navies on the high seas, for there they could out-sail and out-gun him. He always made sure that in any engagement he was close to the shore.

There were two main types of ships in the Maratha fleet — the Ghurab and the Gallivat. The Ghurabs were the heavy armed ships, usually twin-masted, ranging from 150 to 400 tons. Typically they might have two guns firing forward and six along each side. Neither their guns nor their gunpowder were equal to that of the European ships. They were slow and cumbersome.

The much more numerous Gallivats were light and fast. Most were less than seventy tons and had bamboo decks unable to take the weight of cannon. They relied on bows and arrows, and slings until their crews were able to use their curved Maratha swords. The Gallivats had two masts, one with a large triangular sail and one with a small one. They also had forty or fifty oars.

Kanhoji's tactics were simple. His men waited until a potential prize came inshore or was lured there. Ideally, there would be little or no wind. Then, out of their hiding places, the Marathas would attack. The Ghurabs would be towed, or half-sailed and half-towed, into position by a cluster of oared Gallivats. The Ghurabs would then open fire at point-blank range, hoping to bring down a mast or otherwise disable their quarry. Then the Marathas would board. Usually the men on their packed ships would totally outnumber the sailors aboard their enemy. In any event, the Marathas were expert swordsmen and deadly in close fighting.

If possible, the prize would be towed back to one of Kanhoji's forts. It would then be stripped of its cargo and valuables. The Europeans and other wealthy captives would be held for ransom. When repaired, the ship would join Kanhoji's fleet.

———•———

After many successes against the Company, Kanhoji became the diplomat. There were complications in the Maratha succession and he wanted to use his army to influence events. Not wishing to fight on two fronts, he proposed a treaty of friendship with the Company. The Company was keen to agree and a treaty was signed in April 1713. In 1715, Kanhoji signed another treaty of peace – this time with his traditional enemies, the Siddis. With the Maratha succession decided in his favour and at peace with his two main enemies, Kanhoji set about fortifying Khanderi. This small island lay ten miles south of Bombay and three miles off the coast. It had been taken by Shivaji in 1679, but nothing had been done with it. It was ideally placed to gather intelligence on the activities at Bombay port.

Shortly after the peace treaty between the Company and Kanhoji was signed, a new governor arrived at Bombay. Charles Boone was energetic and aggressive. He immediately began to strengthen the defences of Bombay. A tax was imposed on the Indian and other merchants to finance a wall with fortified gates around the township. He also started a large shipbuilding programme. Within six months, he had added three frigates to the Company's fleet. By 1718 he had added another frigate, two fire ships and the *Phram* – a floating battery of guns – the very latest thing in naval architecture. These were not defensive weapons.

Kanhoji soon gave Boone an excuse to act. Firstly, he failed to return the timber and cannon he had appropriated when he had captured the *Anne* and the governor's yacht at Karwar. Secondly, he seized four ships flying the English flag. These ships were Indian-owned, but carried the Company's cargo. Kanhoji insisted that since these ships did not carry his dastak he was within his rights, but the Company maintained that they had immunity. In April 1718, Boone issued secret orders to seize Kanhoji's vessels. Shortly afterwards, one of Kanhoji's ships was taken near

Bombay. 'Our friendship is over,' Kanhoji wrote to Boone, 'and from this day forward, what God gives, I shall take.' Boone then decided to send an expedition against Kanhoji's main base – the fort at Gheria.

It was an excellent time to attack. The monsoon was imminent and Kanhoji's fleet was at anchor. Moreover, many of the sailors had departed to their villages and most of the officers were at Colaba for the wedding of Kanhoji's daughter. The British had another advantage too, for one of Kanhoji's senior advisors, the Portuguese adventurer, Manuel de Castro, had defected to them. He appeared to know a great deal about the Maratha fleet and had assured Boone that it would be easy to float a fire ship into the huddled vessels in Gheria harbour and then take the fort by storm. Nevertheless, a formidable force was assembled, of twenty Gallivats filled with soldiers, 2,500 men in all.

When the English squadron arrived, they found the reality was somewhat different. Kanhoji's ships were there. However, they were not in the harbour by the fort, but in the river. A strong boom had been put across the river mouth, which made it impossible to send in fire ships. The fort was also not as imagined either. Its walls were so high that the British ladders were useless. A two-day bombardment of the fort failed to achieve much. However, since it seemed that there were only a few defenders, a landing was made beneath its walls. The troops were supposed to march to the river and set fire to Kanhoji's fleet. This plan was abandoned when they found themselves in a swamp. As the men tried to regain their ships, they came under heavy fire from within the fort. The British then left for Bombay 'to repair our frigates and take care of our wounded men, of whom we had a considerable number'.

Despite the failure of this expedition and a similar repulse with heavy casualties later in the year at Kanhoji's island fort of Khanderi, Governor Boone determined to attack Gheria again. At the end of the monsoon in 1720 a large fleet set sail from Bombay under the command of a Company official, Mr Walter Brown, who had been made admiral and commander-in-chief for the occasion. His flagship was the *London*, of forty guns. He also had five other large warships, various smaller ships, a fire ship and a bomb ketch, the *Terrible Bomb*. The fleet was to be augmented later by two more ships and the *Phram*. There were 2,000 sailors in all, plus 350 British soldiers and 80 others, mostly Africans.

On arrival at Gheria on 18 September, Brown lined up his ships and gave the order to open fire. Unfortunately, they were still a mile away and all the shots fell into the sea. The *Terrible Bomb* was then sent inshore to blast the fort. It only fired twice before it became apparent that its gun barrels were too weak to use an adequate charge of gunpowder. Four days later, a party of fifty soldiers was put ashore to capture a building on top of a nearby hill. The building turned out to be merely a pile of stones. The men returned and suffered heavy losses as they tried to regain their ships.

Brown was under the impression that his men would fight better if intoxicated. As discipline broke down, some of the officers begged him to stop issuing rum. He refused, saying, 'Let them drink as they please.'

There was a hiatus while they waited for the *Phram*, in which Brown had great confidence, to arrive. Meanwhile, seeing the inaction, the Maratha commander brought in new supplies and new men. The *Phram* arrived on 27 September and was immediately sent into the attack. However, its gun slits were too low and it only managed to fire into the sea twenty yards away. The next day was spent in making modifications.

The Seizure of Bengal

On 29 September, the combined assault began. Brown had assumed that the sailors would be part of the force, but most of them refused. Only 239 men volunteered to take the forty-rupee reward. The *Phram* went into action. It fired shells indiscriminately among friend and foe alike. This resulted in Brown ordering it to go under cover of darkness right beneath the fortress's walls. It was to open fire the next morning. To steady their resolve he sent them 'six dozen each of wine and arrack'. This was well received by the *Phram's* commander, Lieutenant Wise. He became too drunk to take any further part in the action.

Those sober enough to do so opened fire from the *Phram*. Their most devastating salvo went into a British ship. This had the Company's African troops aboard. Half of them were killed; half were 'terribly scorched'. The Marathas then opened fire on the *Phram*, killing fifteen and wounding thirty.

The English withdrew their ships, including the *Phram*, and resumed drinking. Captain Woodward of the *Revenge* reported to Brown that his ship had run aground and was lost. This turned out to be a delusion and he was 'put into irons for cowardness'. There was a fist fight between some of the other officers.

There was then a lull in hostilities for the liquor was running out. Brown sent a ship to Goa for fresh supplies. When the arrack arrived, Brown proposed another assault on Gheria. His officers refused to even consider it – one telling Brown he was mad. To salvage some pride, Brown then took off his fleet to bombard the nearby Maratha fort of Devgad. This had little effect and on 21 October the fleet set sail for Bombay. Then occurred the most extraordinary disaster of all.

Just off Gheria, Brown saw four pirate ships. Frightened by the possibility of an encounter, Brown's flotilla sailed into Gheria harbour hoping the pirates would be nervous of getting too close to the Marathas. At night they crept out to sea again.

In the dark, probably entirely by coincidence, they ran into the pirate fleet. The pirate ship *Victory* then fired across the bows of the Company's ship *Victory*. Brown's flagship, the *London*, then hailed the ship that had fired the shots to ask her name. When, out of the darkness, she replied that she was the *Victory*, the *London* announced her own identity. A pirate broadside then raked her.

The pirate commander was Edward England. Based in Madagascar, he had recently captured and commandeered the Company's ship *Cassandra*, which had been coming to India with the annual injection of cash for investment – some £75,000. Normally, the pirates would have avoided a battle against such a large force, but it was soon apparent that, despite their overwhelming superiority, the Company's fleet was more in fear of them. Admiral Brown gave the order for all the flags of his fleet to be hauled down and then ran for Goa. They were slowed down in their escape by the ungainly *Phram*. It was set on fire and cast adrift.

Before Governor Boone left Bombay, he supervised one more operation against Kanhoji. The Company entered into an alliance with the Portuguese to attack Colaba. Although this fort was on an island, at low tide it was possible to reach it from the mainland by foot. A combined Anglo-Portuguese force of over 6,000 men was assembled. Ten large warships were to pound the fort from the sea. The ineptitude of the commanders and the animosity between the two nations resulted in another failure. The Royal Navy commander, Commodore Mathews, was so incensed that he abused the viceroy and accusing one of the Portuguese generals of treachery 'thrust his cane into his mouth'. Kanhoji took advantage of the situation to make a new treaty of friendship, this time with the Portuguese.

Charles Boone left Bombay in 1722. He had done much to improve Bombay, but wasted much money and many lives on disastrous military adventures. The Royal Navy departed with Commodore Mathews. As a final insult to the Company, Mathews sent a message to the Portuguese viceroy telling him that if he failed to capture every one of the Company's ships he would send him a petticoat.

———•———

The new governor of Bombay, William Phipps, was more levelheaded than Boone. Realizing he could not defeat Kanhoji, he refrained from attacking him. An uneasy truce resulted and there was an exchange of prisoners. In 1729 Kanhoji Angre fell ill and died. Gradually, over three decades, he had built up a formidable Maratha fleet, which had successfully taken on the navies of the Portuguese, the Dutch and the British. He had also made the Maratha coastal forts virtually impregnable.

Kanhoji left five sons. Although they divided Kanhoji's legacy and fought among themselves, the Angre family managed to resist the Europeans for another twenty-five years and often captured their ships. Year after year, however, the British were becoming more formidable.

In 1755, the Angre fort at Suvarnadurg was captured by a small Company fleet under Commodore William James. Handling a bombardment with great skill, James managed to explode the fort's gunpowder magazine, which then set the other buildings on fire. He subsequently captured three subsidiary forts and raised the English flag on all four. This victory was a turning point for the Company. It showed that against competent professional leadership, the Marathas were not invincible. On Shooters Hill near Woolwich Common in London there is an impressive monument to Sir William James – a triangular tower still known as Severndroog Castle.

The attack against Gheria involved a much larger fleet. Commodore James's ships were again involved, together with another Company fleet. They were joined by six ships of the Royal Navy and the landing craft for Robert Clive's 1,400 soldiers. In addition, Clive was to be joined by a Maratha land force. The Maratha leadership had fallen out with the Angres following an incident in which some of their men, who had been sent to collect tribute from the Angres, had been returned with their noses cut off.

When the British arrived at Gheria, they found the Maratha army already besieging the fort. The Marathas had previously captured the Angre leader and they wanted to take the fort without British help. The British, however, were determined to take the fort themselves, even though they were committed to returning it to the Marathas afterwards. It was rumoured that there were great spoils to be had and the British officers had already decided how to divide it among themselves and their men.

The British ships opened up with a massive barrage from over 150 cannon. After two hours of continuous firing, they set one of the enemy ships on fire – actually a Company ship that had been captured earlier and refitted for the Angre navy – and the blaze spread throughout the moored fleet. Soon the buildings inside the fort were also on fire. Clive then took his men ashore a mile or two away from the fort. The Marathas joined him.

Next morning there were surrender talks, but Angre's men fought on. Clive then moved his men closer to the fort and started shelling it from the land side. A powder magazine blew up inside the fort. Shortly afterwards, the Angre flag was lowered to indicate surrender. The Marathas tried to gain entry to the fortress, but Clive's men stopped them and next day took over the fort themselves. Ten British and three Dutch prisoners were found and released. The search for treasure then began. The official value of the seized gold, silver and jewels came to

£130,000 and this was divided as agreed among the British. No doubt, there were other pickings too.

Richer by the £5,000 he had gained from Gheria, Clive reached Fort St David in May 1756. Now he was second in the Company only to the governor of Madras. He arrived at a time of crisis for the Company in Bengal.

A month before Clive's arrival, the Nawab of Bengal, whose territory also included Orissa and Bihar, had died. He had been succeeded by his grandson, Siraj-ud-daula. Calcutta had grown phenomenally since its founding and now was nearly as large as the nawab's capital, Murshidabad. This had alarmed the old nawab who saw it as an abuse of the Company's original authority to merely trade, especially so as Calcutta's fortifications were continually being enhanced. His grandson had the same opinion and was determined to do something about it. He ordered the Company to demolish the latest improvements to Calcutta's fortifications. The governor of Calcutta, Roger Drake, was not suited to diplomacy. He dismissed the nawab's envoy with disdain. The nawab was furious: 'What honour is left to us, when a few traders who have not yet learnt to wash their bottoms reply to the ruler's order by expelling his envoy?'

Siraj-ud-daula moved fast. He occupied the Company's outpost near his capital, at Cossimbazar, and then marched his army towards Calcutta. Governor Drake then made a serious error – rather than bolster up the defences of the fort, he constructed artillery batteries on its approaches. Siraj-ud-daula's army overran these. They set fire to the town and bazaar. Fearing that he had too few men to defend the fort, Drake made the decision to evacuate by boat. In the confusion that ensued, many boats sank and many lives were lost. Drake escaped, having abandoned many of his garrison to the enemy. These were confined in a small dungeon that became infamous as 'The Black Hole of Calcutta'. On the night of 20 June, most of them died from overcrowding and suffocation. Nowhere near as many died as was subsequently alleged (modern estimates vary, from less than twenty to more than forty) but it was, nevertheless, a barbaric event. It is doubtful whether it had any part in the decision to regain Calcutta from Madras.

News of the fall of Calcutta reached Madras on 16 August. After much bickering, command of a relief operation was entrusted to Robert Clive. He finally sailed for Bengal on 16 October. He had 800 European soldiers and 1,000 Indian sepoys. The wind was against them, blowing some of the fleet as far south as Ceylon, and it was December before they began to enter the River Hooghly. On 15 December the fleet anchored at Fulta, forty miles downstream from Calcutta. There, they met up with the British fugitives. Contact was established with Siraj-ud-daula and his commanders, with whom there was a civil exchange of messages. From the British, however, this was probably just a device to gain time while they waited for a tide high enough to enable them to go upstream to Calcutta.

On 27 December the expedition moved towards Calcutta. Halfway, there was a skirmish with a detachment of the nawab's army. Clive had managed to have his artillery dragged overland, which enabled him to inflict heavy casualties on the enemy. The advance to Calcutta continued, with Clive and the European troops aboard the ships and the sepoys marching along the riverbank. They reached Calcutta on the morning of 2 January 1757. There was a brief exchange of fire, then the small garrison of the nawab's troops fled. The town was severely damaged. Large areas of the bazaar had been consumed by fire. The European

The Seizure of Bengal

houses and their church had been destroyed. In a breach in the fort walls, a mosque was under construction.

Clive was determined that Siraj-ud-daula should compensate the Company for its losses. Two British warships were sent up the river to Hooghly, where the nawab's troops who had fled from Calcutta were camped. They were bombarded by the ship's guns and fled again. The British, before they departed, plundered and set fire to the town and its surrounding areas.

Siraj-ud-daula came south with the bulk of his army, about 100,000 strong, through Hooghly and was shocked by the damage the British had wrought. It seemed as though he would meet the British demands for restitution and confirmation of their privileges. As he neared Calcutta, however, he became more belligerent. He camped his huge army just outside Calcutta.

Clive decided to launch a night attack on Siraj-ud-daula's camp, during which he hoped he might incapacitate or take away the Nawab's cannon. Vice Admiral Charles Watson agreed to supply 600 sailors to carry off the cannon. They arrived late, however, and it was dawn before the British attacked. The element of surprise was lost and Clive might have been defeated. However, by good fortune, a fog descended. Clive and his men were able to cut a swath through the nawab's camp, firing as they went. They failed to capture any cannon and lost fifty men. However, they had killed 1,300 of the nawab's men. Perhaps the nawab would have fought on, but he had received intelligence of a greater threat – an Afghan army was marching towards Bengal. He rapidly agreed a peace treaty, giving the British what they wanted, and took away his army.

The Seven Years War had started in Europe. News reached India that Britain and France were once again enemies. Clive was not confident that Siraj-ud-daula would respect the treaty. He worried that the nawab might forge an alliance with the

French in the future to overwhelm the British. There were two possible options for him – either to agree to a treaty of neutrality with the French at Chandernagore or to capture that settlement. There were talks about neutrality but eventually, with the nawab distracted by the menace from the approaching Afghans, Clive decided to attack Chandernagore. The nawab had left some troops behind to aid the French if they were attacked. Clive managed to bribe the nawab's representative, Nundcomar, not to use these in the conflict. The British then captured the town and laid siege to its fort. It was a hard-fought battle. Both sides lost about 200 men. Most of the British losses were sailors, on board the ships that were brought in close to cannonade the French. Their efforts were decisive in the British getting the upper hand. The French surrendered on 23 March. It was a body blow to the French company, for most of its profits came from Bengal.

Siraj-ud-daula had excited much resentment among the financial elite of Bengal. A large proportion of their profits came from dealing with the European exporters. Moreover, the nawab had insulted some of them for not being Muslim. One of the principal businessmen of Calcutta was Omichand. The nawab had used him as an intermediary with the British. Now, Omichand advised Clive that there were powerful bankers at Murshidabad who believed that if the nawab were to show hostility to the British again, it might be politic to have him removed. There were nobles who might be willing to support a coup. The most powerful of these was a military commander and relative of the nawab, Mir Jafar. He was chosen by the conspirators to replace the nawab if the British would support a coup d'état. A committee of the Company, including both Clive and the governor of Calcutta, agreed to proceed. Mir Jafar, if installed, would compensate the Company and its employers, who traded privately, for all losses over the previous year; more land around Calcutta would be granted to the Company; the personnel of the army and navy would divide a gift of Rs 4,000,000; the four members of the committee would divide another Rs 1,200,000.

Clive summoned Omichand, showed him a display of military manoeuvres, and sent him to report to the nawab. Omichand told the nawab that Clive intended to attack his capital next day. The threat from the Afghans had receded and the nawab ordered Mir Jafar to march an army towards Calcutta. Soon afterwards, Clive received a proposal from some Marathas that offered him assistance against the nawab. He sent a bland response, saying that he was friendly with the nawab, and then arranged for the nawab to see the message. The nawab recalled his army.

Omichand then threw matters into confusion by demanding a percentage of Siraj-ud-daula's money and jewels. This would have amounted to millions of rupees. It was suspected that he would reveal the plot if not placated. Clive had two documents drafted – a red one for Omichand, which would give him Rs 2,000,000, and a white one, the real agreement, with nothing for Omichand. Mir Jafar was then told that the white document was the genuine treaty and both parties signed both papers. The Company officials who had been acting as emissaries to the nawab's court made their escape. Next day, on 13 June, Clive marched towards Murshidabad. He was joined by some sailors and some soldiers from Calcutta. In all, Clive had about 1,000 European troops and 2,000 sepoys. They had about eight pieces of light artillery.

Siraj-ud-daula had an army that was many times larger than Clive's. He seems to have had about 40,000 infantry. These were not well trained and many were armed only with pikes or bows. However, he also had 18,000 Pathan cavalry. These competent horsemen mostly had swords or lances. Finally, he had fifty pieces of artillery. These were large guns, much larger than Clive's, and were operated by French gunners who had escaped from Chandernagore. They were eager to avenge that defeat.

Given the disparity between the size of the armies, Clive was entirely dependent on Mir Jafar, who was to command one of the three divisions of the nawab's infantry, and his co-conspirators. The nawab's army lay on an island in the river. Clive would have to take his men across in boats. If Mir Jafar reneged on his promises, Clive would find retreat extremely difficult. There were rumours that Mir Jafar and Siraj-ud-daula had become reconciled. In fact, the nawab had attempted to regain Mir Jafar's loyalty, and the two had pledged friendship on the Quran. On 20 June, a messenger brought a note to Clive from Mir Jafar – he now considered himself bound by his oath of friendship to the nawab. He could not fight against the nawab. However, he and his men would stand aside from any battle.

Heavy rain set in, the river began to swell. This made it even more likely that, if the British crossed the river, they would find themselves marooned on the island with no possibility of escape. With Mir Jafar's support doubtful, Clive began to have doubts about the whole enterprise. He wrote to the other members of the Company's committee asking for their advice. A reply was so delayed that on 21 June Clive convened a council of war with his own officers. Nine senior officers voted – seven of them were against immediate action and two in favour. Eight junior officers also voted – three were against immediate action and five in favour. Clive prevaricated. A letter arrived from Mir Jafar, which gave him hope. It ended:

When you come near I shall be able to join you. If you would send two or three hundred good fighting men the upper road towards Cossimbazar, the Nabob's army would themselves retreat. Then the battle will have no difficulty. When I am arrived near the army I will send you privately all the intelligence. Let me have previous notice of the time you intend to fight.

Clive replied:

Upon receiving your letter I am come to a resolution to proceed immediately to Placis.

That evening, Clive's army crossed the river.

———•———

Clive marched his men in darkness, over the sodden ground, until at 1 a.m. they reached the village of Plassey. They took possession of a large mango orchard. This, surrounded by a ditch and a high bank, was highly defensible. The space between the orchard and the river was taken up by a substantial hunting lodge, which Clive himself occupied.

At dawn on 23 June 1757, Robert Clive stood on the lodge roof and watched the nawab's army of 50,000 men spread across the landscape. Luke Scrafton, a Company factor who was there, described the scene: '... and what with the number of elephants all covered with scarlet cloth and embroidery; their horse with their drawn swords glittering in the sun; their heavy cannon drawn by vast trains of oxen; and their standards flying, they made a most pompous and formidable appearance.'

Clive had heard nothing further from Mir Jafar and was not confident that he would stand aside from the fray. At 7 a.m., he sent him a message:

> Whatever could have been done by me I have done, I can do no more. If you will come to Daudipore I will march from Placis to meet you, but if you won't comply even with this, pardon me, I shall make it up with the Nabob.

In fact, Clive was firm in his belief that an audacious confrontation might win the day.

Clive's troops moved out from the cover of the orchard to form a line facing the approaching army. The nawab's army stretched from the river on Clive's left, along the face of the orchard, and curved around to Clive's right flank. The artillery of both sides opened up a barrage. The Company's guns were too light to damage the nawab's heavy cannon. Although Clive's artillery was killing many of the nawab's infantry, Clive was losing some of his own men. With his much smaller force, he could not afford many losses. He withdrew his troops back into the orchard. Settled behind the protective wall, they continued to fire at the approaching army.

At noon there was a tremendous thunderstorm. Much of the ammunition of the nawab's army was soaked and their firing became intermittent. Thinking that Clive's men were similarly affected, the nawab's best commander, Mir Madan, charged with his cavalry. In fact, the British had protected their ammunition with tarpaulins. They were able to maintain their fire and Mir Madan was hit and fatally wounded.

The nawab was deeply shocked by the loss of Mir Madan. He called for Mir Jafar, threw his turban at the traitor's feet, and entreated him to help. Mir Jafar advised the nawab that it was too late to attack that day and suggested he recall his troops. Another conspirator gave the same advice. Mir Jafar then wrote to Clive (this letter was not received until the battle was over):

> Attack him at 3 in the morning; they will run away, and then will be my opportunity. The forces want to return to the city.

Attack him in the night by all means. We three shall be to the left of the Nabob...We three are ready for your service and will see you by and by.

As the nawab's troops withdrew, Clive went to the lodge to change into dry clothes. Shortly afterwards he was told that, despite his orders to do nothing, a detachment of his troops had moved forward to take control of a reservoir recently abandoned by the French artillery. Angrily, Clive rushed out and threatened to put his second-in-command under arrest. When he calmed down, he realized that it would be folly to give the impression of withdrawing. He summoned up more of his troops and then launched another attack. The nawab's troops, backed up by French artillery, counter-attacked. Clive's cannon were able to cause havoc among the oxen that drew the nawab's huge artillery platforms. Some elephants stampeded. Several of the nawab's senior officers were killed. His troops began to lose confidence.

Until this point Clive, not having received Mir Jafar's message, had been unsure about the intentions of the nawab's army deployed to his right. As they held back from the fight, however, he became sure that they must be the troops commanded by Mir Jafar and his co-conspirators. This prompted him to call up the rest of his army to attack the enemy in front. The nawab's soldiers soon realized they were losing the battle and fled. The Nawab himself had already gone. He took a fast camel back to his capital. By 5 p.m., the battle of Plassey was over.

For such a massive confrontation, there were very few casualties. The nawab lost about 500 men. The British losses were only four Europeans and sixteen sepoys. The treachery of Mir Jafar had won the day.

On the morning after the battle, Mir Jafar visited Clive. The two embraced and Clive hailed him as the new ruler of Bengal. Mir Jafar hastened to his own palace at Murshidabad. Siraj-ud-daula was in his palace across the river. That night, he disguised himself and, together with a favourite wife and daughter and a eunuch, made for Patna where he thought he still had support.

Clive entered Murshidabad two days later, accompanied by a large escort. He went to pay his respects to Mir Jafar. He punctiliously maintained the fiction that Mir Jafar was master of Bengal, Bihar and Orissa, and not himself. Next day they discussed money. The treasury had been partly emptied by Siraj-ud-daula and by looters, so was not as full as had been supposed. It was eventually agreed that Mir Jafar should pay one half of what had been agreed immediately, mostly in cash but some in jewels, silver and goods. The other half would be paid in instalments over three years. Seventy-five boats were loaded up, each carrying a large chest containing Rs 100,000. They headed down the river to Calcutta, escorted by the navy, and serenaded by music and drums. Clive received the money due to himself as commander-in-chief, as a member of the committee and as privately promised by Mir Jafar. Altogether, this came to nearly a quarter of a million pounds sterling. In all, the equivalent of one year's total revenue of Bengal found its way to Britain.

Siraj-ud-daula was brought back to Murshidabad as a prisoner. He had been recognized and then captured by Mir Jafar's brother. Within a few hours he was stabbed to death. Before he was buried, his corpse was paraded around the city on the back on an elephant.

POSTSCRIPT

The role of the East India Company in India was completely transformed by Clive's tactics. The directors of the Company in London were still adamant that peaceful trade should be Company policy. They complained that their men in India were 'so thoroughly possessed of military ideas as they forget their employers [were] merchants and trade was their principal object...Were we to adopt your several plans for fortifying, half our capital would be buried in stone walls.' However, it took many months, sometimes over a year, for correspondence to go back and forth from England to India. London's efforts to control events were further negated when Clive and his friends used their new money to buy large quantities of the Company's shares. Meanwhile, the men in India did what was in their own best interests.

Clive's agreement with Mir Jafar had stipulated that the Company would be allowed to import and export goods without paying any duty. This enabled the Company and its employees to undercut the Indian merchants and seize control of much of the trade. Moreover, their profits were sent back to Britain rather than used to boost local businesses. This, together with the loss to Bengal of the money paid over by Mir Jafar, severely damaged the economy.

In 1760 Clive returned to Britain with a vast fortune. He was given an Irish peerage, became an MP and was given an honorary doctorate by Oxford University. In his absence from Bengal, mismanagement by the officers of the Company became even more rampant. Henry Vansittart, who took over from Clive as governor, wrote:

> A trade was carried on without payment of duties, in the prosecution of which infinite oppressions were committed. English Agents or Gomashtas [native agents], not content with injuring the people, trampled on the authority of government, binding and punishing the Nabob's officers whenever they presumed to interfere.

Bengal's coffers were empty and Vansittart decided to remedy this by installing a stronger nawab. Accordingly, he used the Company's army to depose Mir Jafar and replace him with his son-in-law Mir Qasim. For this, Mir Qasim generously rewarded Vansittart and his colleagues. Furthermore, several districts of Bengal that were adjacent to Calcutta were ceded to the Company.

Mir Qasim was a capable ruler and substantially improved his administration and army. However, the depredations of the Company's men, who were using the Company's right to illegally trade duty-free on their own account and even selling this right on to local merchants, severely hampered Mir Qasim's attempts at reform. He gradually became more hostile to the Company and decided to curtail the Company's activities by abolishing all duties so as to reopen trade on a more equal basis. He further enraged the Company by seizing a shipment of its arms and detaining some of its men. A Company officer took it upon himself to attack Mir Qasim's men at Patna and was captured. The Company declared war, pronounced Mir Qasim unfit to rule and reinstated Mir Jafar as nawab. Once again he paid up for this. In eight years the Company's senior officers had received a total of £3,770,833, this at a time when a British labourer's family might make £37 a year and a Bengali family less than £2.

Mir Qasim retreated west, where he linked up with the viceroy of Awadh and the Mughal emperor. On 23 October 1764, the Company defeated their combined armies at Buxar, a town on the western edge of Bihar, which was a part of the nawab's fiefdom. This victory would eventually result in the Company extending its influence beyond Bengal.

Clive returned to India for the third and final time in 1765. The defeat of Mir Qasim and his allies at Buxar enabled the Company to dictate terms to the losers. Mir Qasim fled to Delhi and died in poverty. Rather than conquer further territories, Clive decided to allow the viceroy of Awadh to resume office, but give some of his land to the Mughal emperor. In gratitude the emperor bestowed the 'Dewani' of Bengal, Bihar and Orissa on the Company. This made them the legal rulers and gave them the right to all the revenue. This momentous document was delivered at Benares by the Mughal emperor himself. He handed it down from a makeshift throne made by taking a chair from Clive's tent and putting it on top of an English dining table that had been covered with an embroidered cloth. It was the beginning of British rule in India.

On his arrival from England, Clive had declared himself shocked as 'such a scene of anarchy, confusion, bribery, corruption, and extortion was never seen or heard of in any country but Bengal; nor so many fortunes acquired in so unjust and rapacious a manner'. He introduced various restrictions on private trade and banned bribes and lavish gifts. He realized, nevertheless, that he would need to augment his officer's modest official salaries. An 'Exclusive Company' was established whose profits would be distributed among the East India Company's senior officers according to seniority. Clive himself was given the largest number of shares. It would have an exclusive monopoly to make what profit it could on tobacco, betel nut and salt. In the three years before London forced its closure, it made a profit of over Rs 6 million, when the basic wage for Bengalis was one or two rupees a month. Once again, these profits left Bengal for Britain. Clive finally left India in 1767 and was succeeded by Harry Verelst who, at the end of 1769, was succeeded by John Cartier. That year and the year that followed were the most traumatic in Bengal's history.

In most of Bengal, there were normally three harvests a year: a small crop of pulses in the spring, a rice crop in September and a bigger rice crop in December. Normally, it was one of the most fertile parts of India. As the widely travelled Italian, Ludovico di Varthema, put it after his visit in the sixteenth century: 'The country abounds in grain of every kind, sugar, ginger, the best place in the world to live in.' However, the harvests of 1768 had been poor, which caused a rise in the price of food that extended into 1769. In that year there was very little rainfall over most of Bengal and the rice crops failed. Food became extremely scarce and the agents of the Company's men cornered the market in such grain as there was and ruthlessly raised its price.

In the thirteen years since the Battle of Plassey huge sums of money had left Bengal for Britain; this had depressed the local economy. Moreover, the land tax had been collected especially rigorously. Traditionally, this tax had been paid by the cultivator to his landlord, either in cash or kind, at a rate that represented around one-third of his crop. As the landlord lived close to his cultivators, he had a good idea of what was a reasonable assessment. If there was a poor crop the landlord should, of course, receive less than in a good year. The landlord, who was in effect merely a tax collector, then passed on nine-tenths of the collected tax to the government, retaining one-tenth for his services. This system required careful supervision by the government, otherwise unscrupulous landlords would squeeze the cultivators. The Company, short of staff, failed to do this effectively and many cultivators were unfairly assessed when their crops failed. As long as the Company received generous revenues, it turned a blind eye to these abuses.

In 1769 the population, having been bled dry over the previous years, had no cash reserve with which to buy in food from parts of India where food was available. The Company could have done this, but chose not to. The famine accelerated, not because there was no food in India, but because the people of Bengal had no money with which to purchase it. The Company made minor arrangements for relief, but continued to ruthlessly collect the land tax and its other revenues. As the famine increased in intensity the loss of life became terrible.

These developments seem to have been hardly noticed by the governor in Calcutta. Verelst retired on 24 December 1769 without giving London any intimation of the approaching famine or of the loss of revenue it would cause the Company. Nor did his successor, Governor Cartier, who took over on that same day, report anything amiss until late January 1770. The principal concern of both men was the land tax. This was despite having been told by Mr Alexander, the supervisor of Bihar, of the 'extremity of immediate distress' and that 'each day lost in deliberation adds to the calamity' and that 'To judge from the city of Patna, the interior of the country must be in a deplorable condition. From fifty to sixty people have died of absolute hunger in the streets every day for these ten days past.'

In February, Cartier reported that he had not 'yet found any failure in the revenue'. Extraordinarily, in April the government increased the land tax by 10 per cent. By May, however, it was beginning to dawn on the administration that something serious was happening. They reported: 'The mortality and beggary exceed all description. Above one-third of the inhabitants have perished in the once plentiful province of Purnea, and in other parts the misery is equal.'

Throughout the hot season the famine continued. Mohamed Ala Khan, the Foujdar (judge) of Purnea, wrote to Calcutta:

> Hardly a day passes without thirty or forty people dying. Multitudes have, and continue to perish from hunger. Seed grain has been sold for food, and cattle and agricultural utensils. Children offered for sale and no buyers.

The Aumil (collector of revenue) of Jessore wrote:

> The people are bringing in the leaves of the trees from the jungles for food; and they offer to sell their sons and daughters. Many of the ryots [tenants] are running away.

Most shockingly, the resident of the Durbar reported:

> The scene of misery that intervened, and still continue, shocks humanity too much to bear description. Certain it is, that in several parts the living have fed on the dead, and that the number that has perished in those provinces that have most

suffered is calculated to have been, within these few months, as six is to sixteen of the whole inhabitants.

And later, in mid-July, after the rains had finally come, he reported to the governor and his council:

> Previous representations are faint in comparison to the miseries now endured ... in the city of Moorshedabad [Murshidabad] alone it is calculated that more than five hundred are starved daily, and in the villages and country adjacent the numbers said to perish exceed belief ... In one month we may expect relief from our present distresses from the new harvest, if people survive to gather it in; but the numbers that I am sensible must perish in that interval, and those that I see dying around me, greatly affect my feelings and humanity as a man, and make me, as a servant of the Company, apprehensive of the consequences that may ensue to the revenues.

The rainfall in the second half of 1770 was abundant. The crops, in places where there were people left to plant them and where seed that had not been eaten to survive, were good. It was, however, too late for many. In 1772, officials toured the Company's territories to ascertain the mortality. They estimated that, out of a population of thirty million, some ten million had died. For many years afterwards great swathes of Bengal remained uncultivated and reverted to wilderness. The land was roamed by desperate bandits.

It is impossible to know what the mortality would have been had the Company not become the rulers of Bengal and Bihar. It seems clear that it would have been much lower since traditionally, in times of drought, the collection of the land tax was enforced less rigidly and certainly not increased. Moreover, all the money collected would have remained within the country, as would the huge sums given by the nawabs to the Company and its men. The administration and the populace would, therefore, have had more money with which to buy in grain from other parts of India. It seems likely that in the first thirteen years of British rule, more harm was done to the people of India than by all the other European invaders of the centuries before.

John Shore, who would later become Governor General of India in 1793, arrived in Bengal to work for the Company in 1769 and a year later was posted to Murshidabad. Nearly forty years later the memory was still with him:

> Still fresh in memory's eye the scene I view,
> The shrivelled limbs, sunk eyes, and lifeless hue;
> Still hear the mother's shrieks and infant's moans,
> Cries of despair and agonizing moans.
> In wild confusion dead and dying lie;-
> Hark the jackal's yell and vulture's cry,
> The dogs fell howl, as midst the glare of day
> They riot unmolested on their prey!
> Dire scenes of horror, which no pen can trace,
> Nor rolling years from memory's page efface.

In Britain the newly acquired fortunes of the Company's men caused envy and alarm among the established families. Moreover, the wealth seemed not to have benefited the Company or its shareholders. The Company paid for the armies in India and the adventures of its soldiers, but any rewards had been seized by the Company's employees. The benefits to the Company that had been supposed to flow from the conquest of Bengal never materialized. The costs of administration and conflict began to eat up any increase in revenue.

In India the Company's men continually expanded the Company's army so as to control more territory. At the beginning of the century it had been a thousand or so strong; by 1794 it had 13,000 Europeans and 57,000 Indian soldiers. With so much money to be made by its employees, the Company in India was beyond control.

In 1767 the East India Company was unable to pay an agreed annual levy to the treasury of £400,000. Parliament forced through some reforms to control the activities of the Company's employees. Administration improved but, nevertheless, in 1773 the Company had to beg for a government loan of £1,500,000. The Company then found itself involved in more wars, this time against the Marathas in central India. Huge sums had to be extorted from Indian rulers to meet the cost. The resulting furore led to the impeachment of the Company's Governor General. In 1784 ultimate control of the Company passed to the British government. Soon, imperial ambitions would make the Company, as an agent of the British government, no longer a business enterprise but the ruler of India. Profitable trade and conquest had proved incompatible.

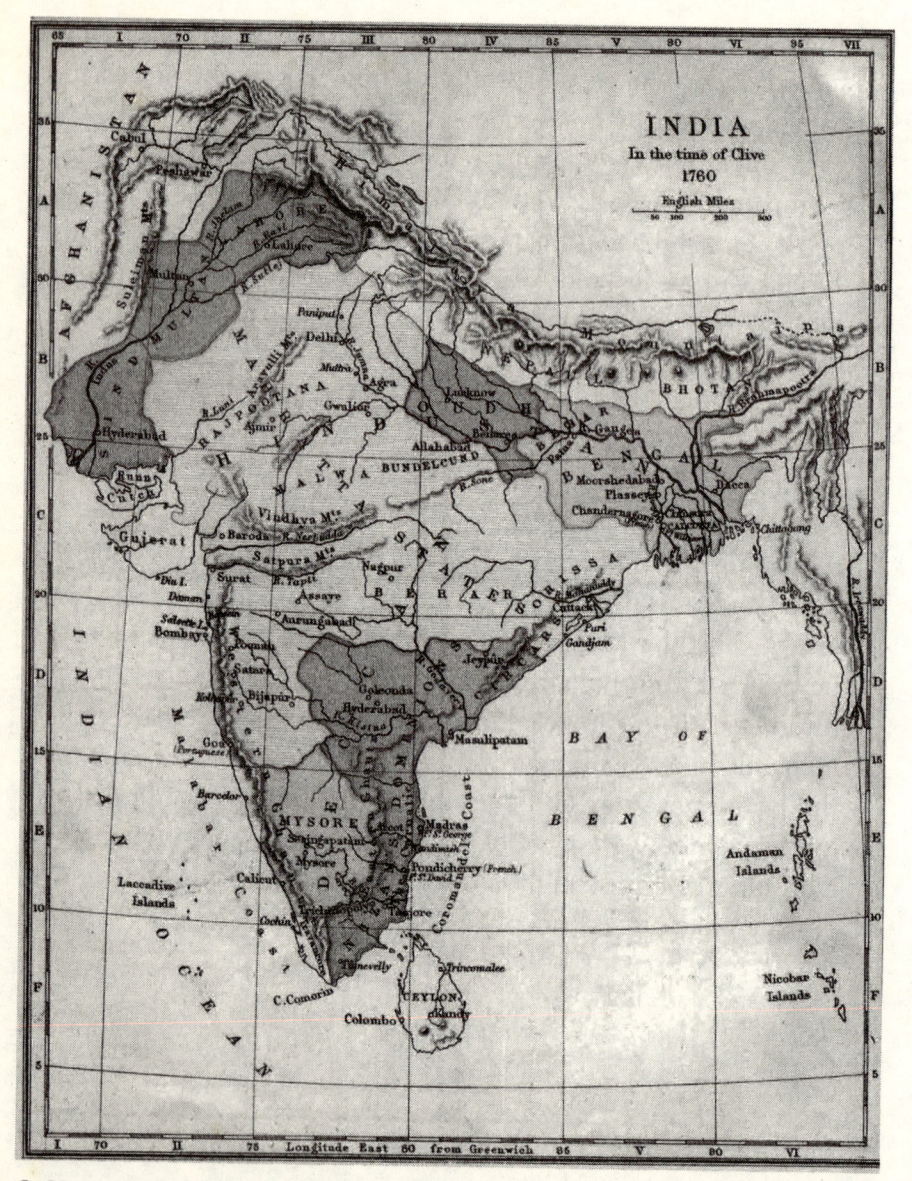

© University of Texas at Austin. Colbeck, C. (ed.), from The Public Schools Historical Atlas, 1905.

BIBLIOGRAPHY

Barlow, Edward, *Barlow's Journal*, Basil Lubbock (transcribed by), London: Hurst and Blackett, 1934.

Bence-Jones, Mark, *Clive of India*, London: Constable and Robinson, 1974.

Biddulph, John, *The Pirates of Malabar*, London: Smith, Elder and Company, 1907.

Bredsdorff, Asta, *The Trials and Travels of Willem Leyel: An Account of the Danish East India Company in Tranquebar, 1639–48*, Copenhagen: Museum Tusculanum Press, University of Copenhagen, 2009.

Boxer, Charles Ralph, *Two Pioneers of Tropical Medicine*, London: Wellcome Historical Medical Library, 1963.

Boxer, Charles Ralph, *The Portuguese Seaborne Empire*, Manchester: Carcanet Press, 1991.

Bruce, John, *Annals of the Honourable East-India Company*, London: Black, Parry, and Kingsbury, 1810.

Chaudhuri, Kirti Narayan, *Asia before Europe*, Cambridge: Cambridge University Press, 1990.

Churchill, Awnsham and John Churchill, *A Collection of Voyages and Travels*, London: Bookseller, 1704–32.

Commissariat, M.S., *Mandelslo's Travels in Western India*, London and Bombay: Oxford University Press, 1931.

———, *History of Gujarat*, Vol III, Ahmedabad: Gujarat Vidya Sabha, 1980.

Gerson da Cunha, J., *The Origin of Bombay*, New Delhi: Asian Educational Services, 1993.

R. de Souza, Teotonio, (ed.), *Essays in Goan History*, New Delhi: Concept, 2002.

Dodwell, Henry, *Dupleix and Clive: The Beginning of Empire*, London: Methuen Books, 1920.

Downing, Clement, *A History of the Indian Wars*, Oxford: Oxford University Press, 1924.

Dutt, Ramesh C., *The Economic History of India*, London: Routledge and Kegan Paul, 1906.

Eraly, Abraham, *The Mughal World: India's Tainted Paradise*, London: Weidenfeld and Nicolson, 2007.

Foster, William, *The English Factories in India*, Oxford: Clarendon Press, 1908–55.

Bibliography

Gokhale, Balkrishna Govind, *Surat in the Seventeenth Century*, London/Malmo: Curzon Press, 1979.

Grose, John Henry, *A Voyage to the East Indies*, London: (printed for) S. Hooper, and A. Morley, 1757.

Hourani, George Fadlo, *Arab Seafaring in the Indian Ocean in Ancient and Early Medieval Times*, Princeton: Princeton University Press, 1995.

Hunter, William W., *The Annals of Rural Bengal*, London: Smith, Elder and Company, 1868.

Jayne, K.G., *Vasco da Gama and His Successors*, London: Methuen Books, 1910.

Krishna, Bal, *Commercial Relations between India and England, 1601 to 1757*, London: Routledge, 1924.

Lawford, James P., *Britain's Army in India*, London: Allen and Unwin, 1978.

Lach, Donald F., and van Kley, Edwin J., *Asia in the Making of Europe*, Vol III, Chicago: University of Chicago, 1993.

Lockyer, Charles, *An Account of the Trade in India*, London: General Books LLC, 1711.

Mainwaring, Arthur Edward, *Crown and Company*, London: Arthur L. Humphreys, 1911.

Malgonkar, Mahohar, *Kanhoji Angrey Maratha Admiral*, London: Asia Publishing House, 1959.

Marshall, P.J., *East Indian Fortunes: The British in Bengal in the Eighteenth Century*, Oxford: Oxford University Press, 1976.

Miller, James Innes, *The Spice Trade of the Roman Empire*, Oxford: Clarendon Press, 1969.

Nairne, Alexander Kyd, *History of the Konkan*, Bombay: Government Central Press, 1894.

Nambiar, O.K., *The Kunjalis*, Bombay: Asia Publishing House, 1963.

Oaten, Edward Farley, *European Travellers in India*, London: Kegan Paul, Trench, Trubner and Company, 1909.

Pagadi, Setu Madhavrao, *Chhatrapati Shivaji*, Poona: Continental Prakashan, 2004.

Pinkerton, John, *A General Collection of the Best and Most Interesting Voyages and Travels*, London: Longman, Hurst, Rees, Orme and Brown, 1808–14.

Poddar, Prem, Rajeev S., Patke, and Lars Jensen, (eds), *A Historical Companion to Postcolonial Literature: Continental Europe and its Empires*, Edinburgh: Edinburg University, 2008.

Poonen, T.I., *Dutch Hegemony in Malabar*, Trivandrum: University of Kerala, 1978.

Priolkar, Anant Karba, *The Goa Inquisition*, New Delhi: A.K. Priolkar, 1991.

Rasmussen, Peter Ravn, *Tranquebar: The Danish East India Company 1616–1669*, available at http://scholiast.org/history/tranarr.html (last accessed on 10 August 2016).

Rawlinson, H.G., *British Beginnings in Western India*, Oxford: Clarendon Press, 1920.

Subrahmanyam, Sanjay, *The Career and Legend of Vasco da Gama*, Cambridge: Cambridge University Press, 1997.

Markus Vink, 'The World's Oldest Trade: Dutch Slavery and Slave Trade in the Indian Ocean in the Seventeenth Century', *Journal of World History*, Vol. 14, No. 2, Hawaii: University of Hawaii Press, 2003.

Welsh, James, *Military Reminiscences*, London: Smith, Elder & Co., 1830.

Whiteway, R.S., *The Rise of Portuguese Power in India 1497–1550*, Westminster: Archibald Constable, 1899.

Goverment Publications, etc.

Gazetteer of the Bombay Presidency, Bombay: Central Government Press, 1880.

Imperial Gazetteers of India, Oxford: Clarendon Press, 1908.

Oxford Dictionary of National Biography, Oxford: Oxford University Press, 2004–05.

Parliamentary Papers: Report of the Indian Famine Commission, Part III, Famine Histories, 18, India, Famine Inquiry Commission, London: Printed for His/Her Majesty's Stationery Office, Darling and Son, 1901.

Hakluyt Society Publications

Burnell, A.C., and P.A. Tiele, (eds), *The Voyage of J. H. van Linschoten to the East Indies*, London: Hakluyt Society, 1885.

Major, R.H. (ed.), *India in the Fifteenth Century: Being a Collection of Narratives of Voyages to India*, London: Hakluyt Society, 1857.

Ravanstein, E.G. (ed.), *A Journal* [by an unknown writer] *of the First Voyage of Vasco da Gama, 1497-1499*, London: Hakluyt Society, 1898.

Stanley, H.E.J. (ed.), *The Three Voyages of Vasco da Gama and his Viceroyalty*, London: Hakluyt Society, 1869.

Gray, Albert and Harry Charles Purvis, Bell (eds), *The Voyage of François Pyrard of Laval to the East Indies, the Maldives, the Moluccas, and Brazil*, London: Hakluyt Society, 1887.

Huntingford, G.W.B. (ed.), *The Periplus of the Erythraean Sea*, London: Hakluyt Society, 1980.

Temple, Sir Richard Carnac (ed.), *The Travels of Peter Mundy in Europe and Asia, 1608–1667*, Cambridge: Hakluyt Society, 1907.

Fryer, John, (Crooke William, ed.), *A New Account of East India and Persia, Being Nine Years' Travels, 1672–1681, by John Fryer*, London: Hakluyt Society, 1909–15.

Foster, Sir William (ed.), *The Voyages of Sir James Lancaster to Brazil and the East Indies, 1591–1603*, London: Hakluyt Society, 1940.

FURTHER READING

Cipolla, Carlo M., *Guns and Sails in the Early Phase of European Expansion, 1400–1700*, London: Collins, 1965.

Cliff, Nigel, *The Last Crusade: The Epic Voyages of Vasco da Gama*, New York: Harper Perennial, 2011.

Farrington, Anthony, *Trading Places*, Exhibition Catalogue, London: British Library, 2002.

Hamilton, Alexander, *A New Account of the East Indies*, London: Argonaut Press, 1930.

Keay, John, *The Honourable Company: A History of the English East India Company*, London: HarperCollins, 1991.

Smith, Vincent A., (Percival Spear, ed.), *The Oxford History of India*, 3rd ed., Oxford: Clarendon Press, 1958.

Spear, Percival, *The Nabobs*, London: Oxford University Press, 1963.

Tindall, Gillian, *City of Gold*, London: Penguin, 1992.

PLACE NAME CHANGES

Many place names in India have been changed in recent years and some of the old place names that have been given either new names or revised spellings are listed below:

Baroda	Vadodara
Bassein	Vasai
Bombay	Mumbai
Broach	Bharuch
Calcutta	Kolkata
Calicut	Kozhikode
Cannanore	Kannur
Cochin	Kochi
Conjeeveram	Kanchipuram
Cranganore	Kodungalloor
Dacca	Dhaka
Devikota	Devkot
Gheria	Vijaydurg

Hooghly	Hugli
Madras	Chennai
Masulipatam	Machilipatnam
Ormuz	Ormus
Panjim	Panaji
Quilandi	Koyilandy
Quilon	Kollam
Tellicherry	Thalassery
Trichinopoly	Tiruchirappalli

ACKNOWLEDGEMENTS

I have received help and hospitality from many in India and the UK while writing this book, for which I am extremely grateful. I would particularly like to thank Dileep Chinchalker, Tejas Desai, Ashvin Naik, C.K. Ramachandran, Premalatha Seshadri, Sharada Srinivasan and Jehangir Vakil.

    I would also like to thank the staff of the British Library's African and Asian Studies reading room for their assistance in my research, Rachel Joy Tanzer for facilitating the publication of this book, and all the staff of HarperCollins India who have striven to make it a success.

INDEX

Akbar, 65, 95, 127
Albuquerque, Afonso de, 22-23, 24-31, 38, 62, 129
Ali, Mohammed, 192, 193-94, 197, 198, 199-200
Angre, Kanhoji (Maratha admiral), 206-08, 209, 215
    and British, 160, 207, 208, 210-14
    and Siddis, 206
    implemented *dastak*, 206-07
    treaty of peace, 210, 214
Anjego, 145-46, 155-57, 158, 161-62, 164, 165
Anwar-ud-din, Nawab of the Carnatic, 191, 192
Arabs, 4, 6, 23, 38, 80, 137
Armenians, 55, 56, 80, 81, 95, 96, 97, 111, 114, 152, 155, 174
Attingal, 145, 156, 157, 158
    Rani of, 145, 156, 158
Aungier, Gerald (English), 94, 97, 98, 100
Aurangzeb, 95-96, 100, 112, 117, 118, 135, 172, 202, 205

Barlow, Edward (English), 103-09, 110
    his ship, the *Experiment*, 104-08

Bengal, British in, 155, 226, 228-35
    trade business in, 125-26, 146, 148-49, 179
East India Company, 87, 92-98, 110, 115, 118, 155, 210, 214, 215
    under Mughals, 152, 154
Boone, Charles (English), 210-15
Boscawen, Admiral (English), 188, 189
Bourdonnais, Mahé de La (French), 178, 182-84, 185
Brown, Admiral Walter (English), 212-14

Cabral, Pedro Álvares (Portuguese), 16-19
Calcutta, British in, 152, 170, 217-19, 221, 226, 229, 232, 233
    trade from, 152, 170, 217
Calicut, 1, 6, 7-8, 11, 12-13, 16, 17, 19, 38, 58, 140, 144
Carnatic, 191, 193
    British in, 88-89, 180, 181
    French in, 179, 181, 182-86, 193, 200
    Marathas in, 180
Caron, Francis (French), 173-74, 175
Carré, Abbé (French), 128, 137-38

Index

Chanda Sahib (Carnatic), 180, 191-94, 195, 196, 197, 198, 199
Chandranagar, 178-79, 181, 220, 222
Charles de Bussy (French), 191, 193
Charnock, Job (English), 150, 151-52
Child, John (English), 115-18, 152
Christianity in India, 5, 9, 11-12, 17, 32-36, 62, 80, 85, 99, 130, 202
Clive, Robert, 194-99, 203, 204, 216-26, 228-31
Cooke, Catherine (married John Harvey, Thomas Chown, and William Gyfford), 158-65
Cooke, Humphrey (English), 94, 159
Courten, Sir William, 73, 74-77, 111

Danish East India Company, 165-67, 170-71
    reborn as Asiatic Company, 170-71
Denmark, 111, 165-71
Devikota, 190, 195
Drake, Roger (English), 217-18
Drake, Sir Francis (English), 47, 53
du Bury, General (French), 186, 187
Dumas, Pierre Benoît (French), 179, 180-81
Dupleix, Joseph François, 178-79, 181-89, 191-93, 200-01
    differences with La Bourdonnais, 182, 183, 184, 185
Dutch
    and Cochin, 140-41, 143
    and English, 63, 81, 104, 144, 146, 166
    and Goa, 143
    and Portuguese, 105, 126, 136, 141
    and religion, 125, 141
    and Zamorin, 139-40, 143
    at Surat, 50, 59, 63, 67
    companies (VOC), 139, 144, 168
East India Company, 106-07, 141-42, 146, 166, 167, 174
    trade by, 57, 59, 67, 139, 140, 141, 142-43, 166-67, 168, 170
East India Company, 47, 49-51, 57, 61-62, 82, 100, 144, 145, 153-54, 186, 228
    and Mughals, 55, 57, 59, 116, 118, 149, 152
    army in India, 98-99, 236
    at Bombay, 94-95, 96, 110, 115, 118, 186, 188
    life of employees, 79-80, 83-87, 91, 98-100, 155-56, 158
    money used for private trade, 159, 161, 163-64, 194-95
    policy of peaceful trade, 50, 62, 87, 140, 144, 155, 228
    policy of religious tolerance, 89, 95, 97, 154-55
    problems they faced, 73, 74-75, 115, 116

Egypt, 2, 3-4, 23, 24, 31, 47
English economy in the sixteenth century, 44-45
Every, Henry (pirate), 111-12
    exports from India, 68, 147
    slaves, 37, 91, 131, 142, 176, 179
    spices, 1-3, 15, 17, 20, 21, 45, 54, 80, 106, 121, 140, 144, 147
    textiles, 58, 80, 81, 82, 88, 92, 125, 146, 148-49, 170

famines, 66-67, 72, 232, 233, 235
Francisco de Almeida, Viceroy, 23, 24-25

Fremlen, William, 68, 71
French
    and British, 177-78, 181-83, 185-86, 188-89, 192, 197, 198, 199, 200
    and Carnatic, 179-80, 181, 182, 183-84, 186, 191, 193, 200
    and Dutch, 174, 175-76
    and Marathas, 180, 200
    and Mughals, 178, 180-81, 184-85, 186, 187, 193
    enterprises, conflict within, 174, 183
    in Bengal, 178, 179
    in Madras, 175, 182-85, 187, 188, 189, 194
    in Pondicherry, 175-77, 179, 180
    trade with India, 173-74, 176-79, 181
    trading company, 173, 175, 176, 177-78, 179, 200, 201
Fryer, John (English), 90, 118-19

Gayer, Sir John (English), 154
Gyfford, William (English), 155-57, 161, 164
Goa, 25-36, 125, 135, 137, 143
    attacked by Adil Shah, 26-29, 30, 31, 32
    Dutch in, 75, 143
    Portuguese in, 25-33, 36, 37, 41-42, 134, 136
Godeheu, Charles (French), 200-01
Golconda, 57-58, 89, 174, 175
Grappe, Roland (Dutch), 166
Gujarat,
    life in, 95, 123
    trade from, 80, 121-22, 124-25

Hamilton, Alexander, 77, 145, 232

Harvey, John (English), 113, 159-60, 161
Hawkins, William, captain of *Hector*, 54-56
Heath, Captain William (English), 151-52
Hindus, treatment given by external powers to, 20, 30, 32-33, 35-36, 68, 69, 93, 96, 155
Honavar, Raja of, 24, 27

Ibn Batuta's account of Malabar, 4, 110
India and Persia, trade between, 29-30, 31, 62, 80, 131
Islam, 10, 15-16, 56, 126

Jafar, Mir, 220-21, 222-23, 224-27, 228, 229, 230
Jahangir, 55, 56, 57, 59, 95, 127
Jains, 78, 82, 95, 122
James, Commodore William (English), 215-16
Jang, Muzaffar, 191, 192, 193
Jang, Nasir, 191, 192, 193
João de Castro (Portuguese), 122, 211

Keeling, William, captain of *Dragon*, 54, 58
Khan, Dost Ali (Carnatic), 179-80
Khan, Mahfuz, 184, 185
Khan, Rumi (Turk), 202
Kawaka Minas, Armenian, 96-97
Kidd, Captain (English pirate), 113-14
Kunjali Marakkar, Mohammad, 39-41
Kunjali Marakkars, 38-40

Lawrence, Major Stringer, 195, 198, 199

Index

Levant Company (English), trade with Turkish Empire, 46-47, 48, 50
Leyel, Willem (Dutch), 166, 167-69

Madan, Mir, 224
Madras, 90-91
    British trade business from, 87, 92, 109-10, 148
    Dutch exported slaves from, 142
Malabar Coast and Romans, trade between, 3, 4
Marathas, 100, 204, 208, 209, 210, 215
    and English, 160, 197, 204, 211, 212-13, 215-16, 221, 236
    and French, 180, 200, 209-10
    and Mughals, 100, 172, 180, 191, 192, 198, 199, 205, 207
Marco Polo, life in India, 4-5, 110
Martin, François (French), 175, 176-177
Mathews, Commodore Thomas (English), 163-64, 214, 215
Morse, Nicholas, 182, 186
Mughal India, 55, 65, 87, 95-100, 115, 152, 172, 190-91, 202
    account of life and work in, 63-65, 70, 95-96
    and trade, 56, 59, 111, 118, 146
    cruelties of the, 64, 68, 69, 70
Mundy, Peter, life in British times, 65-73, 75-76
Muslims, treatment given by Europeans, 10, 20, 24, 26, 27, 30, 34, 62, 83, 122, 124, 155, 156

Nayak, Damarla Venkapapati (Carnatic), 88
Nikitini's, Afanasy, account of India, 6-7

Odoric, life in India, 5
Omichand (Nawab's intermediary), 220, 221
Ovington, Reverend John (English), 83, 97, 119

Paradis, Louis (French), 185, 186, 187, 188, 189
Parsis, 80-81, 95, 97
Pean, Captain (English), 117
Pessart, Barrent (Dutch), 166, 167-68
Phipps, William (English), 215
piracy in India 73-74, 110-14, 125, 153, 207, 214
    laws against, 114-15
    suppression, 114, 163, 204
Plassey, Battle of, 223-26
Pondicherry
    development of, 176-77, 181, 188
    French at, 175-77, 180, 181, 192, 193, 200
    trade from, 176-77, 179-80
Portuguese
    and Hindus, 17, 20, 30, 32, 33, 35-36
    and Islam, 9, 10, 13, 20, 26, 27, 34, 37, 38
    at Diu, 122-23, 124, 137
    contribution to India, 126-27
    conversions to Christianity, 32, 33-34
    in Goa, 26-27, 29, 36, 124, 135
    India, life in, 130-33
    Inquisition, 33, 34, 35, 41, 93
    terror, 1, 16, 18, 19, 24, 26, 27, 29, 34-35, 93, 12
    trade by, 10, 29, 30, 37, 42, 43, 125, 126, 131, 137, 143
Pyrard, Francois (French), 128-35, 173
    fellow soldiers of, 132-33

religious conversions, 32-34, 56, 96, 122, 126
Roe, Sir Thomas, 59-60, 109, 147, 154, 155
Rykloff van Goens (Dutch), 140-41

Sambhaji (Marathas), 204-05, 206, 207
Shah Jahan, 95, 125, 126
Shah, Bahadur (Gujarat), 202
Shah, Yusuf Adil, 25, 26, 27, 28, 30, 31-32, 33, 117, 205
Shivaji, Maratha king, 87, 100, 115, 117, 204, 206, 210
Siddis of Janjira, 100, 112, 116-18, 205-06, 210
Siraj-ud-daula, Nawab of Bengal, 217, 218-20, 221, 222, 226, 227
slave trade, 37, 91, 131, 142, 176, 179
slaves, use of, 33, 37, 69, 78, 91, 97, 116, 120, 130, 131, 133, 137, 142-43
Smythe, Thomas, 49, 50-52, 61, 102
Sodré, Vincente, 21, 22
Stephens, Thomas, 47
sufferings inflicted on Indians by European powers, 1, 16, 19, 24, 26, 29, 34-35, 64, 77, 93, 98, 124, 132, 136, 137, 142, 234
Surat, 80-81

trade centre for
British, 56, 57, 59, 73, 81, 82, 87
Dutch, 40, 59, 67
French, 81, 174

Tanjore, 165-66, 169, 190, 195
Tavernier, Jean-Baptiste (French), 128, 134-36
temples, destruction of, 32, 36-37, 78, 93, 95, 123, 124

Vasco da Gama, 1, 2, 8, 9-12, 14-15, 18, 20-21, 25
Vora, Virji (businessman) and East India Company, 82

Waite, Sir Nicholas (English), 153
Watson, Vice-Admiral Charles (English), 219
Weddell, John (English), 62-63, 75-76, 109

Xavier, Francis, 32-35

Zamorin and
Dutch, 139, 143
English, 58, 143, 144
Portuguese, 10, 11-15, 16, 17, 18-21, 24, 38-41, 58
Raja of Cochin, 16, 22, 23